"Witnessing for Christ with compassion and joy, without fear and guilt—that is the theme of this wonderful book. Christians generally know that Christ commissioned his disciples to baptize people throughout the world in the triune name and to teach them to follow him. The writers of this book recognize that sometimes we feel inadequate for that mission. In winsome, readable prose, they provide wise counsel on how those hesitant to witness for Christ might do so. This is a book for all of us to contemplate in our endeavor to witness for Christ with confidence, compassion, and joy."

John D. Woodbridge, Research Professor of Church History and Christian Thought, Trinity Evangelical Divinity School

"David Dockery has assembled an A-team of scholars and practitioners to contribute to this work. They know the Christian college setting well and speak powerfully into that unique context. Colleges shape leaders for society and the church, and I am grateful students will have this excellent resource from which to glean much wisdom in evangelism and apologetics."

Timothy K. Beougher, Billy Graham Professor of Evangelism, The Southern Baptist Theological Seminary; author, *Invitation to Evangelism*

"The gospel is the best news on the planet—the greatest people-changing, culture-transforming force in human history. It's high time for the church, for this student generation, and for our Christian colleges to rediscover the mutual importance of evangelism and apologetics for the task of re-evangelizing the Western world. *Confident Witness* is a great tool to that end."

Donald W. Sweeting, Chancellor, Colorado Christian University

"*Confident Witness* offers a profound and heartfelt exploration of evangelism's theological roots and practical application, providing valuable insights for believers eager to share their faith effectively. Through engaging contributions from various scholars, this book equips readers with a deeper understanding of the gospel message and deep insight on being an effective witness in today's secularizing society. With an emphasis on theology, evangelism, and cultural engagement, *Confident Witness* inspires Christians to confidently proclaim the good news."

Drew Flamm, President, Grace College and Grace Theological Seminary

T0284679

"David Dockery has collected a rich and diverse trove of perspectives and wisdom on the nature and value of apologetics to equip and encourage a new generation."

Cherie Harder, President, The Trinity Forum

"Jesus's final marching orders to his earliest followers were to make disciples of people in all nations. This Great Commission remains the heart of the church's mission. *Confident Witness* brings together scholar-practitioners, in a variety of academic disciplines and with a wealth of ministry experiences, who together offer a holistic case for a renewed commitment to the advance of the gospel. Readers will see the importance of cultivating postures, embracing practices, and building institutions that reinforce our obedience to the Great Commission in an increasingly post-Christian West—for the glory of God and the advance of his kingdom among all nations."

Nathan A. Finn, Executive Director, Institute for Transformational Leadership; Professor of Faith and Culture, North Greenville University

"We have assigned chapters from *Confident Witness* to our undergraduate evangelism class at Wheaton. The result has been a most animated discussion of key issues and ideas in evangelism. This book is field-tested by students and receives an A+. It is a fantastic introduction, both in scope and in detail."

Greg Anderson, Graduate School Chaplain, Wheaton College

"Beginning with the bedrock of biblical principles and historical observations, and moving to contemporary application, this extensive work presents a unified approach to evangelism and apologetics. Enriched by diverse voices and perspectives of scholars, it conveys indispensable insight tailored to Christian college students, serving as a cornerstone resource for those navigating the intersection of faith and academia. *Confident Witness* is a timely addition to the shelves of any student serious about gospel engagement."

Carl J. Bradford, Dean, Texas Baptist College, Southwestern Baptist Theological Seminary

Confident Witness

Confident Witness

Evangelism and Apologetics for the 21st Century

Edited by David S. Dockery

CROSSWAY®

WHEATON, ILLINOIS

Confident Witness: Evangelism and Apologetics for the 21st Century
© 2024 by David S. Dockery
Published by Crossway
          1300 Crescent Street
          Wheaton, Illinois 60187

Cover design: Jordan Singer

First printing 2024

Printed in the United States of America

Trade paperback ISBN: 978-1-4335-9011-5
ePub ISBN: 978-1-4335-9014-6
PDF ISBN: 978-1-4335-9012-2

Library of Congress Cataloging-in-Publication Data
Names: Dockery, David S., editor.
Title: Confident witness : evangelism and apologetics for the 21st century / edited by David S. Dockery.
Description: Wheaton, Illinois : Crossway, 2024. | Includes bibliographical references and index.
Identifiers: LCCN 2023046939 (print) | LCCN 2023046940 (ebook) | ISBN 9781433590115 (trade paperback) | ISBN 9781433590122 (pdf) | ISBN 9781433590146 (epub)
Subjects: LCSH: Apologetics. | Evangelistic work. | Bible. New Testament—Criticism, interpretation, etc.
Classification: LCC BT1103 .C6448 2024 (print) | LCC BT1103 (ebook) | DDC 239—dc23/eng/20240329
LC record available at https://lccn.loc.gov/2023046939
LC ebook record available at https://lccn.loc.gov/2023046940

Crossway is a publishing ministry of Good News Publishers.

VP		33	32	31	30	29	28	27	26	25	24
15	14	13	12	11	10	9	8	7	6	5	4	3	2	1

With immense gratitude
to
the Mathena family
and
the Witness to Win Foundation

Contents

1

Introduction

David S. Dockery

EVANGELISM IS SHARING the good news of Jesus Christ with men and women, boys and girls, who do not yet know him as Lord and Savior. Evangelism is a work of God as he leads and gifts his people by his Spirit to share the gospel message with others. Those who respond to this good news do so as the Spirit of God enables them and changes their hearts to believe in Jesus Christ, granting them the gift of salvation.

Salvation is a free gift of God, and it cannot be earned by our good behavior (Rom. 3:22–24). Salvation is not the culmination of humanity's quest for God; it is a response to God's initiating love for us. The apostle John writes, "In this the love of God was made manifest among us, that God sent his only Son into the world, so that we might live through him. In this is love, not that we have loved God but that he loved us and sent his Son to be the propitiation for our sins" (1 John 4:9–10). God's grace brings us to him and strengthens us to continue and complete the spiritual pilgrimage (Eph. 1:4–7; Phil. 1:6). In no way does this deny human involvement in salvation, but it does affirm God as taking the initiative.

When men and women receive the grace of God, it is a testimony to the transforming power of grace itself. When humans reject God's grace, it is a sign of the hardness and sinfulness of human hearts (Rom. 1:18–3:20, 23; Eph. 2:1–3). Salvation comes to us through God's agents of grace who share the good news of the gospel with those who are alienated from God, lost in their sins. This spiritual transformation comes to the ill-deserving not because of their own efforts but because of the loving favor of God through the redemptive work of Jesus Christ on the cross and the regenerating work of the Holy Spirit.

Salvation is of God, yet humans must respond to God's grace. As the eighteenth- and nineteenth-century British Christian leaders Andrew Fuller and William Carey made clear, God uses the means of evangelism and the responses of men and women to the gospel message to bring about his desired plan. Only persons who receive divine grace can make a favorable response to God's salvific invitation, but only those who do respond to this good news are transformed by grace.

Thus, we want to affirm the priority of God's initiating grace without neglecting in any way the importance of believers' sharing the good news with others and the responsibility of men and women to believe the gospel message (Rom. 10:9–17; Eph. 2:8–9). When God extends his grace to us, he is the active agent, but he always extends his grace through various means, including the preaching of the gospel, the sharing of personal testimony, the written word of God, the invitation to respond to grace, the prayers of God's people, and the faith of the respondent.

The Bible maintains that faith is the means by which we receive God's salvation, which was purchased for us by the atoning work of our Lord Jesus Christ (Gal. 2:16). Faith includes a full commitment of the whole person to Jesus Christ, a commitment involving knowledge, trust, and submission. Faith is not merely an intellectual assent or only an emotional response but a complete spiritual change of our lives brought about by the work of the Holy Spirit.

Evangelism involves guiding unbelievers to place their faith in Jesus Christ. Though faith is more than doctrinal assent, it must include adherence to Jesus Christ as fully God and fully human (John 1:1, 14, 18), as the one who knew no sin yet became sin for us so that we might become the righteousness of God (2 Cor. 5:21). Unbelievers respond to this evangelistic message by placing their faith in Jesus Christ, acknowledging him as Savior from their sin and Lord of their lives (Rom. 10:9).

God uses our acts of personal kindness and friendship as forms of pre-evangelism, but we must not think that evangelism can take place without a verbal communication of the gospel, either spoken or written. Believers are exhorted to be ready to give an answer for the hope within them (1 Pet. 3:15), doing so with gentleness and respect. The book you hold in your hands is an attempt to help people understand better the meaning of the gospel and the need for taking this gospel message to others, whether across the street or around the world. It is written particularly for college students and for those who serve on college campuses, serving as a reminder of the importance of evangelism and apologetics (making a reasoned defense of Christianity), especially in our pluralistic and secular contexts, in which an implicit form of universalism seems to be prevalent.

Evangelism involves the declaration of God's good news that through faith in Jesus Christ, our sins can be forgiven (Rom.

3:21–26). This message emphasizes complete and total forgiveness (Heb. 10:10–17), as portrayed in the story of the prodigal son (Luke 15:11–32). The means of this forgiveness include our faith and repentance, resulting in the conversion of sinners. Such forgiveness is found only in Jesus Christ (John 14:6; Acts 4:12). Apart from Jesus Christ, there is no hope.

The work of evangelism must be understood within God's overall redemptive work, for God is not merely saving individuals; he is saving a people for himself, the redemption of those from every tribe and language and people and nation (Rev. 5:9; 7:9). As a number of contributors to this volume will note, our evangelistic efforts must reflect an awareness of our context, a lesson provided for us by the apostles in the book of Acts.

The opening chapters in this volume make a concerted effort at closing the gap between theology and evangelism, in keeping with the observations of Michael Green in his *Evangelism in the Early Church* that early church evangelists were theologians and early church theologians were evangelists. Faithful messengers of the gospel will want to be sure their communication faithfully represents the theological truths taught in Holy Scripture. We thus gladly and joyfully acknowledge Jesus Christ as Lord, our prophet, priest, and king, who has completely revealed God, has reconciled women and men to God, and now sits enthroned as ruler of God's kingdom and head of his church. *Confident Witness: Evangelism and Apologetics for the 21st Century* is a testimony to this good news and our shared thanksgiving for what Jesus Christ has done for us. Moreover, it is an expression of our desire to take the gospel to the nations (Matt. 28:19–20) with all boldness and without hindrance (Acts 28:31).

Robert Sloan, president of Houston Christian University, expands on these themes in his chapter, "What Is Evangelism?"

Chris Morgan, dean at California Baptist University, and Erik Thoennes, professor of theology at Biola University, provide thoughtful chapters on the scriptural and theological foundation for evangelism. David Gustafson, from Trinity Evangelical Divinity School, offers an insightful look at "Evangelism in the History of the Church."

David Kotter, dean at Colorado Christian University, traces the New Testament practices of evangelism and apologetics for our readers. Jim Denison and Mark Legg, of the Denison Forum, combine to make us aware of the challenges and opportunities associated with evangelism in a post-Christian context. Travis Dickinson, professor of philosophy at Dallas Baptist University, offers an illuminating look at the role of apologetics in evangelism, while Hal Poe, the Charles Colson University Professor of Faith and Culture at Union University, provides lessons from the life of C. S. Lewis regarding similar themes.

Anna Daub, who serves at Southeastern Baptist Theological Seminary, turns our attention toward global evangelism. Tim McKnight, from Anderson University in South Carolina, offers readers a look at the faithful work of cultivating, planting, and reaping. Susan Booth, of Canadian Baptist Theological Seminary and College, reminds us of the essential ministry of the Holy Spirit and the need for prayerfulness in our gospel proclamation. Daniel DeWitt, currently serving at Southwest Baptist University in Missouri, shows us the importance of both evangelistic and discipleship efforts. Finally, Freddy Cardoza, dean at Grace College and Seminary, connects the dots for us with a summary chapter, "Christian Higher Education, the Church, Evangelism, and Discipleship."

It is our prayer that these combined efforts will provide a symphonic look at the gospel and our calling to be faithful gospel messengers in our various places of service, particularly with application for the context of Christian college and university campuses.

All of the contributors to this volume join me in expressing our heartfelt gratitude to the Mathena family and the Witness to Win Foundation for their generous encouragement for this project. We certainly want to offer our thanks for the support from Justin Taylor, Jill Carter, Thom Notaro, and the rest of the Crossway team for this project. Wang Yong Lee, Kylie Frueh, and Andy Jennings offered valuable editorial assistance at each step of the way. For all who have participated in this effort and for all who have offered prayers and support for this book, we are truly thankful. We pray that the Lord will use this publication for the good of many and that this book will bring glory to our great and gracious triune God.

Questions for Reflection

1. What is evangelism?

2. How does God use human instruments as the means for advancing and proclaiming the gospel?

3. What is the relationship between divine grace and human faith in salvation?

Resources for Further Study

Dockery, David S. "Theology for Evangelism and Missions." In *A Handbook of Theology*, edited by Daniel L. Akin, David S. Dockery, and Nathan A. Finn, 509–20. Brentwood, TN: B&H Academic, 2023.

Green, Michael. *Evangelism in the Early Church.* Rev. ed. Grand Rapids, MI: Eerdmans, 2004.

Packer, J. I. *Evangelism and the Sovereignty of God.* Rev. ed. Downers Grove, IL: InterVarsity Press, 2012.

2

What Is Evangelism?

Robert B. Sloan

EVANGELISM IS THE WORK of God's people in response to Christ's command, with the aid and presence of the Spirit, to announce to all peoples the good news of what God has done in Christ to restore the world (Matt. 28:18–20; Luke 24:44–49; Acts 1:6–9; 2:4–11). It is an act of loving obedience done in the hopeful prospect of evoking in those who hear the message a sincere repentance from the idolatry and worldly wisdom that inflame the pursuit of power, pleasure, money, and fame and replacing them with a life of Spirit-enabled obedience to God. Evangelism is thus the enthusiastic (it is, after all, *good* news) proclamation of what God has done, and conversion is the desired response to the new covenant established by the once-crucified and now-raised-and-enthroned (with bodily immortality) Son of God, the Lord Jesus Christ.

Evangelism and its intended goal of conversion are rightly distinguished, but, taken together, they are a significant, penultimate step in God's plan to judge and restore the world. He has already begun through Christ to defeat the dark powers and gather the nations in submission to himself as the one true God. To complete this inaugurated restoration, he has commissioned his followers to announce his kingship to all the nations and teach them to live in obedience to him—note the parallel between the commissioning of Adam and Eve to extend the frontiers of God's kingship through ruling the earth and Jesus's commissioning of his followers, given his possession of all power in heaven and on earth, after his resurrection (Matt. 28:18). This inaugurated restoration will be completed when God renews all creation at the return of Christ the Lord. But his followers already have significant responsibilities consisting in no small part in the proclamation of the gospel with respect to God's merciful work of bringing the nations into submission to himself (Matt. 24:14; Rom. 11:25–32; 2 Pet. 3:9–13).

The work of evangelism has often been severely reduced to an appeal to individuals to acknowledge sin, repent, and believe in Jesus. Those acts of personal response are necessary and significant moments in the process of conversion, but the work of evangelism and the response to it cannot be limited to these elements. The mission charge of Jesus in Matthew 28:19–20 is grounded in his newly established authority over heaven and earth (Matt. 28:18) as accomplished through his death and resurrection. The commission thus assumes the proclamation of the gospel as the basis for making disciples and baptizing them in the name of the Father, Son, and Holy Spirit, and it seamlessly connects those initial elements of conversion with the need to teach them "to observe all that I have commanded you" (28:20).

Evangelism therefore is a summons to lifelong obedience to the will of God in alignment with his purposes revealed through Jesus

Christ, and it involves participation in God's plans for heaven and earth and all their inhabitants.

The word *evangelism* is closely related as an *activity* (especially verbal acts of preaching, teaching, arguing for, and writing) to the word *gospel* (*euangelion*), which describes the *content* of the message proclaimed and communicated in the work of evangelism. The word *gospel*, and thus the activity of evangelism, is rightly focused on the death, burial, resurrection, and enthronement of Jesus, the long-awaited Messiah/Christ. But as powerful and necessary as those focal points are, Paul reminds us—as did all of the earliest Christian preaching—that those significant events with respect to Jesus were "in accordance with the Scriptures" (1 Cor. 15:3–4; cf. Acts 2:16; 3:18–26; 4:10–11, 23–28; 8:26–35; 13:17–41; 17:11; 26:22–23). That is, they fulfilled a longer story. Evangelism, therefore, in telling the story of Jesus, is announcing a message that is part of the comprehensive story of Scripture—the most dramatic and climactic part thus far, to be sure.

The story of Jesus thus has a backstory—in many instances focused upon the covenant promises God made to Abraham—pregnant with the hints of the forthcoming fulfillment of the hopes for restoration within each scriptural scene and subplot of the longer story (see below). The gospel events, focused on Christ's death, burial, resurrection, and enthronement (ascension) are the surprising fulfillment of the biblical narrative. And while there is a backstory to the historical moments of Jesus—often signaled by brief allusions to Abraham—the gospel also reflects God's deeper, cosmos-wide purposes (Eph. 1:8–10) not only behind those events but also proceeding from them and beyond them. Those purposes are carried forward by the Spirit, involve human agency, and include—through the preaching of the gospel and the witness of the church—the reconciliation of the earth's peoples to one another and to God (both reflected in the church as the body of Christ; see esp. Eph. 2:11–3:13), other restorative works of mercy that are signs of the new creation, and the further administration of God's purposes beyond the return of Christ (1 Cor. 6:2–3; Rev. 7:13–15).

The gospel, therefore, is the story of Jesus's saving deeds, as embedded within the biblical narrative, and the very telling of it as evangelism is a furthering of God's purposes for the world with respect to his heaven-and-earth-embracing, restorative work in Christ.

Depending on the context and the audience, evangelism does not always tell the full scriptural story or elaborate the long account of God's actions and purposes in history. But that longer narrative is always assumed, and it is the basis upon which individual responses of repentance, confession, and faith occur. And it provides, again depending upon the audience, the context and place in the experience of the new convert(s) where discipleship—following Jesus after confessing him as Lord—begins. Evangelism as a witness to the gospel morphs into gospel-shaped discipleship, which repeatedly sheds the "old self" and its practices and "puts on" the "new self," which by the Spirit is being transformed into the likeness of Christ (Eph. 4:22–24; Col. 3:5–14; cf. Rom. 6:5–6; 2 Cor. 4:16).

No doubt the very writing of the Gospels themselves—which took place decades after the earliest Christian preaching of the gospel by the apostles—is partly, if not largely, accounted for by the needs of discipleship. The Gospels told the early followers of Jesus not only how the Jewish Scriptures pointed to Jesus as their fulfillment but also what the life and teachings of Jesus would mean to them and what following him would look like in worship, holiness, and witness in their work as Christ's commissioned agents in the inaugurated transformation of the world.

The earliest apostolic preaching of the gospel as recounted in Acts indicates clearly that the given audience—especially whether mostly Jews, God fearers, or Gentiles—often influenced greatly the level of detail and the rhetorical content and flow involved in the telling of the story of Jesus. Paul's sermon on Mars Hill (17:16–31) started with his noticing the pagan inscriptions, proceeded with a citation from a pagan poet, and finally appealed to the one true God who had created all things and would one day judge the world through a man whom he raised from the dead—namely, Jesus. In many instances, where the Jewish audience possessed sufficient knowledge of the Scriptures, it was not always necessary to provide details of scriptural texts, though the allusions to the Scriptures are many.

So it is in modern-day evangelism. Every act of sharing the gospel need not involve complicated detail, but the longer story of Scripture is the proper frame of reference that needs to inform the work of evangelism (teaching and proclaiming the gospel) and nurture the response of faith to it. Certainly, we spend the rest of our lives as followers of Christ understanding the implications of the scriptural narrative, but the longer story itself must always be understood as the at least implicit background to an appeal for faith in Jesus. To believe in Jesus is to be taken up into the story of how God in history is rescuing and restoring our broken world and thus to become fellow workers under God (2 Cor. 6:1) and coheirs with Christ (Rom. 8:17).

The story that evangelism either tells or assumes begins with God's good creation, the commissioning of the man and the woman to do his work in the world as his priest-kings, and their subsequent rebellion, which left them and God's creation under a curse of corruption and mortality.

The narrative of Scripture in Genesis then progresses from bad to worse and includes murder, a great flood, and eventually the scattering of the nations because of their presumptive attempt to break through—from the ground up—into the heavenly spheres. The peoples of the earth were then dispersed and placed under the control of various heavenly gods (Deut. 32:8—if we translate v. 8c as "according to the number of the people of Israel"), but—as other portions of Scripture show—those gods failed in their task of ruling the nations (Ps. 82). Thus, the nations were given over to false gods, but the Lord chose Israel for himself to be his instrument of reconciliation for the world (Deut. 32:9; cf. 4:19–20).

God's choice of Israel as his people and his national agent of restoration begins, after the scattering of the nations in Genesis 10–11, with the covenant with Abraham (Gen. 12, 13, 15). Through Abraham and his "seed," God promised to establish a nation that would bless (and thus be God's agent to regather) all the nations of the earth. The story of that "seed of Abraham" begins with Abraham's son Isaac, continues with Jacob and the nation of Israel itself, and ultimately culminates in Christ (Gal. 3:15–29).

The Lord confirmed the Abrahamic covenants at Mount Sinai after rescuing the children of Israel from Egyptian slavery, thus constituting them as his nation and people. There he provided for them, through the giving of the law, certain covenantal standards that allowed them to stay in fellowship with him. It was understood that they would sin, but the sacrificial system and the other laws of God given to them were his gracious way of providing for their forgiveness and thus the maintenance of his covenant relationship with them.

But there were no sacrifices or atoning provisions in the sacrificial system for idolatry. When the covenant was established on Mount Sinai, it was sealed with blessings and curses. If Israel remained faithful to the Lord as their God, they would survive and prosper.

But if Israel should go the way of the other nations and worship their gods, they would endure the stipulated curses, be sent into exile, and thus, as part of the Lord's punitive discipline, fall under the dominion of the false gods (Deut. 4:15–19; 28:64; 32:8; 2 Sam. 7:23; 2 Kings 17:7–41; Jer. 16:13; Acts 7:42; cf. Ex. 12:12; Num. 33:4). There was, however, a promise of God—even with the violation of the covenant through idolatry and subsequent exile— that the Lord in his faithfulness would remember his promises to Abraham. If the children of Israel would repent and return to the Lord, confessing truly, as the Shema mandated, that the Lord alone is their God, then he would establish a new covenant with them, restore them from captivity, and give them new hearts that would enable them to obey his will and his law (see Lev. 26:14–45; Deut. 30:1–20; Jer. 31:27–34; Ezek. 36:16–28).

Even at Mount Sinai, with the presence of the Lord powerfully evident through sight and sound (Ex. 19), the children of Israel engaged in a shocking incident of disobedience by building a golden calf, thus foreshadowing their forthcoming history of disobedience (Ex. 32). Their subsequent failure to trust the Lord to capture the land of Canaan brought on military disaster and a punitive wandering in the wilderness that itself anticipated their days of exile centuries later. The rest of the history of the Old Testament is the story of their disobedience and eventual succumbing to worship Canaanite gods, thus forsaking the Lord as their God. After repeated warnings by incursions and military defeat at the hands of their neighbors, Israel was finally sent into exile and handed over to the false gods. In 722 BC Syria scattered the northern kingdom, and in 587 Babylon overcame Judah, the southern kingdom.

The prophets had promised, however, that if Israel would repent and return to the Lord as their God, the Lord would remember his promises and restore his people. But if they continued to rebel, he would multiply the plagues and curses upon them. Eventually, after the seventy years of exile predicted by Jeremiah (25:11–12), the Lord led a small remnant of them out of exile and back to the promised land.

But even that small "tent peg" driven into the ground of the promised land was not the real restoration. As Ezra 9 and Nehemiah 9 both lament, even though some had geographically returned, they were still slaves in their own land. Indeed, had not Daniel been mysteriously told that the calamitous time of desolation and distress would be multiplied into seventy periods of seven (Dan. 9:2–4, 21–24; cf. Lev. 26:21–28)? And thus the Old Testament story, for all practical purposes, ends. It is replete with promises that one day the Lord God would come (Isa. 26:2; 31:4; 40:3–5, 9–11; 59:15–20; 66:15) and suddenly indwell his temple (Mal. 3:1–3), but by the close of the Old Testament narrative, while there remained a great longing for restoration, as witnessed by the Psalms and the Prophets, the day of restoration had not come. Though fervently longed for, Yahweh's kingdom, when he would return and reign over all the earth once the required punitive discipline was exhausted, was not yet.

The coming restoration would have many glorious features, according to the prophets. The Lord himself would return to Israel in the temple, and the people's multiplied punishment, their time under the covenanted curses, would be over and done. An anointed son of David would emerge, and the temple would be restored. The proper priesthood would function, and the Levitical offerings would resume. Elijah would come back, a prophet like Moses would arise, and the last great Jubilee would be announced. The land would be fertile and abundant, families would be large, and joy and flourishing would abound. Indeed, the Spirit of Yahweh would touch all of his people so that all would function as prophets, seeing visions, dreaming dreams, and prophesying in the name and power of the Lord. Hearts would be transformed to obey the law, and then, most glorious of all, the nations would rally to the banner of Jesse. The kings of the earth would flock to Jerusalem, and Yahweh the Lord would reign over all. The dead would be raised, the earth restored, and the glory of the Lord would again fill the temple. Indeed, his glory would cover the earth like the waters cover the sea (Isa. 11:9; Hab. 2:14).

But the Old Testament story declares none of these things as fulfilled. The day of restoration remained a fervent but unrealized hope.

By the time of the birth of Jesus, the expectation of a coming restoration had shown itself in various acts of messianic and militaristic zeal. Would-be messiahs had appeared as the heads of revolutionary movements, fanning the flames of hope for Israel, only to be squashed by Roman power.

But still the fervor remained, and it is, therefore, not hard to imagine the excitement that accompanied the appearance of the rugged, locust-eating, strangely garbed prophet in the wilderness, John the Baptist. He preached a baptism of repentance and called for the confession of sins. The fruit of repentance, just as the prophets had said, would have to take place if Israel was to be restored, so he summoned all who would hear—and there were many—to a ritual immersion in water as a sign of repentance, preparing for the coming day of the Lord, when Yahweh would reign and his kingdom be revealed. John, with prophetic insight, even indicated who the coming Messiah was, pointing to Jesus (John 1:29–36), who likewise preached the advent of the reign of God.

The ministry of Jesus, with his power to defeat the demons of the false gods and his miraculous wonders—including feeding thousands in the wilderness; healing lepers, the lame, and the blind; and even raising the dead—stirred the restoration fervor anew, and on occasion hundreds, if not thousands, followed him, believing that the Messiah had finally come.

But then the dark undercurrent of opposition that had hounded him all his ministry—resulting in conspiratorial rejection by some Jewish theologians, scribes, and political elites—resulted in a shocking plot, in collaboration with the Roman authorities, to put him to death. And instead of being stoned, he suffered the worst Roman means of execution, crucifixion. Beaten and then crucified as a seditious character, according to the Romans, and as one "leading the people astray" (John 7:12), according to the Jewish authorities, Jesus died, and the popular messianic movement he led appeared to be over.

But on the third day after his execution, he was seen alive again, first of all by certain women at his tomb and then by his closest disciples. On one occasion, more than five hundred saw him at the same time.

As Jesus repeatedly revealed himself to be alive, various details of his appearances showed him to possess a new kind of body that could never perish again. At the conclusion of a forty-day period of repeated appearances, he commissioned his disciples to announce to all the nations the news of his life, death, and resurrection in fulfillment of Scripture, thus setting in motion the proclamation of the good news of the restoration of all things.

Prior to his separation from his disciples, he confessed to having all authority in heaven and on earth; he then departed from his disciples in a dramatic ascension that not only separated him from them physically but also exalted him far above all rule, authority, and power, as well as every name for spiritual entities that is named

(Eph. 1:20–23). Lifted up on high, he was enthroned at the right hand of God the Father, where he will rule until he has put all his enemies under his feet, when the last enemy to be defeated is death (1 Cor. 15:25–26).

At his ascension and exaltation, there was the promise of his return (Acts 1:11), at which time the whole world will see him (Rev. 1:7; 19:11–16), the dead will be raised (1 Cor. 15:50–58; 1 Thess. 4:13–18), and God's long-awaited judgment—when he sets all things right in heaven and on earth, the great restoration itself—will be completed (Rom. 14:10; 2 Cor. 5:10; Phil. 3:20–21; 2 Thess. 1:5–10; Rev. 20:11–15).

The restoration has begun through the coming of Jesus, culminating in his death, burial, resurrection, and enthronement at the right hand of God. And it is displayed by the pouring out of his Spirit, empowering his followers to announce to the nations that the Jewish Messiah is the rightful King of all the earth, who now reigns and is completing the work of restoration. The powers of darkness and those of the world who listen to them continue their rebellion against the kingdom of God (Eph. 6:10–12), but God's kingdom will prevail.

The church is the assembly of those who believe the good news of Jesus crucified and risen, and offer God their worship through him. And because he is already enthroned as King over all the earth, his followers strive loyally to do his work. Evangelism is the task of announcing God's triumphant reign through Jesus and, thus, not only expanding the frontiers of his sovereignty but increasing the worldwide giving of thanks that God is rightly due (2 Cor. 4:15). Serving Christ in all the ways he has commanded us is our responsibility because he already reigns and at some point will exact a reckoning over the stewardship we have been given. He is the Lord and King whom heaven must receive until the time of the restoration of all things. But the day will come when God will send Jesus the Messiah, and the "times of refreshing"—days of both joy and distress, when all things are put right—will come to fulfillment (Acts 3:19–21).

Evangelism, by announcing the message of God's reign through Christ, aims to persuade all of us—men and women, young and old—to turn from the corrupt idols to serve the living and true God and to await his Son from heaven while doing God's work in the world resolutely and steadfastly, knowing that our work in the Lord is not in vain (1 Cor. 15:58). The word of God is preached, and the Spirit attends the sharing of the gospel (1 Cor. 2:1–5), and when, accompanied by faith in submission to Jesus as King, conversion takes place, the restoration is furthered. For this gospel of the kingdom must first be preached in all the world for a witness; then comes the end, when the return of Jesus will bring all things to fulfillment and God's purposes regarding restoration will be accomplished (Matt. 24:14). Until then, his people are called to be his agents, his messengers to tell the world that the kingdom of God has come in the person of Jesus Christ.

Questions for Reflection

1. What are the central aims of evangelism?

2. Evangelism has been described as "listening." Is that an adequate definition of evangelism? What role does listening play in evangelism? What else is necessary?

3. If evangelism involves sharing a message, what is it that the work of evangelism communicates?

4. Giving a personal testimony of your own conversion can be a helpful piece of communication when doing evangelism. What are the pluses and minuses of such an approach?

5. How is sharing the gospel connected to the long story of the Bible?

6. Are evangelism and discipleship distinguishable? What do they have in common?

7. Evangelism involves telling the good news of God as accomplished through Jesus. What role does God's coming judgment play in the work of evangelism?

Resources for Further Study

Blaising, Craig A. "Last Things." In *A Handbook of Theology*, edited by Daniel L. Akin, David S. Dockery, and Nathan A. Finn, 409–24. Brentwood, TN: B&H Academic, 2023.

Dockery, David S. "Theology for Evangelism and Missions." In *A Handbook of Theology*, edited by Daniel L. Akin, David S. Dockery, and Nathan A. Finn, 509–20. Brentwood, TN: B&H Academic, 2023.

Duvall, J. Scott. "Biblical Theology." In *A Handbook of Theology*, edited by Daniel L. Akin, David S. Dockery, and Nathan A. Finn, 109–20. Brentwood, TN: B&H Academic, 2023.

Green, Michael. *Evangelism in the Early Church*. Rev. ed. Grand Rapids, MI: Eerdmans, 2004.

Knox, D. B. "Evangelist." In *New Bible Dictionary*, edited by J. D. Douglas, N. Hillyer, F. F. Bruce, D. Guthrie, A. R. Millard, J. I. Packer, and D. J. Wiseman. 2nd ed., 356–57. Wheaton, IL: Tyndale, 1982.

Sloan, Robert B. "The Gospel." In *A Handbook of Theology*, edited by Daniel L. Akin, David S. Dockery, and Nathan A. Finn, 427–34. Brentwood, TN: B&H Academic, 2023.

Wright, Christopher J. H. *The Mission of God: Unlocking the Bible's Grand Narrative*. Downers Grove, IL: InterVarsity Press, 2006.

Wright, N. T. *Simply Good News: Why the Gospel Is News and What Makes It Good*. New York: HarperCollins, 2015.

3

The Nature of Scripture and Our Evangelism

Christopher W. Morgan

FROM THE BEGINNING of the church, believers in Christ have insisted on the necessity of the sharing the gospel. This is evident in the ministries of the apostles Peter and Paul. On the day of Pentecost Peter proclaimed, "Let all the house of Israel therefore know for certain that God has made him both Lord and Christ, this Jesus whom you crucified" (Acts 2:36). When Peter's hearers, convicted by the Spirit, cried out for relief, he called them to turn to Christ and receive forgiveness (Acts 2:38).

It is the same for Paul, who on his first missionary journey declared:

God has brought to Israel a Savior, Jesus, as he promised. (Acts 13:23)

We bring you the good news that what God promised to the fathers, this he has fulfilled to us their children by raising Jesus. (Acts 13:32–33)

Let it be known to you therefore, brothers, that through this man forgiveness of sins is proclaimed to you. (Acts 13:38)

On what authority did the apostle to the Jews and the apostle to the Gentiles preach the gospel? In his Pentecost sermon, Peter cited the Old Testament numerous times, and in the two verses preceding Acts 2:36, he quotes Psalm 110:1. Paul did much the same. In the verse preceding Acts 13:23, he cited Psalm 89:20 and 1 Samuel 13:14. In Acts 13:33–35, he cited Psalm 2:7; Isaiah 55:3 LXX; and Psalm 16:10 LXX. The apostles appealed to biblical authority when they preached the gospel, and we should do the same.

Further, the nature and authority of Scripture shape how we understand and share the gospel. So, after we briefly unpack some preliminary definitions, we will look at key characteristics of Scripture and how they shape our understanding of and approach to evangelism:

- The nature of Scripture reminds us: God is the evangelist.
- The inspiration of Scripture guides us: God speaks through his word.
- The inerrancy of Scripture assures us: the gospel is true.
- The necessity of Scripture emboldens us: God uses his word to save.
- The clarity of Scripture encourages us: the gospel is understandable.

- The sufficiency of Scripture focuses us: the gospel is our message.
- The particularity of Scripture calls us: Christ is the only way.

Preliminary Definitions

1. *Biblical authority.* By authority I mean the right to teach truth and command obedience. By biblical authority I mean the authority of Holy Scripture, the sixty-six books of the written word of God. Being uniquely inspired by God, the Bible is our ultimate authority for theology and ethics, that is, for faith and practice. We are influenced by other authorities, including our reason, the tradition from which we come, and even our experience. But none of these is our supreme authority, for as Christians we submit to biblical authority—that is, God's authority—for what we believe and how we live.

2. *The gospel.* The gospel is the good news of salvation in Christ. The gospel centers on the person and work of Jesus. Who Jesus is enables what he has done. The gospel also calls for a response to him. Paul summarizes the gospel as the message of Christ's death for sinners, his resurrection, and the necessity of people's believing in him for salvation. The gospel thus includes the work of Christ, the need for faith, and God's promises of forgiveness and eternal life (1 Cor. 15:1–4).

3. *Evangelism.* Evangelism is the church's task of spreading the evangel or gospel to the world. Just before his ascension, Jesus instructed his disciples to do the work of evangelism: "You will receive power when the Holy Spirit has come upon you, and you will be my witnesses in Jerusalem and in all Judea and Samaria, and to the end of the earth" (Acts 1:8). As ambassadors for Christ, we are not intruders but sent; we are not inventors

but heralds; and we are not detached but personal witnesses (2 Cor. 5:14–21).[1]

The Nature of Scripture Reminds Us: God Is the Evangelist

Before we explore various aspects of scriptural authority that impact gospel witness, it is good to step back and view the nature of Scripture through its overarching narrative. That story centers on a person, predicted in the Old Testament and appearing in the New Testament—Jesus Christ. Because it centers on the person and work of Jesus, God's revelation in Scripture is fundamentally evangelistic. It culminates in the gospel, evangelism's content. It sets the gospel in its historical and theological contexts. Jesus preached the good news of the kingdom of God, and in the Great Commission Jesus commanded his disciples to do the same. Acts records the apostles' beginning to fulfill that command, and their epistles explain and apply the gospel to churches and individuals.

Scripture tells the truth, and as it does so, it commands evangelism. The Bible as revelation gives us the way of evangelism. And along that way, it also gives God's people the authority for evangelism, authority that resides in God and his word. But behind our evangelism, we see that the whole story of the Bible is about God saving a people for their good and his glory. So God is the evangelist behind our evangelism!

The Inspiration of Scripture Guides Us: God Speaks through His Word

As evangelicals, we hold to an *organic* view of the inspiration of Scripture in which both God and human writers were active.

---

1 For more on these and related terms, see Christopher W. Morgan and Robert A. Peterson, *A Concise Dictionary of Theological Terms* (Nashville: B&H, 2020).

This view is also called *concursus*, highlighting the coauthorship of Scripture, and *confluence*, a picture of two rivers merging to become one. Scripture finds its source in God, who spoke forth his word. It is a mistake, therefore, to speak of the inspiration of the biblical authors but not their words: "All Scripture is breathed out by God" (2 Tim. 3:16). God was Scripture's ultimate author; this is where we begin in our doctrine of Scripture. God directly inspired the autographs, the original texts of the biblical books. In his providence, he also preserved Scripture through the centuries so that our Bibles today are dependable copies.

God worked through human authors to produce his word: "Men spoke from God as they were carried along by the Holy Spirit" (2 Pet. 1:21). The Spirit guided the writers so that they spoke his words. Scripture is thus human and divine. Its divinity is evident in the Bible's uniqueness of content and powerful effects. Its humanity too is evident, for the biblical writers exhibited diverse vocabularies, styles, and emphases. They did research (Luke 1:1–4) and wrote of their experiences (2 Pet. 1:16–18; 1 John 1:1–3). God graciously used humans to communicate his truth to humans.

The writers did not get their ideas from their own minds, apart from God. God used their minds, but they were not the ultimate source of their information, because "no prophecy of Scripture came from someone's own interpretation" (2 Pet. 1:20). Rather, God worked providentially in giving Scripture. He used Moses's Egyptian education and life experiences as he wrote the Pentateuch; he used Paul's rabbinical training and missionary endeavors as he penned his epistles. But God did more than exercise his providence in preparing the writers. He not only guided them; he spoke through them. He worked in a special way when the writers wrote. Our inability to understand fully how God did this should not surprise us, for interaction between God and humans often exceeds our ability to comprehend.

We believe that Jesus Christ is fully divine and fully human, although we cannot fathom the depths of the incarnation. Likewise, we believe that the Bible is God's word without fully understanding God's mode of inspiration. We know that God worked through humans to produce his word. The result is "the sacred writings" (2 Tim. 3:15), the "oracles of God" (1 Pet. 4:11). The ways that God used to do this remain largely hidden, for Scripture stresses the results of inspiration but says little about the means God employed.

We affirm the plenary and verbal inspiration of Scripture on the basis of 2 Timothy 3:16: "*All Scripture* is breathed out by God." *Plenary* means that the whole of Scripture is God's word, including its various parts. *Verbal* means that the words and not just the ideas are God's truth. Inspiration pertains to the writers and the writings, the process and the product of Scripture. Jesus and his apostles affirm verbal inspiration. When Jesus quoted David's words in Psalm 110:1, he said,

David himself, in the Holy Spirit, declared,

"The Lord said to my Lord,
'Sit at my right hand
    until I put your enemies under your feet.'" (Mark 12:36)

David spoke by the Holy Spirit, as did all the biblical authors. David really spoke, and when he wrote psalms, God also spoke through him.

Because Holy Scripture is God's inspired word, its source and authority are crucial for evangelism. *God* spoke through the biblical authors and continues to speak through Scripture as his people faithfully share his word today. Although we cannot say it in the primary sense that Paul and his fellow apostles did, in a derivative sense it is true of God's witnesses today: "Therefore, we are ambassadors for Christ, God making his appeal through us" (2 Cor. 5:20). God himself makes the offer of salvation through believers like us when we present the good news to lost persons.

Furthermore, because inspiration means that "*men* spoke from God as they were carried along by the Holy Spirit" (2 Pet. 1:21), Scripture is God's word in human words. In Scripture God through humans addresses their fellow humans. The humanity of Scripture thus assures us of God's care and desire to communicate his gospel to unsaved persons that they might be saved. Indeed, "God . . . through Christ reconciled us to himself and gave us the ministry of reconciliation" (2 Cor. 5:18). Therefore, we can say with Paul, "We implore you on behalf of Christ, be reconciled to God" (2 Cor. 5:20).

In sum, the inspiration of Scripture clarifies how God speaks through his word, and this guides us. We are not intruding into people's lives with our agenda and our ideas. The gospel is not primarily our message. It is God's, and we are his messengers.

The Inerrancy of Scripture Assures Us: The Gospel Is True

As we just observed, Scripture is inspired by God and consequently is his holy word, as Jesus himself regarded it.[2] That means many things, including that it is inerrant; it speaks the truth in all that it affirms. As D. A. Carson summarizes, inspiration is the "supernatural work of God's Holy Spirit upon the human authors of Scripture such that what they wrote was precisely what God intended them to

---

2 See John Wenham, *Christ and the Bible*, 3rd ed. (Eugene, OR: Wipf and Stock, 2009).

write in order to communicate his truth." He adds, "The definition speaks both of God's action, by his Spirit, in the human author and of the nature of the resulting text."[3]

The claim that Scripture is fully truthful demands clarification. Inerrancy is ascribed to the autographs (the original texts), not to copies of the Bible. We value textual criticism because textual variants are undergirded by an inerrant original text. We value the human characteristics of Scripture. The biblical authors wrote in ordinary form and style, and as such their writings lacked certain things not required for inerrancy.[4] Inerrancy does not imply Scripture's adherence to modern rules of grammar or spelling. Inerrancy is compatible with various literary genres and figurative language. Inerrancy does not require historical precision or completeness. Inerrancy does not imply the technical language of modern science. Inerrancy does not mean that the Gospel writers give the exact words of Jesus, only the exact voice; they give the correct sense of Jesus's words but do not always quote in contemporary forms. This is the same for the speeches and sermons in Acts.

The truthfulness (inerrancy) of the Bible gives us confidence in evangelism. Inspired by God, Scripture is truthful and authoritative over what we believe and how we live (theology and ethics). Giving Scripture and illuminating it in the lives of believers are two ways that God acts in the world to accomplish his mission (2 Tim. 3:15–4:5) so that people glorify him through believing in Jesus, the Savior of the world (John 20:28–31; 1 John 5:12–13). God does so by speaking the truth.

3 D. A. Carson, "Approaching the Bible," in *Collected Writings on Scripture*, comp. Andrew David Naselli (Wheaton, IL: Crossway, 2010), 31.

4 For more, see Christopher W. Morgan, *Christian Theology: The Biblical Story and Our Faith* (Nashville: B&H, 2020), 76–79. See also the Chicago Statement on Biblical Inerrancy, 1978, https://library.dts.edu/Pages/TL/Special/ICBI_1.pdf.

As we share the gospel with those who do not yet know Jesus, we can know that the message is true. It is not the latest fad, self-help technique, or repackaged ideas from an ancient guru. The truthful Scripture recounts the true story of Jesus, and we can retell it over and over with full confidence.

The Necessity of Scripture Emboldens Us: God Uses His Word to Save

Our need for God's written word is an aspect of our need for his special revelation. For two main reasons, we absolutely need both. First, God is infinite, and we are finite. God, the infinite Creator, stands over against us, his finite creatures. By infinite I mean that God is limitless, bound only by his attributes. Scripture points to his measureless power and understanding:

> Great is our Lord, and abundant in power;
>   his understanding is beyond measure. (Ps. 147:5)

Isaiah says:

> The LORD is the everlasting God,
>   the Creator of the ends of the earth.
> He does not faint or grow weary;
>   his understanding is unsearchable. (Isa. 40:28)

This infinite God is great beyond comparison.

> For thus says the One who is high and lifted up,
>   who inhabits eternity, whose name is Holy:
> "I dwell in the high and holy place." (Isa. 57:15)

This can be said of him alone; no one is like him. Compared with this great, infinite God, we are very limited. We would never learn about God or come to know him apart from his taking the initiative. Thankfully, our great God graciously reveals himself to us, his finite creatures, in his written word and Son.

The second reason we need special revelation in the form of Scripture is that God is holy, and we are not. In addition to being limited by finitude, we are crippled spiritually by our sin. Angels proclaimed,

Holy, holy, holy is the LORD of hosts;
the whole earth is full of his glory! (Isa. 6:3)

To this Isaiah cried: "Woe is me! For I am lost; for I am a man of unclean lips, and I dwell in the midst of a people of unclean lips; for my eyes have seen the King, the LORD of hosts!" (Isa. 6:5). We have not seen the Lord as the prophet did, but his words and a glimpse at our lives convince us that our lips, hands, and feet are unclean.

Although we learn certain things about God from the light of nature, including his existence (Ps. 19:1–3) and his "eternal power and divine nature" (Rom. 1:20), we do not learn the gospel from creation. Instead, "faith comes from hearing, and hearing through the word of Christ" (Rom. 10:17). We need the word of God to be saved.

As finite and wayward sinners, blinded by our sin, we need deliverance but cannot deliver ourselves. Mercifully, "God so loved the world, that he gave his only Son, that whoever believes in him should not perish but have eternal life" (John 3:16). We gain eternal life by trusting Christ as Lord and Savior as he is offered to us in the gospel. And the only place to learn of that gospel is in the Holy Scriptures. As we grasp these interrelated truths, our boldness will grow to resemble that of Peter and John. Peter declared. "There is salvation in no one else, for there is no other name under heaven given among men by which we must be saved" (Acts 4:12; see 4:5–32).

The Clarity of Scripture Encourages Us: The Gospel Is Understandable

The clarity or perspicuity of the Bible is one of its traditional attributes, along with necessity, sufficiency, and authority. The clarity of Scripture means that the Holy Spirit enables people to comprehend its basic message. By words and example, parents must teach God's word to their offspring (Deut. 6:1–9). This implies that children are capable of understanding the Scriptures. To be sure, God uses his word to educate the inexperienced in the things of God.

> The testimony of the LORD is sure,
> making wise the simple. (Ps. 19:7)

Evidence of the clarity of Scripture includes the fact that God expects believers to understand it. In obedience to the Jews' request when they returned from Babylonian captivity to Jerusalem, Ezra the scribe brought God's Law before the people, including adults "and all who could understand what they heard" (Neh. 8:2). Again, this implies that the word is clear enough for children to comprehend. Ezra read all morning, "and the ears of all the people were attentive to the Book of the Law" (Neh. 8:3). Levites helped, for they "read from the book, from the Law of God, clearly, and they gave the sense, so that the people understood the reading" (Neh. 8:8). Support for the clarity of Scripture is found in the people's response to Ezra's reading, for they "worshiped the LORD with their faces to the ground" (Neh. 8:6), and "all the people wept as they heard the words of the Law" (Neh. 8:9). Ezra told them that this day was to be a day not of mourning but of celebration. Consequently, "All the people went their way to eat and drink . . . and to make great rejoicing, because they had understood the words that were declared to them" (Neh. 8:12). God who made Adam and Eve in his image, able to speak and understand language, gave his word with clarity so humans could understand it, believe, and grow in their faith.

Scripture's clarity also appears in the New Testament. Believers sent Paul and Silas to Berea to save them from jealous Jews rioting in Thessalonica (Acts 17:10). They went to the synagogue and proclaimed Christ. Luke applauds the Bereans: "Now these Jews were more noble than those in Thessalonica; they received the word with all eagerness, examining the Scriptures daily to see if these things were so" (Acts 17:11). The Bereans diligently studied the Old Testament to test Paul's message. Biblical clarity underlines this episode. The Bereans understood Old Testament messianic predictions, compared them with Paul's message, and found his words to be true. God worked through his word, for "many of them therefore believed" (Acts 17:12).

Scripture's clarity does not suggest that all things in it are equally comprehensible (cf. Rom. 11:33–36; 2 Pet. 3:16). Rather, it means that the gospel and basic scriptural teachings are comprehensible. The same Holy Spirit who inspired the word enables us to embrace its message. Christians read the Bible with God's aid, for illumination is the Spirit's work to enable them to understand, believe, and apply Scripture.

Scriptural clarity impacts evangelism, for Scripture communicates the gospel in culturally clear ways. The Bible both commands evangelism and clarifies our message. Biblical clarity enables us to know God, ourselves, the lost, and the gospel. Indeed, the clarity of the word of God encourages us: as we share the good news, we know that God gave his word to reach the lost and for that reason made it as understandable as he did powerful.

The Sufficiency of Scripture Focuses Us: The Gospel Is Our Message

When we say that Scripture is sufficient, we mean that the word of God supplies all that believers need for eternal life and holiness. As Peter said, God's "divine power has granted to us all things that pertain to life and godliness" (2 Pet. 1:3). God uses his word to grant eternal life to all believers and to promote their godliness. Scripture is sufficient to save and sanctify Christians.

Scripture is also sufficient to guide us, as both Testaments attest. With Old Testament saints we confess to God,

> Your word is a lamp to my feet
>   and a light to my path. (Ps. 119:105)

And with Peter we acknowledge, "We have the prophetic word more fully confirmed, to which you will do well to pay attention as to a lamp shining in a dark place, until the day dawns and the morning star rises in your hearts" (2 Pet. 1:19). Although the world is engulfed in darkness, devoid of a saving knowledge of God, God gave us his word to guide us until Jesus's return. How do we account for Scripture's sufficiency? Peter answers that when they wrote Scripture, "men spoke from God as they were carried along by the Holy Spirit" (2 Pet. 1:21).

When we affirm Scripture's sufficiency, we do not exclude other authorities from our work. The study of the Bible and its teachings involves human reason, experience, and tradition. But here is the key: we acknowledge that we use several authorities, but we deliberately and consistently subordinate them to Holy Scripture, which alone is sufficient. This is what the Reformers meant by *sola Scriptura*. Scripture alone is our highest authority, sitting in judgment on our thinking, life experience, and theological tradition. And *sola Scriptura* means that the Bible alone is our sufficient authority.

Jesus supports the sufficiency of Scripture in his parable of the rich man and Lazarus. An unsaved rich man dies and goes to hell. In torment, he asks Abraham (who stands for God in the parable) to send someone from the dead to warn his unsaved brothers. Abraham replies, "They have Moses and the Prophets; let them hear them" (Luke 16:29). In response, the rich man says no to God! "No, father Abraham, but if someone goes to them from the dead, they will repent" (Luke 16:30). Abraham's reply undergirds Scripture's sufficiency: "If they do not hear Moses and the Prophets, neither will they be convinced if someone should rise from the dead" (Luke 16:31).

We can learn much about evangelistic methods and technique from good books on the subject, gain experience witnessing, and follow good examples, but pride of place belongs to Scripture. God's word is necessary and sufficient for us to know people's need for the gospel, an accurate understanding of Christ and what he did to save us, what lies in store for believers and unbelievers, the Great Commission, and much more.

We should learn all we can from a variety of sound sources, but we should also stay focused on the gospel message. God the evangelist revealed himself in Scripture and clearly communicates his good news through Scripture: God made us; we rebelled; Jesus lived, died, and rose for us; and we can know him through faith. Paul wonderfully summarizes:

"Everyone who calls on the name of the Lord will be saved." How then will they call on him in whom they have not believed? And how are they to believe in him of whom they have never heard? And how are they to hear without someone preaching? And how are they to preach unless they are sent? As it is written, "How beautiful are the feet of those who preach the good news!" But they have not all obeyed the gospel. For Isaiah says, "Lord, who has believed what he has heard from us?" So faith comes by hearing, and hearing through the word of Christ. (Rom. 10:13–17)

Why are we saved? Here Paul stacks several interrelated answers. Because we trusted in Christ, and because someone shared the gospel with us, and because churches sent out witnesses, and because Christ died and rose for us. In other words, Christ is the only way. He is the only Savior, and faith in him is the only way to receive the benefits of his saving work.

The Particularity of Scripture Calls Us: Christ Is the Only Way

As I was finishing this essay, I encountered again a common bumper sticker: "Co-exist." Twenty-first-century philosophical pluralism meets the American bumper sticker. Drivers with this bumper sticker may simply be urging people from all ethnicities, cultures, nations, and religions to relate to one another with civility, kindness, and love. If so, as Christians we heartily agree. After all, we follow a Lord who taught and demonstrated love for the outsider, even enemies. But my suspicion is that many affix the "co-exist" bumper sticker on their cars to preach the gospel of philosophical pluralism (which rejects any notion that a particular ideological or religious claim is intrinsically superior to another).

In such a context, it is hard for many to hear the words of Jesus when he boldly asserts: "I am the way, and the truth, and the life. No one comes to the Father except through me" (John 14:6). Many are appalled at Jesus's declaration that he is the only way. But those who accept biblical authority find his assertion to stand firmly in the broader biblical story and worldview. In several overarching ways, the particularity of Scripture underlines the particularity of Christ.[5]

First, Christ as the only way is grounded on the biblical teaching that there is only one God, the triune God of the Old and New Testaments, who is Creator, Lord, and Judge. If there were more than one God, there would likely be more than one way to the gods. But the particularity of God points to the particularity of how God is known, followed, or embraced.

Second, Christ as the only way is grounded on the biblical teaching that the one true and living God has communicated with humanity. He has communicated truly, even if not exhaustively; and humans can understand, even if partially, who he is and how to relate to him. If truth were merely subjective and not rooted in God or eternal realities, then claims to exclusivity would be a stretch. But if the one true God graciously reveals himself to us, then seeking to understand and follow that revelation is not arrogance but humility and faithfulness.

Third, that all of us are sinners, fall short of God's glory, and stand guilty before God also shapes how we view this issue. The

---

5 For more, see *Faith Comes by Hearing: A Response to Inclusivism*, ed. Christopher W. Morgan and Robert A. Peterson (Downers Grove, IL: InterVarsity Press, 2008); also, see D. A. Carson, *The Gagging of God: Christianity Confronts Pluralism* (Grand Rapids, MI: Zondervan, 1996).

biblical teaching on this is unambiguous: we cannot be our own way to salvation by being sincere, good, nice, or pleasant.

Fourth, that Christ is the only way flows from the biblical teaching that God is the covenant Lord who determines if and how he will relate to humans. He freely and graciously sets the terms of the covenant; he freely and graciously sets forth if and how he will forgive, justify, adopt, reconcile, redeem, or save sinners. Thus, not only can we humans not be our own way to salvation; we also cannot devise our own way.

Fifth, and very much related to the last point, Christ as the only way rests on the important truth that Jesus alone is able to serve as the Savior. As the fully divine and fully human mediator, he is uniquely able to save. As the sinless and obedient second Adam, he is uniquely able to represent us. As the obedient Son and the substitutionary sacrifice for our sins, he is uniquely able to forgive us. As the resurrected one, the firstborn from the dead, he is uniquely able to give us new life. Thus, Christ is the only way because of his uniqueness. Many people died on crosses, but none but Jesus could save.

Sixth, Christ is the only way in the sense of being the unique Savior. And Christ is the only way in the sense that faith in Christ is the only way to receive the benefits of his saving work. The benefits of Christ's saving work do not flow to us through our good works, religious scrupulousness, or relational sincerity. Salvation comes only through Christ's work, by grace through faith. That Jesus is the object of our faith highlights his uniqueness, especially his deity (ultimate faith in someone other than God is idolatry) and utter worthiness. Indeed, that Christ saves through faith underlines both his sufficiency and our dependency, and both glorifies him as the giver and benefits us as the recipients.

Seventh, that Christ is the only way to salvation also assumes that those who do not have faith in Jesus are on another path, and not the one to salvation. All of us have sinned and fallen short of God's glory. And all are justly condemned and punished by God. Thankfully, many embrace Jesus as Lord and will receive the blessings he has gained for them. Sadly, many do not and will not follow Jesus; and Jesus will consign them to hell, a place of punishment, banishment, and eternal death.

Maybe framing these items in reverse would be helpful: if other ways of salvation existed apart from Christ, what could they be or where could they come from?

- Could other gods bring such salvation, however the gods and salvation might be defined?
- Could we humans become good, religious, sincere, and so forth, and thereby become our own way?
- Could we devise our own way?
- Could there be something or someone else besides Jesus who could accomplish this for us? Could something other than faith in Jesus be the means to receive the benefits of his saving work?
- Could people who do not follow Jesus somehow receive salvation anyway?
- Or could the question be dismissed out of hand due to a lack of any real, objective truth?

Interestingly, the biblical portrait disrupts each of these possibilities and asserts that Christ is the only way. It does so by pointing to the oneness of God, the reality of objective truth, the universality of human sin, the nature of God's covenant lordship, the uniqueness of Christ, the necessity of faith in Christ, and the horror of hell.

As the only way to salvation, Jesus is worthy of our love, trust, and worship. He is also worthy of our gospel witness. May our recognition of Jesus's uniqueness burden our hearts for the lost and stir our feet to take the good news about him to our universities and through them to the nations.

Questions for Reflection

1. Why is it important to have clear definitions of biblical authority, the gospel, and evangelism?

2. How does understanding the inspiration of Scripture affect our view of its authority?

3. Why is it important to believe in Scripture's authority in sharing the gospel?

4. How would evangelism be hindered if Scripture were not clear?

5. How does Scripture's sufficiency give us confidence in evangelism?

6. Why is Christ the only way? And how do we communicate this in our pluralistic context?

Resources for Further Study

Carson, D. A. "Approaching the Bible." In *Collected Writings on Scripture*, compiled by Andrew David Naselli, 19–53. Wheaton, IL: Crossway, 2010.

Carson, D. A. *The Enduring Authority of the Christian Scriptures*. 2 vols. Grand Rapids, MI: Eerdmans, 2016.

Dockery, David S., and Malcolm B. Yarnell III. *Special Revelation and Scripture*. Theology for the People of God. Nashville: B&H, 2024.

Morgan, Christopher W. *Christian Theology: The Biblical Story and Our Faith*. Nashville: B&H, 2020.

Morgan, Christopher W., and Robert A. Peterson. *A Concise Dictionary of Theological Terms*. Nashville: B&H, 2020.

Morgan, Christopher W., and Robert A. Peterson, ed. *Faith Comes by Hearing: A Response to Inclusivism*. Downers Grove, IL: InterVarsity Press, 2008.

Packer, J. I. *Fundamentalism and the Word of God*. Grand Rapids, MI: Eerdmans, 1958.

Wenham, John. *Christ and the Bible*, 3rd ed. Eugene, OR: Wipf and Stock, 2009.

4

A Theology of Evangelism

Biblical and Theological Foundations

Erik Thoennes

EVANGELISM IS AT THE HEART of the Christian life because it is at the heart of Christian theology. The main message of the Bible is that the one true God displays his glory primarily by fulfilling his covenant promises and commands through the glorious person and atoning work of Christ, thereby redeeming and restoring his fallen creation. This redeeming work of God is also the main message of the gospel Christians are called to preach to all the nations. Among the many things Christians are called to be, and do, there is nothing more central than knowing Christ and proclaiming him the Savior of the world. That is why the "Prince of Preachers," Charles Spurgeon, would say: "I would rather be the means of saving a soul from death than be the greatest orator on earth. I would rather bring the poorest woman in the world to the feet of Jesus than I would be made Archbishop of Canterbury."[1]

When we understand the extravagantly loving heart of God for lost sinners, and the Spirit shows us that we were truly lost sinners before God saved us, we then love because he first loved us and we are compelled to preach Christ to those who are perishing. Redeemed sinners long for others to know Christ. So we pray, preach, and live so that we may be part of God's redeeming work in the world.

The first college course I taught, in 1995, was called Theology of Evangelism. I was privileged to co-teach it with a great man of God, Robert Coleman. I taught it by myself several times after that and then began teaching courses in the theology department, and have continued to teach systematic theology courses since then. I came to realize that there is not much difference between my Theology of Evangelism course content and that of my courses in theology. This is because all evangelism should be grounded in robust, biblically based theology, and all biblically based theology should lead us to greater evangelistic zeal and commitment to the fulfillment of the Great Commission. Good theology should have a God-glorifying, Great Commission telos. This is true of all Christian higher education. No matter the discipline, a biblically informed worldview will never lose sight of the glory of God worshiped among the nations. The linear progression of history, where everyone who has ever lived will stand before his or her Creator and the Judge of all the earth and give an account, should inform and permeate our understanding of every area of knowledge. The rest of this chapter will focus on a few key theological truths that serve as the biblical foundation for evangelism.

1   C. H. Spurgeon, *The Autobiography of Charles H. Spurgeon* (Chicago: Revell, 1899), 233.

The Glory and Holiness of the Creator

The Westminster Shorter Catechism, at its first question, teaches that the main reason for our existence is "to glorify God and enjoy him." Everything God accomplishes for us in Christ is for that purpose. All the benefits that are ours through faith in Jesus lead us to this supreme goal of communion with and enjoyment of our Creator.[2] If we don't have a radical God-centeredness to our understanding of the gospel, we will miss the whole point. Beholding the beauty and glory of God is the beginning, middle, and end of understanding life as he intends. The character of God is the anchor to all other knowledge. When we understand him rightly, we understand everything else rightly. This is why Stephen Charnock says:

> According to the weakness of our knowledge is the slightness of all our acts toward God. When we do not understand his justice, we shall presume upon him. When we are ignorant of his glorious majesty, we shall be rude with him. Unless we understand his holiness, we shall leap from sin to duty; if we are ignorant of his excellency, we shall lack humility before him. If we have not a sense of his omniscience, we shall be careless in his presence, full of roving thoughts, guilty of vain babbling as if he lacked information. . . . It is impossible to honour God as we ought, unless we know him as he is.[3]

Honoring, worshiping, enjoying, and truly knowing God orient our lives in daily and eternally fulfilling ways. The reason

---

2 See John Piper, *God Is the Gospel: Meditations on God's Love as the Gift of Himself* (Wheaton, IL: Crossway, 2005).

3 Stephen Charnock, *The Complete Works of Stephen Charnock*, 5 vols. (1864–1866; repr., Edinburgh: James Nichol, 1964), 4:27.

God is the center of everything is obvious but still needs to be stated. He is perfectly holy, which means that he is distinct from everything else and perfectly righteous. There's nothing lacking in him and nothing good that we would ever want him to be that he is not. God is the source of all that is good, righteous, holy, and beautiful. When we understand reality correctly, God is our greatest treasure and without competitors for our devotion, love, and delight. When someone sees God for who he truly is, he or she is never the same. The onlooker says with Isaiah, "Woe is me! For I am lost" (Isa. 6:5). I think a good way to define a Christian is someone who has beheld the glory of God in the face of Christ and is never the same. We don't really know who we are until we know who he is. We can't be aware of our sin by comparing ourselves to other fallen humans; we must see ourselves in light of the one holy God.

Gospel preaching seeks to enable people to know the God who created them for himself. We preach God's word, praying that people will come to a life-changing understanding of the being and nature of God. This is God's greatest purpose for his creation. God was the first evangelist. He came to Adam and Eve after they had rebelled against him to seek and save his wayward creatures (Gen. 3:8–11). He met with them in their rebellion and asked spiritually diagnostic questions to awaken in them an awareness of their new sinful condition. And even in his righteous judgment, he covered their nakedness with the first sacrifice and put a redemptive plan in place. There was mercy in his judgment and the promise that, in the seed of the woman, the Savior would reverse the curse and one day triumph (Gen. 3:15). God deserves our worship, and we answer to him for the way we live our lives because he is our Creator.

His all-knowing, divine intention in making us gives our lives meaning. He is the source of our lives and the one who defines the purpose of our lives.

We preach the gospel because we love people, but even more foundational, we preach the gospel so God receives the glory due his name. As John Piper has said, "Missions exists because worship doesn't."[4] Love for people *and* for God motivates us to preach the gospel. We long for people to find life in Christ, but we long most of all for God to be glorified the way he deserves to be through the lives of the people we love.

The Dignity and Sinfulness of Humanity

Knowing God as our glorious Creator is where the Bible begins and where I believe an understanding of the gospel needs to begin as well. When we know that God is the one who made us in his image, to glorify him in relationship with him, then we are able to understand ourselves correctly. Being made in God's image means that every human being is worthy of profound dignity, value, and respect. We are created to reflect who God is through worshipful obedience and devotion. When we understand God's purpose for us in this way, we are then able to assess whether we are fulfilling his intention for us.

The Bible teaches that none of us naturally worships, obeys, or loves God. It tells us that "all have sinned and fall short of the glory of God, and [all who have faith] are justified by his grace as a gift, through the redemption that is in Christ Jesus, whom God put forward as a propitiation [a sacrifice that satisfies God's wrath] by his blood, to be received by faith" (Rom. 3:23–25).

---

4 John Piper, *Let the Nations Be Glad! The Supremacy of God in Missions* (Grand Rapids, MI: Baker, 2010), 35.

We are all born with sinful natures that we inherit from a spiritual lineage that goes all the way back to Adam and Eve when they fell in the garden. Of all the things Christians believe, the easiest one to prove is that we have a profound sin problem. One minute spent reading the news or honestly looking in our naturally selfish hearts will prove that. And God's response to our rebellion against him is exactly what it should be, righteous wrath and judgment.

> For the wrath of God is revealed from heaven against all ungodliness and unrighteousness of men, who by their unrighteousness suppress the truth. For what can be known about God is plain to them, because God has shown it to them. For his invisible attributes, namely, his eternal power and divine nature, have been clearly perceived, ever since the creation of the world, in the things that have been made. So they are without excuse. For although they knew God, they did not honor him as God or give thanks to him, but they became futile in their thinking, and their foolish hearts were darkened. Claiming to be wise, they became fools, and exchanged the glory of the immortal God for images resembling mortal man and birds and animals and creeping things.
>
> Therefore God gave them up in the lusts of their hearts to impurity, to the dishonoring of their bodies among themselves, because they exchanged the truth about God for a lie and worshiped and served the creature rather than the Creator, who is blessed forever! Amen. (Rom. 1:18–25)

You will never read a better description of the core problem of humanity than those words in Romans 1. When we worship the creation rather than the Creator, everything in creation becomes disordered and corrupt, and by nature we incur the wrath of God. Our fundamental problem is a worship problem. Everyone worships; we give our ultimate devotion to something or someone. We must consider whether that object of worship is worthy of it.

So how do we solve our sin problem? The answer the Bible gives is clear. Only God can (Eph. 2:1–3). His mercy and grace alone, through the work of Christ, provide the solution we all need. And this solution comes only through Christ.

The Supremacy, Sufficiency, and Exclusivity of Christ

For Jesus to solve our broken relationship with God, he had to be able to truly represent us as a human being *and* have the ability that God alone has to overcome sin and death. Because Jesus is fully God and fully man with divine and human natures in one person, he is able to accomplish our salvation. He is the only way, because of who he is and what he has done. Jesus is not merely a teacher, wise man, sage, or righteous man, He is the Savior of the world. Jesus is "the image of the invisible God" (Col. 1:15), "in the form of God" (Phil. 2:5–11), and in him "the whole fullness of deity dwells bodily" (Col. 2:9). The disciples came to understand that their friend and teacher from Nazareth was none other than the eternal Son of God. This was Jesus's understanding of himself as well. As John Stott wrote:

> So close was his connection with God that [Jesus] equated a man's attitude to himself with the man's attitude to God. Thus to know him was to know God (John 8:19; 14:7). To see him was to see God (John 12:45; 14:9). To believe in him was to believe

in God (John 12:44; 14:1). To receive him was to receive God (Mark 9:37). To hate him was to hate God (John 15:23). And to honor him was to honor God (John 5:23).[5]

As God the Son, Jesus reveals God to us. He is the definitive revelation of God. "No one has ever seen God; the only God, who is at the Father's side, he has made him known" (John 1:18). He is also the only way to have a restored relationship with God. "Jesus said to him [Thomas]: 'I am the way, and the truth, and the life. No one comes to the Father except through me" (John 14:6). This is not a narrow-minded, arrogant statement for a Christian to make, because it comes from the word of God. Further, it makes sense because if Jesus is God, it follows that the revelation and redemption he provides is the only way. God would have to become something other than God if you could know him through means other than himself. The religious pluralist who says that there are many ways to God sounds tolerant. However, pluralism actually rules out the possibility of a personal, self-revealing God as the major monotheistic religions of the world believe. Jesus is God, and, therefore, through him alone can God be known and through him alone can we be saved from our sin.

Jesus is also fully human, with nothing lacking in his true humanity, which enables him to represent us and provide the righteousness and sacrifice we need to bring us back to God. "Therefore he [Jesus] *had* to be made like his brothers in every respect, so that he might become a merciful and faithful high priest in the service of God, *to make propitiation for the sins of the people*" (Heb. 2:17).

5 John Stott, *Basic Christianity*, 50th anniversary ed. (Grand Rapids, MI: Eerdmans, 2008), 26.

When we go to him, we find nothing lacking and everything we need for life and godliness (2 Pet. 1:2–3). When we behold the glory of God in the face of Christ, we have no option but to fall at his feet in utter dependence and unfettered worship (Luke 7:36–50). This also means that we cannot but tell others "what we have seen and heard" (Acts 4:20).

The Glory of the Gospel

The work of Christ is sufficient because of who he is as the God-man. "For there is one God, and there is one mediator between God and men, the man Christ Jesus" (1 Tim. 2:5). The glory of the gospel is that Jesus takes our place and leaves nothing for us to earn, prove, demonstrate, or contribute. When we realize the sinfulness of our sin, we completely despair of any shred of self-righteousness and say with the hymnwriter,

> Nothing in my hands I bring,
> Simply to Thy cross I cling;
> Naked, come to Thee for dress,
> Helpless, look to Thee for grace:
> Foul, I to the fountain fly,
> Wash me, Savior, or I die.[6]

The atoning work of Christ is central to God's work in the history of salvation (Mark 10:45; 1 Cor. 2:2; 15:3). Because Jesus's righteous life and atoning death on behalf of sinners is the only way for fallen humanity to be restored into right relationship with a holy God, nothing else can be made right until we are reconciled

---

6 August M. Toplady, "Rock of Ages," hymn 315 in *Praise: Our Songs and Hymns*, comp. John W. Peterson and ed. Norman Johnson (Grand Rapids, MI: Zondervan, 1979).

to God. Believers need to be salt and light and be a blessing to the world, but preaching Christ as the only way to be reconciled to God must remain the core of our efforts in ministry.

Jesus gave his life of his own initiative and courageous love.

> I am the good shepherd. The good shepherd lays down his life for the sheep. . . . For this reason the Father loves me, because I lay down my life that I may take it up again. No one takes it from me, but I lay it down of my own accord. I have authority to lay it down, and I have authority to take it up again. This charge I have received from my Father. (John 10:11, 17–18; cf. Gal. 2:20)

The Father's initiative was behind Jesus's atoning work as well. "He who did not spare his own Son but gave him up for us all, how will he not also with him graciously give us all things?" (Rom. 8:32; cf. Isa. 53:6, 10; John 3:16). The fact that we are saved by grace means that we do not deserve salvation. God was under no compulsion to save us. He saves us out of his merciful, sovereign freedom. The grace of God is truly amazing!

All the stages of Christ's work are necessary for him to win our salvation. His preincarnate glory, incarnation, perfectly righteous life, sacrificial death, resurrection, ascension, heavenly session, second coming, and eternal glory accomplish exactly what we need. He fulfills the offices of prophet, priest, and king to perfection so that, in him, we have the true words of God, a perfect mediator, and a reigning King.

Through repentance and faith in Christ, we find forgiveness and life eternal. He is the only way of salvation, as Peter said to the religious leaders in the face of intense persecution: "There is salvation in no one else, for there is no other name under heaven given among men by which we must be saved" (Acts 4:12). That phrase "under heaven" is glorious. God is no respecter of persons and will save people from every tongue, tribe, and nation on earth. "Under heaven" means the whole world. He's the Savior of not just the Jew but also the Gentile, Westerner, Easterner, White, Black, Asian, Latino, American, Iraqi, Russian, rich, poor, and former Buddhist, Hindu, Muslim, and atheist. He is the Savior of convicts, CEOs, wise persons, simple folk, males and females. He is the Savior of the world.

We must aim to see him the way he sees himself. We must see that when we call upon Jesus for salvation, he saves to the uttermost (Heb. 7:25). He is our Savior, who makes our blind eyes see, our lame legs walk, and all our sins go away forever. He gives abundant and eternal life if you bow your knee to him. All we should ever hear from God is "depart from me," but because of Jesus's blood and righteousness, the author of life says to all who repent and believe, "Come to me, all you who labor, and are heavy laden, and I will give you rest" (Matt. 11:28).

The Power and Presence of the Holy Spirit

The primary role of the Holy Spirit is to exalt Christ, and Christ brings us to the Father (John 14:26; 15:26). The Father sends the Son, the Son accomplishes the will of the Father, and the Spirit draws us to Christ. This Trinitarian economy accomplishes gospel realities so that the better we understand the Trinity, the better we will understand the gospel. The Spirit illumines the centrality of Christ in the Bible (Luke 24:27, 44–48); empowers gospel preaching, which proclaims Christ (Acts 1:8); and brings new life in Christ (John 3:5–8). The Spirit then transforms the believer into the image of Christ (Rom. 8:29; 1 John 3:2). He takes the objective truth of the gospel and makes it objectively transformative in the life of the believer.

We humans become like what we adore. The Spirit works to foster adoration of Christ so that people will become like him. Thus, sanctification flows from adoration, and both are accomplished by the Spirit in the believer's life. When the Holy Spirit gives us eyes to see and teachable hearts, we understand that only the one true God is worthy of our undivided devotion and that we will have abundant and eternal life only if the author of life changes us from the inside out. Because salvation is work, evangelism must be grounded in prayer and Spirit dependence. He is the one who transforms hearts, so as we seek to be used by him to bring people to Christ, we must seek to be Spirit-filled and empowered ambassadors.

Church as Prophetic Ambassadors

"Jesus is looking for disciples filled with the Spirit of Christ, burning with Calvary love, who set their course by the priorities of heaven."[7] These words from Robert Coleman, a man who has faithfully given his life to serving Christ and proclaiming the gospel, point us to the throne of God, where one day every knee will bow and every tongue confess Jesus as Lord and join with the angelic hosts saying,

> Holy, holy, holy, is the Lord God Almighty,
>   who was and is and is to come! (Rev. 4:8)

A Great Commission perspective provides the powerfully reorienting perspective of heavenly worship that invades all areas of life.

---

7 Robert Coleman, "Educating Fools for Christ" (unpublished manuscript).

When we behold the glory of God in Jesus, life in a fallen world is reframed by the sure hope that God will one day receive the honor due his name from all creation. This is the foundational biblical motive for all who follow in the footsteps of the Savior. True evangelism and discipleship always have the worship of Christ among the nations as their ultimate goal. Glorifying God and helping others to do the same is the greatest delight of the evangelist. Evangelism and discipleship put us on the path that leads to eternal heavenly worship at the feet of the Lamb who was slain for our redemption. The job of the church is to display eschatological realities now—to give a trailer of coming attractions to the world. We are the ones who see Jesus for who he is before judgment day and are pleading with the world to flee the wrath to come.

God's people represent their King when they work to see kingdom realities spread in the world. When they seek social justice—fighting to relieve the plight of the poor, disenfranchised, or unborn—they are working to spread the values of their King. When they work hard and live as good citizens, they are salt and light in a dark world, ultimately serving the interest of their King. One day, when Christ makes all things new, those who are his subjects will reign with their King.

The saying is trustworthy, for:

> If we have died with him, we will also live with him;
> if we endure, we will also reign with him. (2 Tim. 2:11–12;
> see Rev. 5:9–10)

Exaltation of Christ fuels our proclamation of Christ. He is preeminent in all things. As Robert Clouse says:

Our Lord Jesus Christ is the sun about which the whole mission
of the church revolves. Public worship is the encounter of the
risen Redeemer with his people; evangelism is calling men to
the Savior; publishing the law of God is proclaiming his lordship; Christian nurture is feeding his lambs and disciplining his
flock; ministering to the needs of men is continuing the work
of the Great Physician. In the whole work and witness of the
church, Jesus Christ is to be recognized as Lord, the only King
in Zion. Her business is to obey his will, to proclaim not her
own, but his reign.[8]

Since Jesus Christ is the true and perfect prophet, when we want
to know the truth about the things that matter most—like the
meaning of life, right and wrong, and the truth about who God
is and who we are—we go to Jesus. And when we find his truth
through the Bible, we are then able to see the Great Commission
take effect in our own lives as we become disciples who are baptized
and obey everything he has commanded. Paul certainly saw his own
ministry as speaking for God: "Therefore, we are ambassadors for
Christ, God making his appeal through us. We implore you on
behalf of Christ, be reconciled to God" (2 Cor. 5:20).

It is vital that, as God's representatives, we submit to the authority of his word in our lives and in the message we proclaim. When
Jesus gives the Great Commission, he grounds it in the authority
he has and sends us in that authority (Matt. 28:18). That authority
is given to him by the Father and to us through his word. We go
in the authority of Christ himself because we go with his word,
which teaches us who he is and what it means to obey everything

8 R. G. Clouse, "Church," in *Evangelical Dictionary of Theology*, 2nd ed., ed. Walter A. Elwell
(Grand Rapids, MI: Baker, 2001), 248.

he has commanded. The gospel we preach is based not on our mere opinions or feelings but on God's inspired, inerrant, sufficient word. This is why John Stott said:

> Without the Bible world evangelization would be not only impossible but actually inconceivable. It is the Bible that lays upon us the responsibility to evangelize the world, gives us a gospel to proclaim, tells us how to proclaim it, and promises us that it is God's power for salvation to every believer.[9]

The Bible brings authority and clarity to gospel proclamation, and as the Spirit works, it is the source of God's transforming and saving work.

It is vital to contextualize the gospel for whatever culture we are in. However, while we seek to translate the gospel in intelligible ways, we should never transform it into something other than what it is. It is tempting to make the gospel fit into contemporary sensibilities when certain aspects of it are seen as offensive. But any distortion of the true gospel amounts to idolatry and spiritual adultery. Throughout the Bible God is jealous whenever he or his word is distorted or dishonored. Jealousy is the reason God gives for the second commandment:

> You shall have no other gods before me.
>
> You shall not make for yourself a carved image, or any likeness of anything that is in heaven above, or that is in the earth beneath, or that is in the water under the earth. You shall not

---

9 John Stott, "The Bible in World Evangelization," in *Perspectives on the World Christian Movement: A Reader*, ed. Ralph D. Winter and Steven C. Hawthorne (Pasadena, CA: William Carey Library, 1981), 9.

bow down to them or serve them, *for I the LORD your God am a jealous God,* visiting the iniquity of the fathers on the children to the third and the fourth generation of those who hate me. (Ex. 20:3–5; cf. Ezek. 39:25; Acts 12:23)

Godly people should be jealous for God's honor as well. We should earnestly desire that God be recognized for who he is and that he be responded to accordingly. When we proclaim Christ and his ways, we take God's side and represent his case before others. Many of the great leaders of God's people have exhibited this fervor. It is a primary basis for the courage, boldness, and integrity that characterize the great leaders of God's people. Moses, Phinehas, David, Elijah, Jesus, and Paul are clear examples of men motivated by godly jealousy. A godly perspective causes one to act on God's behalf to bring about covenant fidelity and obedience in the lives of his people.

The jealousy of God has serious implications for evangelism, Christian higher education, and evangelical scholarship in general. The jealous Christian educator will react with godly jealousy whenever the clear teaching of Scripture is violated. We must be charitable, humble, and willing to listen well, but we will nevertheless find it impossible to remain ambivalent when God's word is ignored or distorted. Godly jealousy demands that Christian scholars abhor and denounce false teaching, even if they will be considered divisive, intolerant, and uncharitable. Leaders of the church must hold to the exclusive truth claims that we have treasured throughout the centuries. God, whose name is Jealous, demands that his people remain devoted to the true gospel without compromise. Boldness was one of the main traits of the disciples (Acts 4:13). In this age of the radical affirmation of subjective personal opinions and feelings, Christian educators must have biblical backbone, like the martyred missionary Jim Elliot, who said, "Meekness must be had for contact with men, but brass, outspoken boldness is required to take part in the comradeship of the Cross."[10]

As Christ's ambassadors, we are to have a strong prophetic voice into the world, no matter how much opposition that may bring. God also intends to use the church in a priestly role to usher people into his presence. When we are faithful to ministry and education that is grounded in the Bible and empowered by the Spirit, we function as priests representing our great high priest. Because of Christ's work, all of God's people are viewed as priests with priestly access into his presence and with the privilege of representing people before God (1 Pet. 2:9; Rev. 5:9–10). Prayer, preaching, gospel proclamation, and taking initiative in personal, spiritual ministry are all ways in which God's people can encourage others to seek and know God, and can thereby fulfill their call to represent Christ as a kingdom of priests.

Questions for Reflection

1. What is the main message of the Bible?

2. How would you define the gospel or explain the main reason Jesus came?

3. Why do you think so many people today are offended by the wrath and judgment of God? How would you reconcile God's love and wrath so they are compatible?

10 Elizabeth Elliot, *Shadow of the Almighty: The Life and Testament of Jim Elliot* (London: Hodder and Stoughton, 1958), 80.

4. Do you believe you need forgiveness? If so, what would it take for you to be forgiven by God?

5. Do you believe that Jesus is both God and man and is the only way to a restored relationship with God? What do you think Jesus meant when he said: "I am the way, and the truth, and the life. No one comes to the Father except through me" (John 14:6)?

6. Have you ever trusted Christ for the forgiveness of your sins? If not, what is preventing you from doing that today?

Resources for Further Study

Beougher, Timothy K. *Invitation to Evangelism: Sharing the Gospel with Compassion and Conviction.* Grand Rapids, MI: Kregel, 2021.

Boice, James M., and Philip G. Ryken. *The Doctrines of Grace: Rediscovering the Evangelical Gospel.* Wheaton, IL: Crossway, 2009.

Chantry, Walter. *Today's Gospel: Authentic or Synthetic?* Carlisle, PA: Banner of Truth, 1970.

Coleman, Robert E. *The Master Plan of Evangelism.* 2nd ed. Grand Rapids, MI: Revell, 2010.

Kistler, Don, ed. *Feed My Sheep: A Passionate Plea for Preaching.* 2nd ed. Lake Mary, FL: Reformation Trust, 2008.

Morris, Leon. *The Apostolic Preaching of the Cross.* 3rd ed. Grand Rapids, MI: Eerdmans, 1965.

Murray, John. *Redemption Accomplished and Applied.* Grand Rapids, MI: Eerdmans, 1955.

Packer, J. I. *Evangelism and the Sovereignty of God.* Rev. ed. Downers Grove, IL: InterVarsity Press, 2012.

Payne, Tony. *Learn the Gospel: Deepen Your Understanding of and Trust in the Message of Jesus*. Youngstown, OH: Matthias Media, 2022.

Piper, John. *God Is the Gospel: Meditations on God's Love as the Gift of Himself*. Wheaton, IL: Crossway, 2005.

Root, Jerry, and Stan Guthrie. *The Sacrament of Evangelism*. Chicago: Moody Press, 2011.

5

Evangelism in the History
of the Church

David Gustafson

JESUS INTENDED Christian evangelism to be a defining mark of
the church ever since he told his disciples: "The Messiah will suffer
and rise from the dead the third day, and repentance for forgiveness
of sins will be proclaimed in his name to all the nations, beginning
at Jerusalem. You are witnesses of these things" (Luke 24:46–48).[1]

Christian evangelism began in the first century with the birth
announcement of Jesus of Nazareth. At the beginning of Luke's
Gospel, the Virgin Mary testified to the great things God did for
her and his people (1:49–55). Then an angel of the Lord announced

---

1   Portions of this chapter have been adapted from David M. Gustafson, *Gospel Witness through
    the Ages: A History of Evangelism* (Grand Rapids, MI: Eerdmans, 2022). Used with permission.
    Scripture quotations in this chapter are from Christian Standard Bible®, copyright © 2017
    by Holman Bible Publishers. Used by permission. Christian Standard Bible® and CSB® are
    federally registered trademarks of Holman Bible Publishers.

to shepherds in the field near Bethlehem: "Don't be afraid, for look, I proclaim to you *good news* of great joy that will be for all the people. Today in the city of David a Savior was born for you, who is the Messiah, the Lord" (2:10–11).

The announcement that Jesus is the Messiah continued with the public ministry of John the Baptist. When he saw Jesus walking toward him, he said, "Look, the Lamb of God, who takes away the sin of the world!" (John 1:29). On the next day, after Andrew heard John the Baptist say, "Look, the Lamb of God!" he followed after Jesus. Then, he found his brother Simon Peter and said, "We have found the Messiah" (John 1:36, 41).

When Jesus was crucified on the hill outside Jerusalem, a Roman centurion exclaimed, "Truly this man was the Son of God!" (Matt. 27:54). After Jesus was buried in the tomb of Joseph of Arimathea, an angel appeared to the women who had come there to visit on the third day. The angel said to them: "Why are you looking for the living among the dead? . . . He is not here, but he has risen!" (Luke 24:5–6). The women, including Mary Magdalene, Joanna, and Mary, the mother of James, left the tomb and "reported all these things to the Eleven [apostles] and to all the rest" (Luke 24:9).

From the beginning of the church, Christians shared the gospel in their places of influence. They testified of Christ, whether to family, friends, or strangers (Acts 1:8; 2:42–47; 8:4–6). The story of Philip and the Ethiopian—an official in charge of all the treasury of the "queen of the Ethiopians" (Acts 8:27)—illustrates the early practice of evangelism. Prompted by the Spirit, Philip approached the Ethiopian official, who was sitting in a chariot reading the words of Isaiah 53:7–8. Philip asked him, "Do you understand what you are reading?" "How can I," the official replied, "unless someone guides me?" The man then invited

Philip to sit with him and asked, "Who is the prophet saying this about—himself or someone else?" Then "Philip proceeded to tell him the good news about Jesus, beginning with that Scripture" (Acts 8:30–31, 34–35).

The book of Acts says that the apostles taught and proclaimed "the good news that Jesus is the Messiah" in "the temple, and in various homes" (5:42). Decades later, the apostle Paul said to elders of the church at Ephesus: "You know that I did not hesitate to proclaim anything to you that was profitable and to teach you publicly and from house to house. I testified to both Jews and Greeks about repentance toward God and faith in our Lord Jesus" (Acts 20:20–21).

A home provided an informal and hospitable environment that made it a natural setting for evangelism.[2] A household (*oikos*) in the ancient Near East consisted of relatives and close friends.[3] In addition to family, the *oikos* included household slaves and freedmen. When someone turned to God in repentance and placed his or her faith in the Lord Jesus, whether a father, wife, child, slave, or household worker, that person shared the gospel along relational lines from household to household—along social networks.

Despite religious pluralism within the Roman Empire that included many gods, the gospel made exclusive claims on those who believed in and followed Jesus. Christians belonged exclusively to Christ as Lord (*kyrios*).[4] The gospel summoned a response that was costly; Jesus said, "Whoever does not bear his own cross and come after me cannot be my disciple" (Luke 14:27). This became an

---

2 Michael Green, *Evangelism in the Early Church* (Grand Rapids, MI: Eerdmans, 1970), 207–8, 322.

3 Roger W. Gehring, *House Church and Mission: The Importance of Household Structures in Early Christianity* (Peabody, MA: Hendrickson, 2004), 8.

4 Green, *Evangelism in the Early Church*, 42–43.

increasing challenge for Christians socially, especially with the rise of the imperial cult, which required all Roman citizens to worship the emperor as a god.

With this exclusive commitment to Jesus Christ, Christians (while viewed initially as part of Judaism) soon became a threat to the Roman Empire. The Roman authorities were tolerant of all religions as long as adherents paid token allegiance to the emperor as a deity. The unwillingness of Christians to compromise the claims of the evangel, however, led them to face persecution and death.

Persecution at the hands of the Roman government took place in AD 64 under Emperor Nero, who unfairly accused Christians of setting a fire in the capital city of Rome. The historian Tacitus wrote: "Before killing the Christians, Nero used them to amuse the people. Some were dressed in furs, to be killed by the dogs. Others were crucified. Still others were set on fire early in the night, so that they might illumine it."[5] According to tradition, at this time the apostle Paul was beheaded and the apostle Peter was crucified upside down.[6]

In the year 91, Emperor Domitian expanded persecution against Christians beyond the city of Rome. Under his reign, the apostle John was exiled to the island of Patmos. In 112, Emperor Trajan set a policy that remained in force for more than a century. In a letter sent to the governor of Bithynia, he wrote: "Christians are not to be sought out. Do not go looking for them. But if someone denounces someone as a Christian, then bring that person in and

5 Justo L. González, *The Story of Christianity: The Early Church to the Present Day*, 2 vols. (Peabody, MA: Prince, 2010), 1:35.
6 Bernard Green, *Christianity in Ancient Rome: The First Three Centuries* (New York: T&T Clark, 2010), 46–48.

question them. And if that person refuses to recant and worship our gods, then they should be punished."[7]

Martyrdom, as a form of Christian witness, started with John the Baptist, Stephen, and Jesus's apostles. For this reason, the Greek word for *witness* (*martyria*) took on the meaning of *martyr*, because Christians witnessed to the gospel by their deaths.

Polycarp of Smyrna (69–156) was a disciple of the apostle John. Another disciple of John, named Ignatius, exhorted Polycarp to press on in the faith despite threats of persecution.[8] Heeding this advice, when Polycarp was required to offer sacrifices to the Roman imperial cult, he refused. He was brought before the Roman authorities and given the chance to recant and worship the imperial gods. An eyewitness wrote that the Roman governor asked Polycarp to identify himself, saying whether or not he was indeed Polycarp, the overseer of the church of Smyrna. After hearing that he was, the governor within a public arena tried to dissuade Polycarp, saying, "Have respect for your old age; swear by the fortune of Caesar; repent and say, 'Down with the Atheists!' "[9] The Roman polytheists viewed Christians as atheists because they did not worship the Roman gods.[10] Despite the governor's appeal, Polycarp turned the gesture in the opposite direction and waived his hand in the air, pointing toward the pagans in the arena and said, "Down with the Atheists!" because *they* did not believe in Jesus, the Son

---

7 Epistles 10.96, in Everett Ferguson, *Church History*, vol. 1, *From Christ to Pre-Reformation* (Grand Rapids, MI: Zondervan, 2005), 65.

8 Ignatius, *Epistle to Polycarp* 1 (Syrian), in *The Ante-Nicene Fathers: The Writings of the Fathers Down to A.D. 325*, ed. Alexander Roberts, James Donaldson, and A. C. Coxe, 10 vols. (Grand Rapids, MI: Eerdmans, 1978–1979), 1:99; hereafter *ANF*.

9 *Martyrdom of Polycarp* 9 (*ANF* 1:41).

10 Ferguson states, "An atheist was someone who did not observe the traditional religious practices, regardless of the faith he professed." Ferguson, *Church History*, 1:67.

of God. Again, the governor urged Polycarp, saying, "Renounce Christ and I will set you free." However, Polycarp responded by saying, "Eighty and six years have I served Him, and He never did me any wrong; how then can I blaspheme my King and my Saviour?"[11] With his refusal to recant, Polycarp was tied to the stake and burned publicly.

Persecution against Christians such as this was sporadic and local rather than empire-wide and directed mostly toward leaders or highly visible Christians. Seasons of relative peace came, however, which gave Christians opportunities to evangelize more freely. But when they faced the choice of denying Christ, they refused and received torture or death, simply stating, "I am a Christian."[12]

The Christian theologian Tertullian (ca. 160–235) wrote a work titled *Apology* to the provincial governor as a defense (*apologia* in Latin) of the Christian faith, and as a plea for religious toleration of Christians. He argued that the Roman government should protect its Christian citizens, not persecute them. He claimed that putting Christians to death did not dissuade them; it only gave them additional opportunities to spread their beliefs. He wrote, "The more often we are mown down by you, the more in number we grow; the blood of Christians is seed."[13] His observation was that persecution of Christians gave them a public witness that did not destroy the Christian movement but expanded it.[14]

In 313, Emperor Constantine met with Emperor Licinius, and together they agreed to end the persecution of Christians by signing the Edict of Milan. With this act, Christianity received legal status

11 *Martyrdom of Polycarp* 9 (*ANF* 1:41).
12 Milton L. Rudnick, *Speaking the Gospel through the Ages: A History of Evangelism* (St. Louis, MO: Concordia, 1984), 35.
13 Tertullian, *Apology* 50 (*ANF* 3:55).
14 Tertullian, *To Scapula* 5.4 (*ANF* 3:108).

from the Roman state.[15] In the following years, the church received favorable treatment by Constantine as he enacted legislation to benefit the church.[16] This introduced a new era—the Constantinian era—and the advance of Christendom, which brought significant changes to the relationship between the church and the state.

While Christians benefited from their new status, the change brought negative consequences too. As Christianity became favored by the Roman government, vast numbers of people streamed into Christian congregations. As could be expected, many people identified as Christians because of the civil, social, and political advantages, and *not* for spiritual or biblical reasons.

Thus, evangelism became not merely a matter of preaching the gospel to those ignorant of the gospel but also a matter of convincing nominal ("in name only") Christians that they needed to be converted to Christ. Often the latter proved more difficult than the former, especially as Christianity became increasingly identified with the Roman Empire, Christian rulers, and majority Roman culture.

The reaction of some true Christians to the influx of nominal Christians into the church was to flee from the church and Roman society altogether. As they saw insincerity, lack of spiritual devotion, and in some cases blatant worldliness in their local congregations, they concluded that the church was becoming apostate.[17] Although they were critical of what they observed and did not want to break fellowship with the broader church, they did so for

---

15 Henry Bettenson and Chris Maunder, eds., *Documents of the Christian Church* (New York: Oxford University Press, 2011), 17.

16 Eusebius, *The Life of Constantine* 1.28–38, in *A Select Library of the Nicene and Post-Nicene Fathers of the Christian Church*, ed. Philip Schaff, vol. 1 (Grand Rapids, MI: Eerdmans, 1979), 494–95.

17 John Mark Terry, *Evangelism: A Concise History* (Nashville: B&H, 2014), 41.

a life of prayer, meditation, and self-denial. They took up the life of "white martyrdom," as monks who lived in isolation, in contrast to "red martyrdom," which referred to persecution and bloodshed earlier at the hands of the state.[18]

For centuries Christians had emphasized helping the poor and destitute among them. The teachings of Jesus and the apostles had led them to build refuges for the lame, construct dispensaries for the poor, and rescue orphans from drowning and exposure. Christian charity was symbolized in sculptures of *Caritas* (Latin, signifying an *agapē* love) that portrayed a Christian wet nurse who cared for orphaned and abandoned children by nursing them to health.[19]

Such Christian acts of *agapē* love toward one's neighbors continued in the fourth century. This included communities of monks who practiced holistic evangelism by proclaiming the good news and caring for others. With this outward direction, the monastic movement became the leading evangelistic force of the church for several centuries.

Basil of Caesarea (330–379) led in this outward development. He established a monastery in Pontus of Cappadocia, modern-day Turkey, which included a complex of buildings known as a *basileas* that contained a home for the poor, a hospital for the sick, a workshop where the poor developed job skills, a storehouse with food supplies, and a hospitality house for travelers.[20] He challenged the

18 Timothy George, "The Challenge of Evangelism in the History of the Church," in *Evangelism in the Twenty-First Century*, ed. Thom Rainer (Wheaton, IL: Shaw, 1989), 12; Rodney Stark, *The Rise of Christianity: How the Obscure, Marginal Jesus Movement Became the Dominant Religious Force in the Western World in a Few Centuries* (New York: HarperOne, 1997), 183.

19 Alvin J. Schmidt, *How Christianity Changed the World* (Grand Rapids, MI: Zondervan, 2009), 126–28.

20 Edward L. Smither, *Mission in the Early Church: Themes and Reflections* (Eugene, OR: Cascade, 2014), 132–39.

rich to remember their obligation to give to the poor and thereby show gratitude to God for all he had given to them.

While Basil was burdened for the poor and sick, he regarded preaching the gospel as the central task of his ministry.[21] He was well known as a defender of sound doctrine and preached twice a day, expounding the gospel as summarized in the Nicene Creed. Moreover, he knew the importance of instructing Christians in evangelism and sending them to reach pagans (from the Latin *paganus*, meaning "unlearned") with the good news.[22] The gospel witness that Basil and the Christian community practiced did not go unnoticed. Emperor Julian, known as "the apostate" owing to his pagan beliefs, testified grudgingly to the charitable acts of Christians.[23]

While Augustine of Hippo (354–430) is considered by many to be the greatest theological influence of the church since the apostle Paul, he also proclaimed the word of God and cared for the poor. In addition to Augustine's biography, titled *Confessions*, which told of his journey to faith in Jesus, he wrote *On Catechizing Seekers* as a guide for Christians to instruct inquirers in the Christian faith.[24] He wrote this disciple-making manual for a "brother" named Deogratias, a deacon in Carthage. This book describes ways to instruct and encourage a seeker along the way to conversion.

In addition to apologetic and disciple-making resources, other writings were employed for evangelism. After her conversion to Christ, the fourth-century poet Faltonia Betitia Proba arranged a type of Latin poem called a *cento* in which she drew from poems

---

21 Smither, *Mission in the Early Church*, 139.
22 Basil, *Morals* 70.5, 11–12, 24, 27, 31, 33, in *Saint Basil: Ascetical Works*, trans. M. Monica Wagner (Washington DC: Catholic University of America, 1962), 166–82.
23 Roland H. Bainton, *Christianity* (Boston: Houghton Mifflin, 2000), 100.
24 Ferguson, *Church History*, 1:271–72.

of Virgil, such as the *Aeneid* and the *Georgics*, to tell the gospel.[25] Her work titled *Concerning the Glory of Christ* (*De laudibus Christi*) selectively used excerpts from Virgil's writings that began with creation in the Bible's narrative. She described the events of the fall of Eve based on the story of Dido from book 4 of Virgil's *Aeneid*.[26] She employed lines from book 2 of the same work, specifically about Laocoön's death, in order to describe the words of the serpent in the garden of Eden. In telling about the birth and crucifixion of Jesus, she selected lines that related originally to Dido and Venus. The final section of her poem focused on Christ's ascension and return in glory. Copies of Proba's *cento* were produced as plentifully as the writings of Augustine.

The work of evangelism continued by lay Christians, as well as those in monastic communities. Preaching, hospitality, teaching, and charity proved instrumental in converting numbers of people to Christian faith.[27]

Ansgar of Bremen (801–865)—known as the "apostle to the north"—was commissioned with a band of missionaries northward to found a monastery in Westphalia in Germany. Seven years later, he was appointed as a missionary to Scandinavia. As he traveled north, he knew full well that he was risking his life in an attempt to evangelize the barbaric Norsemen, also known as Vikings.[28]

Despite the perceived dangers, Ansgar and his assistant, Witmar, were received and saw Norsemen convert to faith and baptized

25 Josephine Balmer, *Classical Women Poets* (Newcastle, UK: Bloodaxe, 1996), 111.
26 Sigrid Schottenius Cullhed, *Proba the Prophet: The Christian Virgilian Cento of Faltonia Betitia Proba* (Leiden: Brill, 2015), 142, 145.
27 Rudnick, *Speaking the Gospel*, 44.
28 Ruth Tucker, *Parade of Faith: A Biographical History of the Christian Church* (Grand Rapids, MI: Zondervan, 2015), 149.

at the marketplace of Birka near modern-day Stockholm. Ansgar also began a hospital and worked to ransom captives, including Christians, who had been brought to Sweden from raids and held by Viking chieftains.[29] Ansgar himself purchased Scandinavian slave boys in Sweden, taking them with him to Bremen in order to educate them so that they would return to Sweden as redeemed missionaries, able to speak the Nordic language.[30]

Beginning with Ansgar, missionary monks in northern Europe used the *Biblia pauperum* to communicate the gospel. A *Biblia pauperum*, or in English, "Paupers' Bible," was a collection of graphic illustrations of the life of Christ and corresponding images of prophetic types from the Old Testament.[31] Books of this kind were designed for common people, especially useful for the vast numbers of illiterate people in northern Europe during the medieval period.[32] The illustrations were a simple and effective means to communicate the story of Jesus's life, death, and resurrection, and how Jesus fulfilled Old Testament prophecies and biblical images that pointed to him.

Each illustration had three scriptural images.[33] The central figure came from an event in the Gospels and was accompanied by two images of Old Testament events that prefigured the central one. For example, the crucifixion of Jesus was associated with Abraham's

29 Anders Winroth, *The Age of the Vikings* (Princeton, NJ: Princeton University Press, 2014), 201.
30 Winroth, *Age of the Vikings*, 110, 203.
31 Pia Bengtsson Melin and Christina Sandquist Öberg, *Biblia pauperum (de fattigas bibel): En rik inspirationskälla för senmedeltiden* (Stockholm: Kungl. Vitterhets historie och antikvitets akademien, 2013), 12–14.
32 Anke te Heesen, "Within the Tradition of the Biblical Image," in *The World in a Box: The Story of an Eighteenth-Century Picture Encyclopedia*, trans. Ann H. Hentschel (Chicago: University of Chicago Press, 2002), 65.
33 See *Biblia pauperum*, Library of Congress, https://www.loc.gov/item/49038879/.

call to sacrifice Isaac (Gen. 22) and Moses's lifting up the serpent on a pole in the wilderness (Num. 21:4–9).[34] Ansgar's method of evangelism had a formative impact so that those who heard the message could easily repeat it to others, making this method of evangelism highly transferable.

Also, during the medieval period, the Waldenses were an emerging free-church movement in Europe known for their bold witness to the gospel and life of discipleship. They were led by Waldo, or Vaudès, (ca. 1140–ca. 1218) of Lyons, France, who began his career as a wealthy merchant from the burgeoning class of medieval merchants. In 1175, he had a profound conversion and committed his life to proclaiming the gospel while living in apostolic poverty, following Jesus's words literally: "If you want to be perfect . . . go, sell your belongings and give to the poor, and you will have treasure in heaven. Then come, follow me" (Matt. 19:21).[35]

Because Waldo was not able to read the Latin Bible, he asked two priests to translate the New Testament into French, which formed the basis for his evangelism. He memorized large portions of the Scriptures. With the Scriptures in hand and mind, he preached sermons that included long scriptural quotations from memory. Soon he attracted a band of followers who called themselves the "poor men of Lyons."[36] They imitated his apostolic poverty and devoted themselves to memorizing the Scriptures and to lay preaching.

---

34 Jean Philibert Berjeau, *Biblia pauperum: Reproduced in Facsimile, from One of the Copies in the British Museum; with an Historical and Bibliographical Introduction* (London: John Russell Smith, 1859), 33.

35 Scott W. Sunquist, *Understanding Christian Mission: Participation in Suffering and Glory* (Grand Rapids, MI: Baker Academic, 2017), 39.

36 David S. Schaff, *History of the Christian Church*, vol. 5, *The Middle Ages from Gregory VII, 1049, to Boniface VIII, 1294* (Grand Rapids, MI: Eerdmans, 1981), 162.

The evangelistic strategy of Waldo and his followers was generally to go out two by two among the people.[37] At first, they presented their message on street corners and in the market squares. Their evangelism was both simple and personal. They preached the gospel, believing that their authority came not from the pope of the Roman Church but from Jesus Christ. Waldo said, "God commanded the apostles to 'preach the Gospel to all creation' " (Mark 16:15), and "we must obey God rather than men!" (Acts 5:29).[38] With these words from the lips of the apostle Peter, Waldo became known as "Peter" Waldo. Several Waldenses traveled to isolated valleys in the Alps, and from there they preached the gospel in Italy, Germany, Bohemia, Spain, and the Netherlands.[39]

A wave of persecution came against the Waldenses in 1211, in which some were burned at the stake in France and in Germany, and others were martyred in northern Italy.[40] They carried out activities nevertheless, holding "conventicles" (from the Latin *conventiculum*, meaning "small gathering") in homes for worship, witness, and the care of souls.[41] In subsequent decades—and even centuries—the Waldenses existed as a free-church movement, independent or "free" of the Roman Church.

With the coming of the Renaissance and its emphasis to return "to the sources" (*ad fontes*), church Reformers began to draw upon

37 Mendell Taylor, *Exploring Evangelism: History, Methods, Theology* (Kansas City: Nazarene, 1984), 83.

38 Kevin Madigan, *Medieval Christianity: A New History* (New Haven, CT: Yale University Press, 2015), 193.

39 Robert G. Tuttle, *The Story of Evangelism: A History of the Witness to the Gospel* (Nashville: Abingdon, 2006), 206.

40 Gunnar Westin, *The Free Church through the Ages*, trans. Virgil A. Olson (Nashville: Broadman, 1959), 28.

41 Joel Comiskey, *2000 Years of Small Groups: A History of Cell Ministry in the Church* (Morena Valley, CA: CCS, 2014), 62, 67–68, 103.

the Scriptures as their authority, along with the writings of church fathers.[42] They affirmed from their study that salvation is based wholly upon the work of God in Jesus Christ and in no sense upon human merit through good works or paying money to the church to earn merit for salvation.

As these church Reformers recovered the gospel, those in Germany became known as *evangelische*, meaning "evangelical," for their eagerness to share the evangel with others.[43] Martin Luther (1483–1546) used the word *evangelical* to reaffirm the apostle Paul's teaching of the evangel as the indispensable message of salvation, as well as to describe the view of salvation by faith alone in Christ.[44] Leaders of this movement—the Protestant Reformation—claimed they recovered the evangel that was long obscured by the medieval church.

Luther considered himself to be an evangelist and signed his letters with the words "by the grace of God, Evangelist at Wittenberg."[45] He was adamant that pastors preach the gospel; it was their divinely given vocation. Yet he was just as concerned that laypeople engage in the evangelical work. He said, "Every Christian is also an evangelist, who should teach another and publish the glory and praise of God."[46] In several statements Luther emphasized the need to proclaim the gospel to pagans of Europe and elsewhere.[47]

42 Erwin W. Lutzer, *Rescuing the Gospel: The Story and Significance of the Reformation* (Grand Rapids, MI: Baker, 2017), 49–50, 109–12.
43 Mark Hutchinson, *A Global Faith: Essays on Evangelicalism and Globalization* (Sydney: Sydney Centre for the Study of Australian Christianity, 1998), 156–57.
44 John D. Woodbridge and Frank A. James III, *Church History*, vol. 2, *From Pre-Reformation to the Present Day* (Grand Rapids, MI: Zondervan, 2013), 118.
45 Ewald M. Plass, *This Is Luther* (St. Louis: Concordia, 1948), 339, cited in Taylor, *Exploring Evangelism*, 155.
46 Luther, *Luther's Work*, 17:13–14, cited in Michael Parsons, *Text and Task: Scripture and Mission* (Eugene, OR: Wipf and Stock, 2012), 74.
47 David J. Bosch, *Witness to the World: The Christian Mission in Theological Perspective* (Eugene, OR: Wipf and Stock, 2006), 121.

It is estimated that between the years 1522 and 1546, approximately ninety-five editions of Luther's German New Testament were printed, totaling a minimum of 285,000 copies.[48] These editions were mass-produced using Gutenberg's newly developed movable-type printing press. In these editions of the Scriptures, Luther included woodcut illustrations by Lucas Cranach the Elder (ca. 1472–1553). One illustration painted by Cranach in 1529 was titled *The Law and the Gospel*. It depicts Luther's understanding of the gospel.[49] Two identical nude male figures appear on opposite sides of a tree. The left side of the tree is barren and dying, representing the law of Moses or Ten Commandments. The right side of the tree is living, representing the gospel of Jesus Christ, which brings life. On the law side, Adam and Eve are eating the forbidden fruit from a separate tree, and the serpent is wrapped around this tree. Death and the devil pursue the male figure, who is condemned by the law. On the gospel side, one of the four Evangelists—authors of the Gospels—is pointing to Jesus Christ on the cross, who crushes the serpent's head. Jesus also is depicted as risen from the grave and ascending to heaven. This illustration, along with its written explanation, comprised a simple presentation of the gospel. While the law condemns and brings death, the gospel promises forgiveness of sins through faith in Jesus Christ, who triumphs over death and the devil. In this illustration, the gospel is framed within God's redemptive story.[50]

Katharina von Bora (1499–1552), of Saxon descent, became the wife of Martin Luther. Martin spent time teaching, preaching,

48 Plass, *This Is Luther*, 331, cited in Taylor, *Exploring Evangelism*, 149.

49 See Bonnie Noble, "Lucas Cranach the Elder, *Law and Gospel (Law and Grace)*," Smarthistory, August 9, 2015, https://smarthistory.org/.

50 Bonnie Noble, *Lucas Cranach the Elder: Art and Devotion of the German Reformation* (Lanham, MD: University Press of America, 2009), 27–49, 180.

and writing, while Katharina ran the family business and raised their six children and four orphans. The family lived in the former monastery of Augustinian friars at Wittenberg. Katharina turned the monastery into a dormitory and meeting place for resident students and visiting scholars at the University of Wittenberg. During times of widespread illness, she transformed the dormitory into a hospital and ministered to the sick alongside nurses.[51]

As the Protestant Reformation moved across Europe, the Luthers' home served as the movement's epicenter. After dinner, Martin and house guests sat at the table to discuss theology and politics. The "table talks" were possible, of course, because of Katharina's work. She regularly joined discussions herself. Her knowledge of theology in the Latin language eventually earned her the honorary title "Katharina of Alexandria," after the patron saint of the faculty of arts at the university.[52] She played a vital role in promoting the spread of the gospel. Her devotion to Christ remained steadfast, as evidenced by her whispering on her deathbed, "I will stick to Christ as a burr [sticks] to cloth."[53]

When it seemed that some successors of Luther were more interested in debating theology than seeking the conversion of sinners to living faith, some Lutherans known as Pietists grew in number and influence. August Hermann Francke (1663–1727) attended the University of Leipzig, where he became associated with a group of Christians who desired to know the Bible better and formed a campus society for Bible study and its application to daily life.

51 Ruth A. Tucker, *Katie Luther: First Lady of the Reformation* (Grand Rapids, MI: Zondervan, 2017), 97–100.
52 Martin Treu, "Katharina von Bora, the Woman at Luther's Side," *Lutheran Quarterly* 13, no. 2 (1999): 161.
53 Roland H. Bainton, *Women of the Reformation in Germany and Italy* (Boston: Beacon, 1974), 42.

While preparing a lesson on the topic of faith, he converted to faith in Jesus, recalling later:

> In great fear I knelt before God on Saturday night and called out to the One whom I yet neither knew nor believed, for rescue from such a miserable state. . . . While I was still on my knees, He [God] suddenly heard me. Then, just as if one were to turn over one's hand, my doubts were all gone. My heart was sealed to the grace of God in Christ Jesus.[54]

In 1688, Francke launched a full-time ministry to university students. Under this work at Leipzig, students were enthusiastic to read the Scriptures, and in so doing they experienced a spiritual revival that spread to others. Later, Francke became professor of the Greek language at the University of Halle in Germany. While there, he reoriented the theological faculty toward evangelical pietism by establishing conventicles—small group Bible studies. In addition, he not only taught theology in the classroom but lived it before his students by inviting them to join him in his various ministries in the town of Halle.

They began in the neighborhood of Glauchau, known for its deplorable conditions and economic blight.[55] This section of the town contained a row of "degrading beer huts and dance houses" that were frequented regularly by people for entertainment. Francke considered Glauchau to be a "den of iniquity" but also a mission field in which to test the transforming power of the gospel.[56] In

54 Paulus Scharpff, *History of Evangelism: Three Hundred Years of Evangelism in Germany, Great Britain, and the United States of America* (Grand Rapids, MI: Eerdmans, 1966), 29.

55 Gary R. Sattler, *God's Glory, Neighbor's Good: A Brief Introduction to the Life and Writings of August Hermann Francke* (Chicago: Covenant, 1982), 38.

56 Taylor, *Exploring Evangelism*, 231.

this neighborhood, he and his students preached the gospel and engaged in discussions in the street and in homes, generally on Saturday nights and Sunday afternoons. His approach was never to preach a message without including the gospel of repentance and forgiveness so that if anyone heard him once, he or she could receive salvation. For a time, Francke distributed bread to the poor every Thursday and invited those who received it to join him for a fifteen-minute gospel message.

The influence of the Pietist movement spread in Europe to Moravian Brethren refugees who settled on the estate of Nikholaus von Zinzendorf in Germany, and to John and Charles Wesley and the Methodist movement in England. Among the Moravian missionaries was Rebecca Protten of St. Thomas.

Rebecca Freundlich Protten (1718–1780) was born a slave on the Caribbean island of Antigua, the daughter of an African mother and European father.[57] When about six years old, she was kidnapped from Antigua and sold to a plantation owner named Lucas van Beverhout on the island of St. Thomas.[58] She worked for the Beverhout family as a house servant and learned from them—members of the Dutch Reformed Church—the gospel of Jesus Christ and subsequently converted to faith. At twelve years of age, shortly after Lucas's death, the family set her free.

In 1736, when more Moravian missionaries arrived in St. Thomas, Rebecca met Friedrich Martin, who noted in his diary: "I spoke with a mulatto [sic] woman who is very accomplished in the teachings of God. Her name is Rebecca."[59] The Moravian missionaries

---

57 Jon F. Sensbach, *Rebecca's Revival: Creating Black Christianity in the Atlantic World* (Cambridge, MA: Harvard University Press, 2005), 30.

58 Sensbach, *Rebecca's Revival*, 31–32.

59 Malcolm McCall, *Aspects of Modern Church History, 1517–2017: From an African Perspective* (Bloomington, IN: Westbow, 2018), 54. Cf. Sensbach, *Rebecca's Revival*, 45–46, 52–53.

taught her how to read and write, and involved her in evangelism to the slaves. Despite the hostile environment by slave masters, including violence toward the slaves and verbal abuse toward the missionaries, Rebecca and the Moravian missionaries walked "daily along rugged roads through the hills in the sultry evenings after the slaves had returned from the fields" in order to converse with them about Jesus.[60]

Rebecca's evangelistic ministry "took her to the slave quarters deep in the island's plantation heartland, where she proclaimed salvation to the domestic servants, cane boilers, weavers, and cotton pickers whose bodies and spirits were strip-mined every day by slavery."[61] Despite the challenges, she shared the gospel with hundreds of slaves, and along with the Moravian missionaries, saw hundreds convert to faith in Christ.[62]

In addition to evangelism, Rebecca taught at the church located "at the end of a rugged road through the hills of St. Thomas known to the enslaved as 'The Path.' "[63] In 1738, she and the Moravian missionary Matthäus Freundlich were united in marriage.[64] A few weeks later, Rebecca was named a deaconess of the Moravian community.

In 1742, Rebecca and Matthäus set sail for Germany with their daughter, Anna Maria. Matthäus needed to return to his homeland because of his failing health. Sadly, he died just after arriving in Germany. Rebecca remained at Herrnhut, where two years later her daughter also died. Despite the grief, Rebecca became a respected

60 Sensbach, *Rebecca's Revival*, 3.
61 Sensbach, *Rebecca's Revival*, 3.
62 Woodbridge and James, *Church History*, 2:459.
63 David Hempton, *The Church in the Long Eighteenth Century* (New York: Tauris, 2011), 85.
64 Sensbach, *Rebecca's Revival*, 102–5.

member of the community and assumed leadership in the Moravian women's ministry.

In 1746, she married Christian Protten, similarly noted for his lineage of having an African mother and European father.[65] Eventually, Rebecca and Christian moved to Christiansborg, on Africa's Gold Coast in modern-day Ghana and, with the blessing of the Moravian community, taught African children at the Christiansborg Castle School. The children not only learned how to read and write but also learned the gospel of Jesus Christ.[66]

Newly converted to faith, John Wesley (1703–1791) prepared to launch a new ministry. Although he had earned the master's degree at Oxford and lectured in Greek, in 1738 he traveled to Germany to learn from the Moravian community about mission and evangelism.[67]

He then returned to Britain to reach his countrymen with the gospel. He began preaching in churches but soon agitated nominal Christians. In response to their spiritual condition, he exclaimed, "Oh, who will convert the English into honest heathens!"[68] Wesley, like other evangelicals, saw himself as recovering a core doctrine of the gospel, justification by faith alone. He stressed conversion to Christ, the authority of the Bible, and living out the gospel in works of mercy, which included doing good, visiting the sick and prisoners, feeding and clothing people, and earning, saving, and giving all one can.[69]

---

65 Sensbach, *Rebecca's Revival*, 162.

66 Sensbach, *Rebecca's Revival*, 217–18.

67 Howard A. Snyder, *The Radical Wesley and Patterns for Church Renewal* (Eugene, OR: Wipf and Stock, 1996), 29; Tuttle, *Story of Evangelism*, 285.

68 John Wesley, *The Journal of the Reverend John Wesley*, vol. 1 (New York: Mason and Lane, 1837), 546.

69 Kenneth J. Collins, *The Theology of John Wesley: Holy Love and the Shape of Grace* (Nashville: Abingdon, 2007), 267–68.

When Wesley entered a new area to evangelize, he took his stance at a favorable spot, usually in the town center, then he would "preach the law in the strictest of terms" or "preach a fifteen-minute sermon" on the topic of "death or hell," and only when his listeners were clearly under conviction of sin would he "bring out the medicine of the gospel."[70] His coworkers circulated among those who responded, signing them up to attend a Methodist meeting later that day. The Methodist meetings and classes proved to be effective means for the participants to convert to faith in Jesus. It was calculated that 70 percent of those who converted to Jesus Christ under Wesley's ministry did so during these meetings, often speaking to a Methodist coworker one-on-one.[71]

Evangelistic renewal in the eighteenth century stemmed not merely from Pietism on the European continent and from its Methodist stream in the British Isles but also from the Great Awakening in America. Among those who came to the American colonies, especially to Massachusetts, Rhode Island, and Connecticut, were Congregationalists and Baptists from England.

John Mason Peck (1789–1858) was an American Baptist. He came to faith at a revival meeting at the Congregational church in his hometown of Litchfield, Connecticut. He married Sallie Paine and, shortly after the birth of their first son, joined a Baptist church.[72] After meeting Luther Rice (1783–1836), Peck became interested in mission work and traveled to Philadelphia for further study.

With secured funding, Peck became a Baptist missionary to Missouri Territory in 1817. He began preaching the gospel, and

---

70 Taylor, *Exploring Evangelism*, 261.
71 Tuttle, *Story of Evangelism*, 285.
72 William H. Brackney, "John Mason Peck," in *Biographical Dictionary of Christian Missions*, ed. Gerald H. Anderson (Grand Rapids, MI: Eerdmans, 1999), 524.

in the following February, he baptized two converts in the frigid Mississippi River. Peck soon founded the United Society for the Spread of the Gospel, taking up the work of traveling evangelist, as well as establishing Bible societies and Sunday school associations in St. Louis and the surrounding area.

In 1822, Peck moved to O'Fallon, Illinois, just east of St. Louis, Missouri, where he traveled a circuit to visit the societies and Sunday schools he established. During this time, he helped to form the African Baptist Church of St. Louis, known today as First Baptist Church. Of the original 220 members, 200 were slaves.[73] Peck ordained a young freedman named John Berry Meachum (1789–1854) as pastor. Peck was invited to preach sermons on various occasions and seized every opportunity to share the gospel. On one particular occasion, the title of his sermon was "The Snares of Sin. A Discourse Delivered from the Gallows in Edwardsville, Illinois, February 12, 1824, at the Execution of Eliphalet Green, for the Murder of William Wright."[74]

Under Peck's leadership, in 1832, the American Baptist Home Mission Society was organized. This society was directed toward reaching settlers, Native Americans, and slaves. Peck also helped to establish the Illinois State Baptist Convention in 1834 and served as its first president. He published widely in the areas of agriculture, Illinois history, geography, and Native Americans. In 1843, he founded the American Baptist Publication Society and published a weekly religious journal titled *Western Pioneer*. During his tenure, he contributed to planting nearly nine hundred Baptist churches,

---

73 Harriet C. Frazier, *Runaway and Freed Missouri Slaves and Those Who Helped Them, 1763–1865* (Jefferson, NC: McFarland, 2004), 66.

74 John Mason Peck, *The Snares of Sin: A Discourse Delivered from the Gallows in Edwardsville, Illinois, February 12, 1824, at the Execution of Eliphalet Green, for the Murder of William Wright* (Edwardsville, IL: Hooper Warren, 1824).

ordaining six hundred pastors, and seeing thirty-two thousand people convert to faith. In 1852, Harvard College awarded him an honorary degree.

————

Much more could be said about evangelism in the nineteenth and twentieth centuries that shaped evangelism globally. The evangelism of Francis Asbury of the Methodists and Charles Finney and Dwight Moody of the Congregationalists profoundly transformed contemporary ideas of evangelism. In addition, the ministries of Billy Sunday, Billy Graham, and Bill Bright in the twentieth century altered practices of gospel witness in the twenty-first century. For many Christians today, especially those of the evangelical Protestant tradition, the thought of evangelism may conjure up thoughts of Billy Graham preaching to thousands of listeners at an evangelistic crusade or of someone sharing Bill Bright's "Four Spiritual Laws." These methods have colored our perception of evangelism today.

However, my hope is that this chapter's survey of evangelistic practices since the first century will broaden our perceptions. When we see the centrality of the gospel among followers of Christ throughout the history of the church, we are invited to share in the gospel identity of Christians from previous centuries who announced the evangel. The variety of people and approaches from history may serve to expand our understanding of evangelism and how it can be carried out today.

Questions for Reflection

1. Why was the community of Basil in Caesarea effective at evangelism? What elements of his evangelism might be useful today?

2. Faltonia Betitia Proba found a way to share the gospel that both was creative and fit her cultural context. How might we share the gospel in creative ways while maintaining the integrity of the gospel? What examples have you seen?

3. Ansgar of Bremen was sent into an area of the world that was considered hostile. Why was he effective? How do you respond to people or groups who threaten you? What steps can you take to share the gospel with them?

4. Of the evangelists mentioned in this chapter, from whom do you draw the most inspiration for evangelism today, and why?

Resources for Further Study

Gustafson, David M. *Gospel Witness through the Ages: A History of Evangelism.* Grand Rapids, MI: Eerdmans, 2022.

Hunter, George G., III. *The Celtic Way of Evangelism: How Christianity Can Reach the West Again.* Nashville: Abingdon, 2000.

Sunquist, Scott W. *Understanding Christian Mission: Participation in Suffering and Glory.* Grand Rapids, MI: Baker Academic, 2017.

Terry, John Mark. *Evangelism: A Concise History.* Nashville: B&H, 2014.

Tucker, Ruth A., and Walter Liefeld. *Daughters of the Church: Women and Ministry from New Testament Times to the Present.* Grand Rapids, MI: Zondervan, 1987.

Tuttle, Robert G. *The Story of Evangelism: A History of the Witness to the Gospel.* Nashville: Abingdon, 2006.

6

New Testament Practices of Evangelism and Apologetics

David Kotter

AFTER SERVING AS A PASTOR for many years, I now have the privilege of being a professor of New Testament studies and living across the street from Colorado Christian University. On Friday nights my wife and I enjoy having students walk over to our house to eat ice cream and talk about anything on their minds related to the Bible.

Recently one dear student asked whether it was a sin that she had never shared the gospel with coworkers at the restaurant where she was a waitress. Before answering, I asked more questions to better understand her situation. Apparently, some of her coworkers were Muslims, and others had militant LGBTQ+ beliefs that made her fear an antagonistic response. Others were just pursuing a life of sexual freedom and had no interest in talking about spiritual things (which they considered silly). And although my friend became acquainted with many people during busy shifts of serving food, she had little chance to engage deeply in their lives.

Reflecting on her question reminded me that Christians often find it easier to obey negative commands from the Bible (what a believer must avoid) than positive commands (what a believer must do). For example, most understand that a Christian should not commit murder or adultery and are able to avoid such sins. Believers can often obey trickier prohibitions, like to not quarrel or speak evil of others (Titus 3:2). But the positive commands from the Bible can be tough to obey consistently. For example, many struggle with the command "Count it all joy, my brothers, when you meet trials of various kinds" (James 1:2). Others work hard to even understand positive commands, such as "rejoice always" or "pray without ceasing" (1 Thess. 5:16–17).

From my days as a pastor, I remembered that one of the most challenging positive commands to obey is the Great Commission. At the end of the Gospel of Matthew, the resurrected Christ gave final instructions: "Go therefore and make disciples of all nations, baptizing them in the name of the Father and of the Son and of the Holy Spirit, and teaching them to observe all that I have commanded you" (28:19–20). Even at the end of his ministry, Jesus emphasized the importance of making disciples and teaching new believers about obedience. Another command that is tough to follow is Peter's call to be ready to defend the faith, "Always being prepared to make a defense to anyone who asks you for a reason for the hope that is in you" (1 Pet. 3:15). If you are a Christian who struggles with obeying either of these positive commands, let me assure you that you would not be alone on the campus of CCU or in most parts of the church.

In fact, I have asked many college students whether they have shared the gospel with anyone in the last month, year, or ever. Sometimes my question is answered with an excited yes, followed by a quick story of a recent evangelistic encounter, along with gratitude to God for providing such a glorious opportunity. The vast majority of times, however, my questions about evangelism are greeted with an uncomfortable silence or remorseful admission of never actually having shared the good news of Jesus Christ with anyone.

I have learned that sometimes Christians avoid pursuing evangelistic encounters out of fear of being rejected or dread of being unable to answer questions with specific Bible verses. Others avoid evangelism because a hostile culture considers sharing the good news an act of intolerance or violence against others. While I can identify with such feelings, I suspect that such fears might flow from a fundamental misunderstanding of New Testament teachings on evangelism and apologetics.

I was, and am, confident that the New Testament holds answers for my student friend's question. When I looked at biblical passages on evangelism, I found that Christians from the earliest churches left examples for us to follow and timeless principles that can be adapted to any culture. Even more than today, New Testament Christians faced militant religions, rampant sexual immorality, and violent persecution against evangelistic efforts. Even in a hostile culture, the earliest Christians successfully shared their faith in Jesus Christ, and the gospel advanced across the empire from Jerusalem to Rome.

The rest of this chapter will summarize what I shared with my Friday night friends about early church practices of evangelism and apologetics. From the writings of the New Testament, it is clear that early believers deeply understood several essential things, and this understanding created in them an incredible motivation for evangelism. Specifically, they understood the heart of Jesus for people, their clear mission from Jesus, the reality of the gospel, the unspeakable joy of being saved, the eternal consequences of being lost, and the power of prayer and the Holy Spirit. Such thoughts motivated the earliest Christians to be intentional in evangelism and apologetics while persevering despite hostile situations.

My prayer is that this review will be helpful for any Christian who wants to grow into a lifestyle of evangelism based on the ideas and practices of the New Testament church. Beyond that, I am confident that God will be pleased to answer our prayers and equip any believer who wants to be obedient in evangelism. The first part of this chapter will examine the thoughts and feelings that motivated early Christians to evangelism, and the second part will examine how the motivated church put evangelism into practice.

What Motivated Early Christian Evangelism?

Early Christians Understood the Heart of Jesus Christ

Not just the apostles, but thousands of people in the earliest church personally spent time with Jesus, heard his teachings, and experienced his miracles. Through his life and teachings, Jesus made it clear that he was seeking lost people.

For example, Luke records a day in Jericho when a tax collector named Zacchaeus climbed a tree to see Jesus (19:1–10). In this account we can be tempted to focus on the "wee little man" and his desire to find out about Jesus. More accurately, it was Jesus who was seeking to see Zacchaeus. Passing through Jericho on the way to Jerusalem, Jesus looked up, spoke first, called Zacchaeus by name, and insisted that the two of them meet that very day. While Zacchaeus had an interest in Jesus, Jesus had already prepared to meet Zacchaeus on that day at that place. After sharing a meal and hearing the repentant speech of the tax collector, Jesus declared, "Today salvation has come to this house," and stated his purpose: "The Son of Man came to seek and to save the lost" (v. 10).

On another occasion, Peter found Jesus praying in a solitary place outside of Capernaum, but Jesus was reluctant to return to the town, where he had healed many people. Instead, he announced, "Let us go on to the next towns, that I may preach there also, for that is why I came out" (Mark 1:38). Further, the joy of Jesus at recovering lost sinners was expressed in his parables about recovering the lost coin, the lost sheep, and the prodigal son (Luke 15:1–32). Over time the disciples came to know the heart of Jesus to save lost people and had a growing desire to follow in his footsteps.

Early Christians Understood Their Mission from Jesus

The Great Commission in Matthew 28 was the last command of Jesus's ministry, but for several years he had been developing in the disciples a mindset of outreach. Jesus told them, "As the Father has sent me, even so I am sending you" (John 20:21). Accordingly, early in his ministry Jesus sent out the twelve apostles to the lost people of Israel, and later he sent out seventy-two disciples in pairs to bring the good news of the kingdom of God (Luke 9:1–6; 10:1–17). Jesus's vision was not limited to Israel, however, so he informed his disciples that "this gospel of the kingdom will be proclaimed throughout the whole world as a testimony to all nations" (Matt. 24:14). Jesus reminded his disciples of this mission just before he ascended into heaven: "You will be my witnesses in Jerusalem and in all Judea and Samaria, and to the end of the earth" (Acts 1:8).

This mission continued when Jesus appointed Paul to preach throughout the world, saying,

I have made you a light for the Gentiles,
  that you may bring salvation to the ends of the earth.
    (Acts 13:47)

Christian history shows that the earliest believers understood the heart of Jesus in seeking the lost and also understood the mission from Jesus to tell the good news to the whole world. If you are a follower of Christ, then Jesus is calling you to be part of this ongoing mission, and grace from God is available to help you along the way. The challenging question is how each of us will respond to this positive command from the Lord.

Early Christians Understood the Gospel Message

In addition to the mission from Jesus, the earliest Christians also understood the gospel itself. The term *gospel* means "good news" and is the central message of Christianity. This good news is that Jesus Christ is the Son of God, who lived a sinless life, died on the cross to pay the penalty for our sin, and rose from the dead to offer forgiveness of sins and new life to all who put their trust in him. The essence of this message is that through faith in Jesus Christ, people can have a personal relationship with God and experience eternal life with him.

To be precise, this message consists of six essential truths or key components necessary to proclaim the whole gospel. First, God is the perfect Creator of all the world, including human beings, made in his own image, and that God is worthy of praise for his creation (Rev. 4:11). Second, everyone has rebelled against God, and the Bible labels such rebellion "sin" (Rom. 3:10–12). Third, God is a great King who will not tolerate this ongoing revolt and will justly punish every sinful rebel for eternity (2 Thess. 1:8–9). Fourth, God is just, but also infinitely loving and merciful. For this reason, God sent his own Son, Jesus, to live as a man who never sinned in anything he ever thought, said, or did. Amazingly, Jesus voluntarily chose to die in the place of rebels so that God could legitimately punish sin while extending mercy to sinners (1 Pet. 3:18). Fifth, God raised Jesus from the dead to demonstrate in historical time and space that sins were forgiven, and a way has been opened to a right relationship with God (1 Pet. 1:3). Sixth, every person faces a choice either to live in obedience to God according to the perfect design of the original creation or to continue in rebellion and suffer the consequences of everlasting punishment (John 3:36).[1]

This gospel message is not only true but also amazing and life-changing. As the world heads toward chaos and hell, Christians need to remember that the gospel is the ultimate solution to every cultural and spiritual problem. Before undertaking the path of evangelism in obedience to Jesus's commands, every believer needs to review and understand the gospel well. Taking an easier path of urging people "to become friends with God" or to "allow Jesus into your heart" skips over important parts of the gospel message and often leads to more harm than good.

Undoubtedly the earliest Christians knew that effective evangelism was driven by an intellectual understanding of the mission and the gospel but also included important emotional components as well. We will look at those emotional motivators in the next section.

---

1   This paragraph follows the helpful structure of "Two Ways to Live" found at https://two waystolive.com/.

Early Christians Were Glad to Be Saved and Grieved for the Lost

Christians in the New Testament church were motivated by gratitude that they themselves had been saved. The apostle Peter expressed this well: "You believe in him and rejoice with joy that is inexpressible and filled with glory" (1 Pet. 1:8). The apostle Paul rejoiced, saying, "The grace of our Lord overflowed for me with the faith and love that are in Christ Jesus" (1 Tim. 1:14). This gratitude motivated every aspect of his life such that Paul wrote, "The life I now live in the flesh I live by faith in the son of God, who loved me and gave himself for me" (Gal. 2:20). The apostle John understood this direct connection between receiving from God and giving to others: "If God so loved us, we also ought to love one another" (1 John 4:11). Love was the ultimate motivation for early church evangelism; so Paul wrote: "For the love of Christ controls us" (2 Cor. 5:14). I am afraid that many Christians today view evangelism as an unpleasant but necessary chore. I fear that such people do not feel the anticipatory joy of being with Jesus forever or perhaps lack enough love to help others escape unimaginable punishment.

The earliest Christians grieved for the fate of lost people, and their sorrow spurred evangelism. Paul told the Thessalonians of "flaming fire, inflicting vengeance on those who do not know God and on those who do not obey the gospel of our Lord Jesus. They will suffer the punishment of eternal destruction, away from the presence of the Lord and from the glory of his might" (2 Thess. 1:8–9). Since God himself is the source of light, love, and everything hopeful, to be shut out from his presence will be a hellish existence in the absence of any love and in utter despair. Such a future for any human being is unthinkably tragic, but the Bible assures us that it will become a reality for everyone who does not know God and obey the gospel of Jesus Christ. Realizing this, Paul wrote: "I have great sorrow and unceasing anguish in my heart. For I could wish that I myself were accursed and cut off from Christ for the sake of my brothers" (Rom. 9:2–3). In other words, Paul's love for the lost was so great that he was willing to take their place in hell if that were a possible way to save them.

The New Testament church found great motivation for evangelism both from gratitude for the wonders of salvation and from an appalling grief over the fate of lost people. Christians today would be more motivated toward evangelism if we better understood that there are only two options for the eternal state of every person we meet.

Early Christians Understood the Power of Prayer and the Holy Spirit

Despite the incredible personal motivation we have seen in the previous section, early Christians understood that something beyond themselves was needed for the monumental task of world-wide evangelism. Accordingly, Paul asked, "Pray for us, that the word of the Lord may speed ahead and be honored, as happened among you" (2 Thess. 3:1). Indeed, Paul continually pleaded for prayers for boldness: "[Pray] also for me, that words may be given to me in opening my mouth boldly to proclaim the mystery of the gospel" (Eph. 6:19–20). The earliest believers recognized that the spread of the gospel was driven not by human power or ingenuity but by God glorifying himself in answer to the prayers of his people.

Jesus earlier taught about the necessary role of the Holy Spirit in evangelism, "You will receive power when the Holy Spirit has come upon you, and you will be my witnesses in Jerusalem and in all Judea and Samaria, and to the ends of the earth" (Acts 1:8). On the day of Pentecost, the new believers were "filled with the Holy Spirit and began to speak in other tongues as the Spirit gave them utterance" and declared "the mighty works of God" in many languages (Acts 2:4, 11). Three thousand people were added to the number of believers that day, but the work of the Holy Spirit grew and has continued until today. Before Peter preached the gospel to a hostile Jewish council, he was "filled with the Holy Spirit" (Acts 4:8), and likewise all the earliest believers were "filled with the Holy Spirit and continued to speak the word of God with boldness" (Acts 4:31). The church understood that evangelism was not simply a human venture but a joint work empowered by prayer and the Holy Spirit from beginning to end.

To summarize what I shared with my Friday night friends up to this point, the earliest believers were motivated to share the good news with lost people by their deep understanding of the heart of Jesus, the mission, and the gospel itself. Also, a sense of gratitude for salvation and grief for the lost led to reliance on prayer and the Holy Spirit for evangelistic success. Sharing the good news was a joyful opportunity rather than a mere duty to be endured, and this can still be true for Christians today if we learn from the examples of the New Testament church.

These examples include the strategies and methods used to systematically identify receptive unbelievers and effectively present the gospel. Specifically, the New Testament shows that the earliest Christians were intentional in evangelism, apologetics, and perseverance. The rest of this chapter will examine New Testament accounts of each of these in turn, then conclude with a consideration of how these truths can be applied in the life of every believer.

Putting Evangelism into Practice

Early Christians Were Intentional in Evangelism

The New Testament shows that early Christians were consistent in sharing the good news with individuals and households, as well as proclaiming the gospel in public squares and through the written word. These believers were intentional in utilizing natural relationships with the people that God brought into their lives for evangelistic opportunities.

One of the best illustrations of the one-on-one method of bringing people to Jesus can be found in the first chapter of the Gospel of John. One day John the Baptist pointed two of his disciples to Jesus as the Lamb of God, and both began to follow Jesus (1:36–37). One of John's former disciples was named Andrew, and he immediately went to find his brother Peter and personally brought him to Jesus (1:40–42). The next day, Jesus called Philip to follow him as a disciple, and then Philip found Nathaniel, who met Jesus and accepted him as the Messiah (1:43–51).

This personal approach was not a one-time phenomenon but rather an ongoing pattern in the lives of Andrew and Philip. When Greek men in Jerusalem asked to see Jesus, it was Andrew and Philip who introduced them to the Lord (12:21–22). When five thousand people were hungry, it was Andrew who brought a little boy and his lunch to Jesus, with miraculous results (6:8–14). Finding himself alone in Samaria, Philip had no hesitation in approaching a man in a chariot to explain the good news about Jesus Christ (Acts 8:26–40). These are just a few of the innumerable examples of individual encounters throughout the history of the church, and they show how every Christian needs to be prepared for personal conversations to introduce another person to Jesus Christ.

The New Testament church also recognized the value of evangelism in households. In the first century, some believers already were married when they accepted Christ. Paul instructed them to stay in their marriages, if possible, because there was hope that the unbelieving spouse would be saved (1 Cor. 7:10–16). Peter also recognized that the conduct of a respectful and pure wife could be a powerful witness for saving her husband (1 Pet. 3:1–2). In the same way, the home was a strategic evangelistic opportunity for raising children "in the discipline and instruction of the Lord" (Eph. 6:4). Even slaves could witness to unbelieving masters through sincere service, and Christian masters could represent Christ to unbelieving bond servants (Eph. 6:5–9). In other words, the earliest church understood extended households (or any long-term relationships) as opportunities to express the love of God and share the gospel.

The earliest church was also committed to the public proclamation of the gospel, and some Christians are still called to such open-air and street evangelism to this day. The New Testament records many examples of believers preaching publicly in synagogues and marketplaces (e.g., Acts 2:14–40; 9:20; 13:13–43; 17:19–34). While not every Christian is called to such public proclamation, every believer can encourage pastors to include the gospel regularly in expository sermons.

Early Christians also composed literature to broadcast the teachings of Jesus and persuade people to believe. Many examples abound in the letters of Paul, as well as the four Gospels. John wrote that the purpose of his Gospel was to inform and persuade: "These [things] are written so that you may believe that Jesus is the Christ, the Son of God, and that by believing you may have life in his name" (20:31). Today the Internet has exploded the opportunities to write and publish the reasons for the hope that Christians have in Christ, with gentleness and respect. In fact, when choosing evangelistic methods, the answer for many Christians should be "all of the above."

Early Christians Were Intentional in Apologetics

The earliest Christians did not just proclaim the good news of Jesus Christ; they also provided apologetics to support the gospel. In this sense, the word *apologetic* means "a reasoned defense" (not to be confused with the English word *apology* or saying "I'm sorry"). Peter wrote, "Always be prepared to make a defense [*apologia*] to anyone who asks you for a reason for the hope that is in you; yet do it with gentleness and respect" (1 Pet. 3:15). Other chapters in this book will examine apologetics for Christians today, so this brief section simply reviews the strategic use of apologetics in the New Testament church.

The earliest Christians understood the culture and beliefs of their audiences and shaped their messages about Jesus to attract the most receptive listeners. For example, Stephen found himself in front of a Jewish council composed of elders and scribes and began his speech with an account of the history of Israel to tell them about Jesus Christ (Acts 7:1–60). Peter, on the day of Pentecost, spoke to Jews from all over the world and used Old Testament prophets to point to Jesus (Acts 2:14–40). Paul went into the synagogue in Thessalonica, and "on three Sabbath days he reasoned with them from the Scriptures" (Acts 17:2). Later, in Ephesus, Paul secured the "Hall of Tyrannus," where he reasoned daily with Gentiles for two years until all the residents "heard the word of the Lord, both Jews and Greeks" (Acts 19:9–10).

Evangelism coupled with apologetics was a key part of Paul's intentional outreach. When he arrived in Athens, Paul encountered

Epicurean and Stoic philosophers and reasoned "in the marketplace every day with those who happened to be there" (Acts 17:17). To better identify with his Gentile audience, he intentionally quoted pagan poets instead of Jewish Scriptures (Acts 17:17–34). Paul summed up his strategy of personal apologetics:

> I have made myself a servant to all, that I might win more of them. To the Jews I became as a Jew, in order to win Jews. . . . To those outside the law I became as one outside the law. . . . To the weak I became weak, that I might win the weak. I have become all things to all people, that by all means I might save some. (1 Cor. 9:19–22)

One of the easiest apologetic explanations for the hope within a believer is to give a personal testimony of encountering Jesus, and examples of this abound in the New Testament. When Paul spoke to a king named Agrippa about his faith, he began by describing his life before he encountered Jesus when he was a strictly religious man filled with raging fury (Acts 26:1–12). Paul next described meeting Jesus on the road to Damascus. Though Paul's eyes were blinded by a bright light, in his heart he understood the gospel message for the first time (Acts 26:13–18). Paul's final statement was to describe his life after becoming an obedient follower of Jesus Christ (Acts 26:19–23).

I especially appreciate Paul's example and would encourage all believers to think in advance about dividing their personal testimony into the same three parts: What was your life like before Jesus? What was it like for you to encounter Jesus and understand the gospel for the first time? What has your life been like since you were forgiven and have peace with God? In any personal testimony, remember to use simple words and avoid "Christianese" or technical religious jargon. It is also helpful to be able to deliver a testimony in exactly one minute for impatient listeners (a stopwatch for testimony training has been used on my campus), and about five minutes for someone who has a greater interest in your story.

Early Christians Were Intentional in Perseverance

The New Testament church knew the heart of Jesus Christ and the eternal tragedy of being lost, and this motivated them to persevere in sharing the gospel even in hostile situations. When Paul was saved, "immediately he proclaimed Jesus in the synagogues, saying, 'He is the Son of God'" (Acts 9:20), and he felt a joyful obligation to preach the good news to Gentiles (Rom. 1:14–15). Stephen walked through the history of Israel to proclaim Jesus even as his audience prepared to kill him (Acts 7:2–60).

The author of Hebrews describes the experience of some believers in the earliest church who "suffered mocking and flogging, and even chains and imprisonment. They were stoned, they were sawn in two, they were killed with the sword. They went about in skins of sheep and goats, destitute, afflicted, mistreated—of whom the world was not worthy" (Heb. 11:36–38). Despite this tribulation, persecution in the church only led to more opportunities for evangelism as "those who were scattered went about preaching the word" (Acts 8:4).

The earliest believers were not surprised by persecution for sharing the gospel in a world hostile to God, and their confidence flowed from Jesus's final statement in the Great Commission, "Behold, I am with you always, to the end of the age" (Matt. 28:20). Christians today should not be dismayed by a hostile culture but rather should expect increasing persecution from proclaiming the gospel of Jesus Christ. Even to the end of the age, we can share the good news with confidence as we remember that Jesus has promised to be with us.

Recommendations for Christians Today

I hope you have found it profitable to read the essence of what I told my friends at our home while eating ice cream on a Friday night, and I pray you will be motivated to take intentional steps to develop a lifestyle of evangelism. Times change, but Jesus Christ and the human heart remain the same. So the examples of the New Testament church and the ideas that motivated them are timeless. The Holy Spirit is still ready to empower believers to reach the lost.

As I answered my student friend's question, Christians are commanded to evangelize, and failing to obey that command over a long time is sinful. But if we confess our sins, Jesus "is faithful and just to forgive us our sins and to cleanse us from all unrighteousness" (1 John 1:9). Jesus Christ died for sinners like us, and this makes the gospel such good news for us and for others whom God has brought into our lives.

What does this mean for us today, and what steps should we take to develop a lifestyle of evangelism? I am still on this journey myself (along with the students who come to my home on Friday nights), but here are five recommendations:

First, evaluate whether you are a Christian who has accepted the gospel and who personally knows Jesus Christ. Sometimes people do not evangelize because they are not saved and are simply going through the motions of being cultural Christians from Christian homes or living on a Christian campus. Also, you will want to consider if you are genuinely happy to be saved, like the earliest Christians. If sharing the gospel seems more like a chore than an amazing opportunity, then consider again the unspeakable joy of being saved and the appalling tragedy of being lost.

Second, be intentional and plan for evangelism in the future. Memorize a presentation of the gospel (or perhaps more than one). Practice one-minute and five-minute versions of your testimony that explain in everyday language what your life was like before being saved, how you heard the gospel and encountered Jesus Christ, and what your life has been like since you became a follower of Jesus.

Third, study the Scriptures daily for your personal devotions and learning, but also to be prepared to give a defense. Pray for opportunities for evangelism with friends, family members, neighbors, classmates, and coworkers. Be confident that God is delighted to answer such prayers.

Fourth, love the people God brings across your path by sharing your life with genuine friendship and warm hospitality. Talk about Jesus openly, and share how he is working in your life through your struggles and joys. Invite unbelievers along with other friends into the events of your life, including hobbies, sports, small groups, and worship services.

Finally, present the gospel of Jesus Christ when the time is right, and defend the hope that is in you, with gentleness and respect. Ultimately, evangelism is a work of the Lord in which we can joyfully participate. Indeed "when the Gentiles heard this [good news], they began rejoicing and glorifying the word of the Lord, and as many as were appointed to eternal life believed" (Acts 13:48).

Questions for Reflection

1. Which of the motivations for evangelism in the early church did you find most compelling?

2. What scares you the most about following the example of the New Testament church?

3. Are you saved? Are you glad that you are saved? Why?

4. Do you grieve about the future of lost people in your family and in your life?

5. When was the last time you shared the gospel with an unbeliever, and are you regularly praying for opportunities to present the gospel to lost people?

6. From the recommendations at the end of the chapter, what would be your first step to prepare for evangelism?

7. What would it look like for you to trust God the next time you are given an opportunity to share the gospel?

Resources for Further Study

Coleman, Robert E. *The Master Plan of Evangelism*. 2nd ed. Grand Rapids, MI: Revell, 2010.

Green, Michael. *Evangelism in the Early Church*. Rev. ed. Grand Rapids, MI: Eerdmans, 2004.

Koukl, Gregory. *Tactics: A Game Plan for Discussing Your Christian Convictions*. Grand Rapids, MI: Zondervan, 2019.

Packer, J. I. *Evangelism and the Sovereignty of God*. Rev. ed. Downers Grove, IL: InterVarsity Press, 2012.

Schnabel, Eckhart. *Early Christian Mission*. 2 vols. Downers Grove, IL: InterVarsity Press, 2004.

7

Evangelism in the Post-Christian West

Marrying Truth with Compassion

Jim Denison and Mark Legg

A RUMBLING SOUTHERN VOICE echoes across Madison Square Garden in 1957. A calloused farmer's fist shakes from behind the pulpit, the air is suffused with the gospel, and thousands of people lean in with rapt attention. Thousands kneel, tears streaming down their faces, as they profess faith in God. Jesus accepts them all, and Billy Graham steps off the stage.

Billy Graham's evangelism represents a golden age of Spirit-led opportunity. Graham's humility, conviction, and simplicity in presenting the good news shook the world. He is the most prolific evangelist in Christian history, preaching face-to-face to

05

an estimated eighty million people. Around three million came forward during altar calls to give their lives to Christ.[1]

That type of movement may come again. Our culture feels ripe for revival, but not necessarily through the same method as Billy Graham's spiritual crusades. In those days, America remembered Sunday school and thought highly of the church, but many neglected their faith and fell away.[2] When Graham's preaching swept through the country, Jesus swept those lost sheep into the fold.

Back then, evangelism usually meant inviting coworkers, friends, and family to church. Get them through the doors, and the pastor would do the rest. "Professional" Christians took on the bulk of preaching the gospel.

Now, much of the West views the church as a backward, untrustworthy place of judgment that clings to outdated sensibilities. At best, we're irrelevant or a curious part of some people's spiritual "journey." At worst, we are literally dangerous to LGBTQ+ folks and a serious threat to moral progress.

Young Christians dread the odious stamps of social stigma: "intolerant," "homophobic," "racist," "transphobic," "hateful," and even "dangerous." They fear finding themselves out of their depth in philosophical challenges or feeling embarrassed, ostracized, or canceled. Their worries are often unfounded, but sometimes not.

In an increasingly post-Christian West, saturated with postmodernism and lacking a shared understanding of truth, Christians struggle to share *the* truth. So, under the threat of being labeled

---

1   "Billy Graham: Evangelist to Millions," *Christianity Today*, August 8, 2008, https://www.christianitytoday.com/.

2   Sam Chan, *How to Talk about Jesus (without Being That Guy): Personal Evangelism in a Skeptical World* (Grand Rapids, MI: Zondervan, 2020), 19.

"intolerant, irrelevant, oppressive, and dangerous," how do we evangelize?[3]

In a culture cynical of our claims, we must *show* them Jesus. He says to us, "Let your light shine before others"; he says of himself, "I am the light of the world," promising that his followers will "not walk in darkness, but will have the light of life"; and says to others, "Believe in the light, that you may become [children] of light" (Matt. 5:16; John 8:12; 12:36).

So how do we shine our light?

Truth

Christianity stands on objective truth claims such as Jesus's self-description "I am the way, and the truth, and the life" (John 14:6). Paul said of Jesus's historic resurrection, "If Christ has not been raised, your faith is futile and you are still in your sins" (1 Cor. 15:17).

However, to shorten a very long story, the seventeenth- and eighteenth-century Enlightenment called into question inherited beliefs and truth claims, whether they were derived from Scripture, church tradition, or any other source. Immanuel Kant (1724–1804) spoke for many with his famous injunction "Use your own reason!" The German philosopher Friedrich Nietzsche (1844–1900) claimed that all humans are motivated by the "will to power" and that speech acts are mere means to this end.

Postmodernism, the claim that all truth claims are personal, individual, and subjective, has been the result. Michel Foucault (1926–1984) agreed with Nietzsche that we must reject all claims to objective knowledge and focus instead on our personal experiences.

3   Jim Denison, *The Coming Tsunami: Why Christians Are Labeled Intolerant, Irrelevant, Oppressive, and Dangerous—and How We Can Turn the Tide* (Nashville: Forefront, 2022).

Jacques Derrida (1930–2004) encouraged us to "deconstruct" objective truth claims. Richard Rorty (1931–2007) viewed truth as pragmatic descriptions of the way the world works for us in community with others.

The result is a "post-truth" culture that is paradoxically convinced of no truth except that there is no truth. As D. A. Carson notes in *The Intolerance of Tolerance*, tolerance used to mean that people have the right to be wrong. Now it means that there is no such thing as wrong.

Of course, if you disagree, you are "intolerant."

God's Truth

Jesus obviously disagreed. One of his most famous declarations, a statement seen over many libraries around the world, announces, "You will know the truth, and the truth will set you free" (John 8:32). However, most expressions of this claim leave out its foundational precursor: "If you abide in my word, you are truly my disciples" (John 8:31). Only then can we know the truth, since the truth is found in the one who is "the truth" (John 14:6).

Jesus added that "the Spirit of truth . . . will guide you into all the truth" (John 16:13). Praying for his followers, he asked his Father, "Sanctify them in the truth; your word is truth" (John 17:17). And he calls us to "worship in spirit and truth" (John 4:24).

To summarize: The Bible views truth as objective and based on the authority of Scripture. The Spirit will lead us to understand the objective meaning of biblical truth so we can apply it to our lives and thus experience personal sanctification and genuine worship.

Jesus's invitation to experience such a true and loving God is the good news we call the "gospel."

What Is the Gospel, Plain and Simple?

So, what *is* the good news? God created humans and everything else as good. Tragically, humans choose to trust themselves rather than what leads to flourishing: God's wise instruction. Whether out of selfishness, pride, lust, or something else, we choose to do what seems good in our eyes. When we miss the mark of true goodness, we sin. The brokenness we see in the world results from sin. All of us sin, and God will hold us accountable, judging our thoughts and actions.

Thankfully, he loves us and still wants to partner with us in caring for his creation. So God will re-create the world into a sinless, sorrowless new place where we live in a thriving relationship with him that lasts forever.

For God to bring us close to himself so that he might transform us, we must first get rid of sin and overcome death. We cannot do that in our own power; we have to trust him for it. Jesus, who is also God, humbled himself by becoming a man and living a perfect life. He willingly gave his life up as a sacrifice to cover our sins so that we can become close to him. He defeated death by rising from the dead. He offers new life to anyone who takes him up on his offer. That offer is a gift: it is by grace. However, if we do not trust Jesus, his judgment will find us wanting, sending us to a place of darkness and fire—eternal death, separated from him. But when we trust and follow Jesus, which leads to looking to the Bible for wisdom and instruction, committing ourselves to bringing his kingdom on earth through love and being led by the Holy Spirit, he will give us new, eternal life that starts now.

Through his undeserved gift, we become adopted sons and daughters of God.

Simple Apologetics

Our personal story, or "testimony," is probably our most powerful evangelistic tool, especially in this relativistic culture. However, some unbelievers affirm objective truth but reject the gospel, claiming that evidence and argument is on their side. For this reason, if for no other, we should study apologetics, defending the faith based on rational merits.

Interestingly, even in these cases, rational barriers are often not the underlying reason for unbelief. So listen attentively to people's stories before engaging in this kind of discussion, and always keep the conversation loving and civil.

Instead of reproducing what is more fully developed elsewhere, let me direct you to the "Resources for Further Study" at the end of this chapter. In addition, many brilliant thinkers discuss apologetics online, which anyone can access for free.

Rational arguments are like candles, not floodlights. While they help illuminate the truth, they cannot dissipate all uncertainty.[4] Even when evidence convinces us of Christianity, we need to trust Jesus; we must not only mentally acquiesce to his existence but must also pledge our allegiance (James 2:19).

To reach skeptics, we cannot stop at lighting the candles of rational argument. We must shine our light by compassionately reflecting Christ's light in our lives.

Compassion

In the twenty-first century, the digital marketplace of ideas produces a constant runoff of vitriol, creating a sullied public dis-

---

4 I borrowed this image from Bruce B. Miller, *The Seven Big Questions: Searching for God, Truth, and Purpose* (Dallas: Global Media Outreach, 2022).

course.[5] In the West, where chasms run so deep that some equate conservatives with the KKK and others equate progressives with Stalinists, how can we hope to talk lovingly about something even deeper than politics—religion?

To begin, this poisoned public discourse is disconnection from people and reality. It springs from the false safety of castigating others behind a digital mask and saying things we would never say to people's faces. We allow the extreme fringes of society to grip our attention when our neighbors are not beyond hope, even if they do disagree with us.

Paranoia and fear often keep us from sharing our faith. We sit in tribes, huddled together with people who look and think like us, weathering one purported existential crisis after another.[6]

But God's kingdom overrides this rampant tribalism when we, his ambassadors, fear God and live to the beat of "compassionate hearts" (Col. 3:12). Compassion allows us to see through the acts of a criminal to his broken, traumatized childhood and feel compassion; compassion produces tears at the sight of violence; compassion slices through dividing walls because, no matter what, the people involved are beautiful individuals created by God.

What about righteous anger against the evils of our degrading culture? Brokenness should break our hearts and inflame our souls.

---

5   Jonathan Haidt's insights on social media and America's modern public square are particularly illuminating. See Jonathan Haidt, "Why the Past 10 Years of American Life Have Been Uniquely Stupid," *The Atlantic*, April 11, 2022, https://www.theatlantic.com/; Haidt, "Yes, Social Media Really Is Undermining Democracy," *The Atlantic*, July 28, 2022, https://www.theatlantic.com/.

6   For more on overcoming political tribalism, we recommend the *Truth over Tribe* podcast, as well as the book *Truth over Tribe*, and subscribing to Denison Forum's content, where we strive to view current events through a nonpartisan, biblical lens. See Patrick Keith Miller and Keith Simon, *Truth over Tribe: Pledging Allegiance to the Lamb, Not the Donkey or the Elephant* (Colorado Springs: Cook, 2022).

JIM DENISON AND MARK LEGG

Yet, always, we must say to ourselves, "There but for the grace of God go I," or we become a religious "brood of vipers" that keeps people from Jesus because of our illusion of moral superiority (Matt. 12:34). Compassion is not easy. In fact, compassion is often harder when we get to know people—because they are sinners like us. In Dostoevsky's *The Brothers Karamazov*, Ivan, the intellectual atheist, remarks: "I could never understand how one can love one's neighbours. It's just one's neighbours, to my mind, that one can't love, though one might love those at a distance."[7]

So how do we allow Spirit-led compassion to overwhelm our cultural divisiveness? We *see, serve, befriend, pray for, fear and weep for, evangelize,* and *disciple* our neighbors.

See Your Neighbors

The most powerful stories of Jesus's redemptive love begin with him noticing people whom others ignored. He extended love to an outcast with leprosy, to a sexually promiscuous woman who, as a Samaritan, was his bitter cultural rival, and to rough, poor, backwater fishermen.

But lest one characterize our Messiah as preferential to the "working class," he also extended love to Zacchaeus, a chief tax collector for the oppressive Roman regime who received kickbacks as he extorted the poor.

Jesus reserved his harshest words for hypocritical, legalistic religious leaders. But he loved even them. He met in the night with Nicodemus to explain the mystery of the good news.

The tribalism of the first century differed from ours in content but not much in form. Samaritans and Jews held on to centuries-old hatred and prejudicial grudges, which is precisely why Jesus used

7 Fyodor Dostoevsky, *The Brothers Karamazov*, trans. Constance Garnett (New York: Macmillan, 1926), 248–49.

them as characters in his parable answering the question "Who is my neighbor?"

Joshua S. Porter once put it to me like this: If Jesus began his ministry today, he might walk into the fray of a 2020 protest in Portland and grab an ANTIFA rioter in a ski mask and say, "Follow me." Then, he would cross the street to find a counterprotester in a MAGA hat and say, "Follow me."[8] When Jesus called Matthew the tax collector and Simon the zealot, for all intents and purposes, he did exactly that.

We must see through the political, cultural, and economic divides. If we love others radically enough to give up our lives, we must put everything on the block for sacrifice, even our own opinions.

Elliot Clark, in *Evangelism as Exiles*, provides an example. When Clark talked with a few of his Muslim professor friends, they would occasionally bring up 9/11 conspiracies. Clark made the hard call that "I couldn't allow my national pride or a commitment to 'the facts' to jeopardize my greater commitment—to humbly present the gospel."[9]

See *through* the broken beliefs of others; we will stand naked of our opinions when we reach judgment day.

Jesus exemplified a new way in seeing the unseeable and noticing the unnoticed. He overrode prejudice to present the truth of himself. In love, we must lay our opinions, our finances, our safety—everything—on the altar to God, so that we are freed from ourselves so that we *see* others.

You have neighbors. Notice them.

8   "'Death to Deconstruction': How Orthodoxy Is Radical: A Conversation with Joshua S. Porter," *Denison Forum* (podcast), episode 54, December 19, 2022, https://www.denison forum.org/.

9   Elliot Clark, *Evangelism as Exiles: Life on Mission as Strangers in Our Own Land* (n.p.: TGC, 2019), 74–76.

Serve Your Neighbors

We cannot forget that good deeds are an essential part of sharing the good news, especially since acts of service resonate with a young generation that puts all institutions under a microscope to test their bona fides.[10]

Good deeds do not make for good news nowadays; mainstream media does not often talk about good news, especially good deeds by Christians. So, while the cultural perception that the church does not benefit society is false, we must still recognize that many people see the church as doing more harm than good.[11]

But we can unite with our neighbors around something we agree on: helping others. For example, churches outnumber public schools two to one in America.[12] How much would our influence spread if each of our churches "adopted" a struggling school, giving it supplies, volunteer hours, mentoring, after-school programs, renovations, and so on, without strings attached?

Kevin Palau, a Christian evangelist, partnered with the mayor of Portland, who is gay, to help schools through CityServe, which established a friendship and partnership in service. Palau encourages us to reach out by "joining hands with community leaders and our literal neighbors to build a healthy community, strong public schools, a safe and clean environment for everyone."[13]

10 Mark Legg, "What Does Gen Z Value? 4 Truths about What Gen Z Believes," Denison Forum, September 12, 2022, https://www.denisonforum.org/.

11 "In study after study, religious practice is the behavioral variable with the strongest and most consistent association with generous giving." Karl Zinsmeister, "Less God, Less Giving?," *Philanthropy Roundtable*, December 23, 2021, https://www.philanthropyroundtable.org/. That does not even account for the countless hospitals and charitable ministries, like the Red Cross, that exist because of Christian charity.

12 Kevin Palau, *Unlikely: Setting Aside Our Differences to Live Out the Gospel* (New York: Howard, 2015), 99.

13 Palau, *Unlikely*, 41.

There are countless ways for us to shine our light by serving in our communities. We can extend the gospel not only to those we help but also to those who help alongside us.

Befriend Your Neighbors

Rosaria Butterfield writes in *The Gospel Comes with a House Key*: "In post-Christian communities, your words can be only as strong as your relationships. Your best weapon is an open door, a set table, a fresh pot of coffee, and a box of Kleenex for the tears that spill."[14] Our best strategy to "make strangers neighbors and neighbors family of God" is ordinary but selfless hospitality.[15]

Butterfield is an example of God's work through hospitality. Once a feminist, an open lesbian, and a tenured professor of English and women's studies at Syracuse University, she herself came to find Jesus through an ordinary pastor and his family's persistent love and reliable hospitality.

Everyone eats, and everyone enjoys a good meal. Most people, in America at least, also enjoy a good cup of coffee. Drinks, meals, and kindness open conversations and hearts.

At the cusp of the twenty-first century, Alan Putman, in *Bowling Alone*, explored how America lost the art of making friends of strangers and developing a broader sense of community. Here's a rule of thumb for every Christian: Don't "bowl" alone. Find something you enjoy doing and make friends around that common interest.

For instance, I (Mark Legg) am making friends with my neighbor in a local rock-climbing gym (under a literal LGBTQ banner).

---

14 Rosaria Champagne Butterfield, *The Gospel Comes with a House Key* (Wheaton, IL: Crossway, 2018), 40.

15 Butterfield, *The Gospel Comes with a House Key*, 31.

When I *saw* him, I invited him to coffee. Then, I invited him to rock climb. Then, I invited him into my home, and he invited me into his. Now we're becoming *friends*. Friends trust each other, and they talk about their faith (or, in his case, the lack thereof).

Palau writes: "Our impact can be measured by the quality and depth of our relationships. They're not incidental to our mission. They are the mission."[16]

J. I. Packer writes: "If you wish to do personal evangelism, then—and I hope you do; you ought to—pray for the gift of friendship. A genuine friendliness is in any case a prime mark of the man who is learning to love his neighbour as himself."[17]

Pray for Your Neighbors

We are convinced that ranks upon ranks of people will arrive at home with Jesus because of teary, sincere prayers of children for their jaded grandparents and, conversely, because of fervent, elderly heroes praying for their estranged grandchildren.

C. S. Lewis wrote: "I have two lists of names in my prayers, those for whose conversion I pray, and those for whose conversion I give thanks. The little trickle of transference from list A to list B is a great comfort."[18]

Through studying the world's Great Awakenings, one of us (Jim Denison) found a common denominator: committed prayer. Dutch Reformed pastor Theodore Frelinghuysen, after coming to the New World, said he prayed for seven years for all his church deacons to become Christians, then continued praying for spiritual awakening

---

16 Palau, *Unlikely*, 81.

17 J. I. Packer, *Evangelism and the Sovereignty of God* (Downers Grove, IL: InterVarsity Press, 1979), 82.

18 C. S. Lewis, *Yours, Jack: Spiritual Direction from C. S. Lewis*, ed. Paul F. Ford (New York: Harper Collins, 2008), 136.

to sweep colonial America. His prayers and those of others were used to birth the First Great Awakening.

The Second Great Awakening was born out of Baptist pastor Isaac Backus's call to prayer for a genuine movement of God's Spirit. The Third Great Awakening began in what became known as the "Businessmen's Prayer Meeting" movement. The Fourth Great Awakening was birthed in Wales out of Evan Roberts's call for confession and repentance in prayer.

Prayer does not sprinkle our evangelism with good luck; prayer is a desperate plea with God to move in the hearts of our friends. "Evangelism is man's work, but the giving of faith is God's."[19] Talking to God is *essential* for talking to others about Jesus.

Fear and Weep for Your Neighbors

In the book of Romans, Paul pours out his heart for his Jewish kin: "I have great sorrow and unceasing anguish in my heart. For I could wish that I myself were accursed and cut off from Christ for the sake of my brothers, my kinsmen according to the flesh. . . . Brothers, my heart's desire and prayer to God for them is that they may be saved" (9:2–3; 10:1). Sadly, most of Paul's fellow Jews missed the Messiah after waiting for centuries.

How many of us can say we weep for the lost? When we live in Jesus's presence, we'll adopt his heart for compassion. Bonhoeffer wrote: "So few are granted the pitying eyes of Jesus, for only those who share the love of his heart have been given eyes to see. And only they can enter the harvest field."[20] May God fill our eyes with hot tears over those "progressing quietly and comfortably" toward hell.[21]

19 Packer, *Evangelism and the Sovereignty of God*, 40.
20 Dietrich Bonhoeffer, *The Cost of Discipleship* (1959; repr., New York: Touchstone, 1995), 203.
21 C. S. Lewis, *The Screwtape Letters* (1942; repr., New York: Macmillan, 1959), 49.

Without love, compassion, and fear of the Lord, we will not fear for the state of our neighbors' souls. We authors wrestle with the doctrine of hell as much as anyone, but God's wrath stands whether we want it to or not.[22] Truth can feel terrifying, and rightly so. It moves inexorably and without respecting our sensibilities or concerns.

Brennan Manning, in *The Ragamuffin Gospel*, relates a story of a congregant talking to his pastor:

When I look at . . . the God of Abraham, I feel I'm near a real God, not the sort of dignified, businesslike, Rotary Club God we chatter about here on Sunday mornings. Abraham's God would blow a man to bits, give and then take a child, ask for everything from a person, and then want more. I want to know *that* God.[23]

As C. S. Lewis wrote about Aslan, the Christlike character in Narnia, he is "not like a *tame* lion."[24] Recognizing God's overwhelming holiness should never bring us to despair; it should lead us to heartfelt urgency in presenting the gospel and, indeed, prayer. This aspect of the gospel will be the most uncomfortable and difficult to talk about in our current climate.

God's judgment does not need to be the point of the spear in our conversations, but neither can we neglect it.

22 Scripture attests to eternal fire and darkness for those who live outside of God's saving grace. See the accessible, poignant treatment of this topic in Francis Chan and Preston Sprinkle, *Erasing Hell: What God Said about Eternity, and the Things We've Made Up* (Colorado Springs: Cook, 2011).
23 Brennan Manning, *The Ragamuffin Gospel: Good News for the Bedraggled, Beat-Up, and Burnt Out* (Sisters, OR: Multnomah, 2005), 39 (emphasis original).
24 C. S. Lewis, *The Lion, the Witch and the Wardrobe* (1950; repr., New York: HarperTrophy, 2002), 200 (emphasis original).

Evangelize Your Neighbors

As we make strangers into neighbors and neighbors into friends, we share the good news.

A method of evangelism that focuses on relationships does not rule out street evangelism, church evangelism, or other manners of reaching unbelievers. Woe to the one who hinders the Holy Spirit's good and multiple ways of reaching those in darkness. But under the shadow of our post-truth, post-Christian culture, where people believe street evangelists are crazy and churches are backward, relationships present the strongest, most God-honoring way forward.

So, how do we talk about the good news?

First, take heart. Although today's climate feels hostile, young people are twice as open to discussing spirituality than in previous generations.[25]

In conversations and friendships, we can move through a natural course: interests to values, then values to worldviews.[26] Sam Chan gives a tailored list of ways to share the gospel, depending on what kind of crises your friend might be going through.[27] For example, try to "ditch the jargon." I (Mark) recently presented the gospel by talking about my personality (how Jesus is healing my rampant perfectionism). During that conversation, I brought up "Christ's blood" and got a strange look. I laughed, backtracked, and was privileged to discuss the meaning of Christ's shed blood in plainer terms.

Talking about the gospel usually means listening more than anything else. Do not lie in ambush for "gotcha" moments. The best way to share Jesus is to listen to your conversation partner's

---

25 Barna, *Gen Z: The Culture, Beliefs and Motivations Shaping the Next Generation* (Ventura, CA: Barna Group, 2018).

26 Chan, *How to Talk about Jesus*, 36.

27 Chan, *How to Talk about Jesus*, 71–73.

story first, *carefully and attentively*. Listening is a skill—hone it. Then humbly present the beautiful truth of Jesus.

While evangelism is one of the Spirit's good and varied gifts, that does not preclude every Christian from practicing it. Ryan Denison categorizes this gift as a "paradigm" gift, something that every Christian should practice but that the Spirit empowers some to do more compellingly.[28]

Talking about the gospel varies in entry points based on hundreds of factors, but at the end of the day, how can people know about Jesus if we do not tell them? How can they understand the Bible if we do not help explain it (Acts 8:31; Rom. 10:13–15)?

Evangelism is not going to be a neat and perfect affair. If God wanted it done perfectly, he would do it himself. And in a way, he does—though through us broken vessels. So take heart and start somewhere.

Disciple Your Neighbors

"[We have] gathered like eagles round the carcass of cheap grace, and there we have drunk of the poison which has killed the life of following Christ."[29] So wrote German theologian Dietrich Bonhoeffer in *The Cost of Discipleship* during the rise of Nazism. He would eventually die in a concentration camp.[30]

What is cheap grace? It is the good news preached like this: "Of course you have sinned, but now everything is forgiven, so you can stay as you are and enjoy the consolations of forgiveness." Bonhoeffer counters, "It is under the influence of this kind of 'grace' that

---

28 See Ryan Denison, *What Are My Spiritual Gifts? How to Discover, Understand, and Apply Your Spiritual Gifts* (Dallas: Denison Forum, 2022).

29 Bonhoeffer, *The Cost of Discipleship*, 53.

30 Eric Metaxas, *Bonhoeffer: Pastor, Martyr, Prophet, Spy* (Nashville: Thomas Nelson, 2020), 531–32.

the world has been made 'Christian,' but at the cost of secularizing Christianity as never before."[31]

We have peddled cheap grace for too long. It collapses under the Western church before our eyes. When following Jesus becomes costly, those who have claimed him by cheap grace will abandon biblical convictions or leave the faith altogether, becoming, at best "cultural Christians" (a repugnant oxymoron). An ironic upside to our post-Christian culture, D. A. Carson writes, is that "nominal Christianity is becoming obsolete: it costs too much, with no real advantages."[32]

We must focus on making *disciples*, not just "converts." Of course, that's what Christ called us to do from the beginning (Matt. 28:19). Disciples profess that Jesus is Lord. And if he is indeed your Lord, you will obey—you will follow. You have a high calling, whether you are a new or old Christian; our Lord calls us *all* to a holier place. Growing closer to Jesus through ups and downs has a name in the Christian tradition: *sanctification*.

We cannot pretend to have achieved perfection—we lie if we say we do not sin (1 John 1:8)—but following Jesus entails growth and fruit, like that of a healthy tree in its season (John 15:5). Following Jesus requires denouncing our sinful minds and hearts with the help of Christian fellowship and the Holy Spirit. Christians growing in the fruit of the Spirit, as they submit to the Spirit, will in turn attract more lost sheep to Jesus.

Faith, Hope, and Love

God is working across the globe as millions are coming to faith in Christ. Seeing his hand at work and remembering our hope, we are compelled to share the truth with compassion.

31 Bonhoeffer, *The Cost of Discipleship*, 50.
32 D. A. Carson, foreword to Clark, *Evangelism as Exiles*, 10.

Non-Western Christianity Is Growing

We have examined the challenges of evangelism in post-Christian Western culture, but what about in the East? In Asia, countless lost people are coming to know Jesus every day. In predominantly Muslim countries, only a few thousand had converted to Christianity for hundreds of years. Now, in the past couple of decades, hundreds of thousands flock from Islam to know Christ.

Even in the West, Soong-Chan Rah argues, soft persecution will help Christ's true church shed cultural Christianity. Rah delves into how Western culture has slowly emptied the gospel of its content, rendering it captive to culture. The "tyranny of individualism, leading to personalism and privatism . . . reflects the narcissism of American culture rather than the redemptive power of the gospel message."[33] Yet he finds great potential for God's work through immigrant communities in the West.

Even if Christianity were in decline globally, we would not lose hope, but it is not in decline. On the contrary, Christianity grows under the haze of persecution in Eastern countries, even while it loses influence in the privileged, prosperous West.

Ripe for Awakening

We are always one generation away from an awakening. The biblical call is still God's invitation to us: "If my people who are called by my name humble themselves, and pray and seek my face and turn from their wicked ways, then I will hear from heaven and will forgive their sin and heal their land" (2 Chron. 7:14).

We are not waiting on God; he is waiting on us.

---

33 Soong-Chan Rah, *The Next Evangelicalism: Freeing the Church from Western Cultural Captivity* (Downers Grove, IL: InterVarsity Press, 2009), 33.

Rather than measuring success by budgets and attendance numbers, consider the practicality of relational evangelism. If one believer pours out his or her heart to several friends, and just one friend follows Jesus in the course of a year, one believer becomes two. And if each leads another friend to Jesus in the next year, two become four. Four then become eight, and so on.

If this trend continued, it would take less than thirty-three years to reach the entire eight billion people on the earth. And that is starting from one person. The point of these numbers is not to cast shame on the church or to reduce evangelism to numerical notches on one's belt. Instead, we are saying something simple: relational evangelism seems slow, but in fact its potential is exponential.

Marry Truth with Compassion

Whether you are a pastor or a layperson, wealthy or poor, look at the people around you. Make strangers into neighbors and neighbors into friends, then friends into a family through adoption by Jesus Christ.

We are not advocating a cookie-cutter way of leading people to Christ. For every million testimonies, we find a million ways of coming to know him. God might call someone to faith through a short conversation on an airplane, through decades of patient debates, through a miraculous vision of Jesus,[34] through a YouTube video, or through years of persistent, godly hospitality. But in the post-Christian West, we must refresh our understanding of how we should proclaim the gospel. By keeping truth in the forefront and radically demonstrating compassion in a culture deprived of both, we take a two-pronged approach that Jesus took.

34 Mark Legg, "How Dreams and Visions of 'Isa' Are Awakening the Islamic World," Denison Forum, September 8, 2021, https://www.denisonforum.org/.

To put it even more plainly: *show* people the light of Jesus and *tell* them about the truth of his marvelous light. Marry truth with compassion.

Questions for Reflection

1. In the late twentieth century, how did the Western church promote evangelism? Was that way inherently wrong? What do you think were the weaknesses of that approach?

2. Why is the concept of truth so important in today's world? Why must we not take that idea for granted?

3. Do you feel confident talking about the gospel and Jesus? If not, why not?

4. How is Jesus relevant to your life? Without this conviction, it will be hard to share Jesus with others.

5. Why do you think sharing the gospel by your own testimony is important in today's culture?

6. Why should we lead with compassion? What are tangible ways you can move toward compassion?

7. Why does the gospel presentation need to be accompanied by love and good works?

8. Is Christianity in decline? Does a lack of political influence mean a real decline for a Christian? Why do you think Christianity is growing so rapidly in non-Western countries?

9. Is there one "right way" to spread the gospel? What ways might be wrong or unhelpful?

Resources for Further Study

Barna. *Gen Z: The Culture, Beliefs, and Motivations Shaping the Next Generation.* Ventura, CA: Barna Group, 2018.

Denison, Jim. *Between Compromise and Courage: The Choice Every Christian Must Make.* Dallas: Denison Forum, 2021.

Denison, Jim. *The Coming Tsunami: Why Christians Are Labeled Intolerant, Irrelevant, Oppressive, and Dangerous—and How We Can Turn the Tide.* Nashville: ForeFront, 2022.

Trueman, Carl R. *The Rise and Triumph of the Modern Self: Cultural Amnesia, Expressive Individualism, and the Road to Sexual Revolution.* Wheaton, IL: Crossway, 2020.

8

Putting Christian Apologetics in Its Place

The Role of Case-Making in Evangelism

Travis Dickinson

A FEW YEARS AGO, a few colleagues and I had lunch with a retired evangelist who was then in his eighties, having spent his entire ministry career as a vocational evangelist. Someone at the table asked him why we see so few vocational evangelists today. His answer was that in today's culture, things are quite different. It used to be that, with a clear gospel presentation, people were often ready to come to faith, and evangelistic ministries were often very successful. But today people have more objections.

Our world has become much more hostile toward Christian faith. While Christianity was once a central part of our cultural identity, it no longer is. To engage a hostile world with the gospel, we need Christian apologetics in its proper place. Indeed, apologetics—the reasoned defense of the hope we have in Christ—ought to play a critical role in our being faithful witnesses to a world that desperately needs hope.

Misunderstanding Apologetics

To understate the matter, not everyone has a high view of apologetics, especially as it relates to evangelism. At least two groups look askance at the discipline. The first group thinks of it as a waste of time or even contrary to evangelism. Apologetics is time diverted from sharing the gospel. The second group sees the value of apologetics but thinks it is not for them. It is for the pastor, professor, or large-brained parishioner, they may say. Normal people have other roles and interests.

I have to admit that the bad reputation of apologetics is in some ways deserved. Sometimes apologists spend all their time arguing, with seemingly no shred of evangelistic urgency for getting to the gospel. They get bogged down in the minutiae of some line of evidence as if the only goal were to win that argument. And to be honest, apologetics presentations are often more than a bit dusty and technical, leaving the average person behind. One wonders what advanced degree one would need to follow the discussion. While the popularity of apologetics has grown in recent years, especially in the wake of increased hostility, it has remained largely academic and esoteric.

But these are misunderstandings (or perhaps misapplications) of apologetics. Christian apologetics is neither contrary nor tangential to evangelism, nor is it only for academics. Let us look at each confusion in turn.

Misunderstanding 1: Apologetics Is Contrary to Evangelism

What seems to fuel the sometimes strained relationship between apologetics and evangelism is the larger and older debate about the compatibility of faith and reason. The church father Tertullian famously asked, "What indeed has Athens to do with Jerusalem?"[1] Many read Tertullian as thinking that reason and evidence have, at best, a questionable value for faith. Since apologetics has a lot to do with reason and evidence, if we doubt that reason and evidence have value for faith, then we will likely doubt that apologetics has value for evangelism.

This view has much to do with how we understand the nature of faith. If faith is blind acceptance of the truth of Christianity, then of course reason and evidence will have little value. Some hold to what I call the *seesaw view* of faith and reason: one has faith only when one lacks reason. The more reason and evidence someone has, the less faith he or she has, and vice versa. On this view, a person cannot have a lot of evidence *and* a lot of faith. So you can imagine why apologetics would be avoided. If apologetics is the *reasoned* defense of Christianity, it cannot fan the flames of *faith*.

But this cannot be a right understanding of faith, because the Bible sees reason and evidence as appropriate grounds for faith. Take, for example, God's command that Abraham sacrifice his son Isaac (Gen. 22:1–14). Was this a call to blind faith? Far from it! By this time in Abraham's life, he had a clear view of who God was, having experienced God's miraculous providence in a variety of events. The clearest example is, of course, the miraculous birth of Isaac. Sarah had spent her adult life suffering with barrenness and was, at this point, in her early nineties. And yet she conceived

---

1 Tertullian, *Prescription against Heretics* 7.

and bore this promised child. Given this experience, Abraham came to know God as a God of power and authority. It is worth noting too that in commanding Abraham to sacrifice Isaac, God *spoke* to Abraham (Gen. 22:1–2). So did Abraham have good reason to believe? When the God whom you know to be the God of the universe gives a clear command, the rational thing to do is obey! Abraham's obedience was certainly not a case of blind faith.

Jesus had a very public ministry that included a variety of miraculous signs and wonders. Why? I suggest it was to demonstrate his divine identity and provide reasons and evidence for people to believe. He did not ask people to believe blindly. When John the Baptist found himself in prison, he had some of his followers come to Jesus and ask if he really was "the one." Jesus's reply is instructive. He did not say that John just needed to accept this by faith. He said, "Go and tell John what you have seen and heard: the blind receive their sight, the lame walk, lepers are cleansed, and the deaf hear, the dead are raised up, the poor have the good news preached to them" (Luke 7:22). Jesus pointed John and his disciples to the evidence to believe.

When it comes to the apostles, Paul's custom was to reason with the Jews in the synagogue (Acts 17:1–2; 19:8). Paul also reasoned with the Greeks. According to Acts 17:17, he "reasoned . . . in the marketplace every day with those who happened to be there," and this included Epicurean and Stoic philosophers. When they took him to the Areopagus, he made a compelling case using only reason (i.e., no scripture references) and the words of their own poets (Acts 17:28).

Christian faith always has its reasons. If this sounds odd, it may be because we have an overly narrow view of reason and evidence. We may think of evidence as synonymous with formal academic arguments. Those things, of course, count as evidence and have their place, but we do not typically look to them for most of our rational decisions. Most people believe in God not because of formal academic arguments but because God has revealed himself in some way in their lives.

The evidence upon which we believe is often rather mundane, and we typically pick it up unreflectively. For our purposes, something constitutes evidence for a claim if it points to the truth of that claim.[2] While this may include formal academic arguments, it is far broader than that. Seeing a car speeding toward you, as you step into a crosswalk, is terrific evidence of your need to jump out of the way. Spending time with someone who is kind and reliable gives you good reason to trust him or her as a friend.

Christians have a great variety of evidence, understood broadly, for Christian faith. Again, all the formal arguments one might learn in an apologetics classroom count as evidence, and these can have powerful effect. These include the many arguments for God's existence,[3] the historical evidence for Jesus's resurrection,[4] and a variety of fields that point to the reliability and truthfulness of the biblical record, including science, history, textual criticism, and archeology, among others.[5] But there are far more mundane

---

2   For more on this, see "Evidence," in Travis Dickinson, *Logic and the Way of Jesus: Thinking Critically and Christianly* (Nashville: B&H, 2022).

3   See, for example, J. P. Moreland, Chad Meister, and Khaldoun A. Sweis, *Debating Christian Theism* (New York: Oxford University Press, 2013); Gavin Ortlund, *Why God Makes Sense in a World That Doesn't: The Beauty of Christian Theism* (Grand Rapids, MI: Baker, 2021).

4   See, for example, W. David Beck and Michael R. Licona, *Raised on the Third Day: Defending the Historicity of the Resurrection of Jesus* (Bellingham, WA: Lexham, 2020); N. T. Wright, *The Resurrection of the Son of God* (Minneapolis: Fortress, 2003).

5   See Steven B. Cowan and Terry L. Wilder, *In Defense of the Bible: A Comprehensive Apologetic for the Authority of Scripture* (Nashville: B&H, 2013); Craig L. Blomberg, *The Historical Reliability of the New Testament* (Nashville: B&H, 2016).

reasons why people believe, including answers to prayer, religious experience, miraculous events, and Christian testimony. When someone gives a testimony of how her life was transformed by the power of the gospel, that person is offering powerful evidence for the truth of the gospel.

There need be no tension between faith and reason, or between evangelism and apologetics.

Misunderstanding 2: Apologetics Is Only for the Learned

The clearest call to apologetics comes in 1 Peter 3:15. Peter tells his readers, "In your hearts honor Christ the Lord as holy, always being prepared to make a defense to anyone who asks you for a reason for the hope that is in you; yet do it with gentleness and respect." This injunction is clearly not only for the "smart" people in the church. Peter's epistle was addressing Christians from all walks of life who were spread out across modern-day Turkey and were experiencing significant hostility. Thus, being ready to give a defense is no mere hobby for the specialized few but is a call for every Christian.

That is not to say that all Christians must do graduate-level work in apologetics. On my view, there are many ways one can fulfill the call to be ready to defend the faith. For a trained academic, that will look very different from how it looks for a businessperson, a stay-at-home mom, a police officer, or a plumber. As I have argued above, there are many reasons why we believe. Our task is to reflect on those and to be ready to articulate those reasons when the opportunity arises.

A problem we need to confront before moving on is that our contemporary culture, Christians included, tends to be averse to the intellectual life. This is not to say people are not smart. People today are often highly specialized in their particular vocations.

However, most people have spent little time contemplating their values and the deep things of life. J. P. Moreland puts it bluntly:

> Our society has replaced heroes with celebrities, the quest for a well-informed character with the search for flat abs, substance and depth with image and personality. In the political process, the makeup man is more important than the speech writer, and we approach the voting booth, not on the basis of a well-developed philosophy of what the state should be, but with a heart full of images, emotions, and slogans all packed into thirty-second sound bites.[6]

Another way to make this point is that many have not considered and evaluated their worldviews. A worldview is the set of assumptions and the commitments of the heart that shapes our values and affects how we think about reality.[7] We all have one, but many in our culture have not questioned or even contemplated their worldviews.

Unfortunately, the situation in the church is not much better. Christianity has its own set of assumptions and commitments. But many Christians have not deeply considered and evaluated these assumptions and commitments. Many cannot even articulate the claims of Christianity beyond a few slogans. Moreland sees this as a trend of anti-intellectualism in the church.[8] A person who cannot explain what he believes will have a hard time recommending those beliefs to others.

6 J. P. Moreland, *Love Your God with All Your Mind: The Role of Reason in the Life of the Soul*, rev. ed. (Colorado Springs: NavPress, 2012), 14.
7 James Sire, *The Universe Next Door: A Basic Worldview Catalog*, 5th ed. (Downers Grove, IL: InterVarsity Press, 2009), 20.
8 Moreland, *Love Your God*, 15.

This anti-intellectualism is deeply out of step with the Christian way of life, and it cuts the legs out from under any apologetic efforts. We have already seen that Paul and the other apostles had the capacity to engage in rational debate with people. Jesus was also an intellectual. Challenged often by the elite Jewish scholars of the day intellectually, he met these challenges with a stellar use of logical reasoning and argumentation (see, e.g., Matt. 22:15–46).

Jesus also commands us to love God with all of who we are, and he explicitly includes loving God with all our minds (Matt. 22:37). What does it mean to love God with all our minds? Part of being in love with someone is being curious about that person. We naturally want to know things about our beloved. It happens every semester on my campus as students form into couples. They fall deeply in love, and the world effectively stops when they are together. To the dismay of all their friends, they spend the bulk of their waking moments together talking about *everything*! Along with deep emotion, there is deep curiosity. They ask questions, questions, and more questions. They are loving each other with their minds as they pursue each other intellectually. Similarly, the pursuit of God should include a significant intellectual dimension as we seek to know him deeply. It is incumbent on the Christian to cultivate his or her intellectual life.

While apologetics is just one part of this picture, it is a significant part. In fact, I suggest below that wrestling with the deep and difficult apologetic questions ourselves, thus loving God with all our minds, is the best preparation for making a defense to others.

What Is Apologetics?

With those misunderstandings out of our way, it is time to say more fully what apologetics is.

The term *apologetics* comes from the Greek word *apologia*, which means "a defense." The term is used in 1 Peter 3:15, where Peter calls us to be ready to make an *apologia*, or a defense of the hope that is in us. The term was typically used in a legal context where one made a case for one's innocence. The Greek philosopher Socrates was once on trial for the charges of impiety and corrupting the youth of Athens. The account of his response to these accusations is titled *The Apology of Socrates*. From that title one might think that Socrates was apologizing or sorry for his actions, but that could not be further from the truth. In fact, after a rigorous defense of his innocence, Socrates willingly drank a hemlock cocktail as a death sentence, refusing to concede the charges.

So, what is Christian apologetics? Apologetics is defending the truth, goodness, and beauty of Christianity without assuming the unbeliever subscribes to biblical authority. Let us break this down.

1. *Defending.* In making the case, one both gives positive reasons to believe (e.g., arguments for God's existence or historical evidence for the resurrection) and responds to objections (e.g., the problem of evil or challenges from contemporary science). Even though the apologist is giving a defense, it is not only defensive. It spells out reasons in favor of Christianity and also addresses claims against Christianity. The defense will typically consist in offering evidence, understood broadly. This may include formal academic arguments but also things like testimonies of personal experiences.

2. *Truth, goodness, and beauty.* Truth is, of course, crucial to the apologetics task, and therefore most contemporary apologetics focuses exclusively on providing reasons to believe that Christianity is true. But the problem with making this our sole focus is that one can believe that a claim is true but treat it with apathy, even hostility. Consider the fact that most people believe that careful

eating and regular exercising are important for health. While we generally agree on this, many of us do little about it, unwilling to give up the pleasures of unhealthy living.

In his letter to the Romans, the apostle Paul speaks of those who "knew God" yet "suppress[ed] the truth" and "exchanged the truth about God for a lie" (1:18, 21, 25). People's suppression of what "is plain to them" (1:19) can be more or less explicit. Some may know and even admit to the truth but be tacitly unwilling to give up the pleasures of their lifestyles for its sake. Others explicitly reject Christianity, but their rejection is not on factual grounds. They contend that Christianity is not true, good, or attractive.

We need to make the case for each of these. Truth, goodness, and beauty are arguably the objective values of reality that we all need. Peter Kreeft once said:

> [Truth, goodness, and beauty] are the three things we all need, and need absolutely, and know we need, and know we need absolutely. . . . For these are the only three things that we never get bored with, and never will, for all eternity, because they are attributes of God, and therefore of all God's creation.[9]

I am convinced that Christianity satisfies all three—it is true, good, and beautiful. As Paul Gould puts it, "What we find in Christianity is a perfect blending together of reason and romance, a comprehensive understanding of reality that speaks to both head and heart, rationality and experience."[10] I am further convinced that there

9 Peter Kreeft, "Lewis's Philosophy of Truth, Goodness and Beauty," in *C. S. Lewis as Philosopher: Truth, Goodness and Beauty*, ed. David J. Baggett, Gary R. Habermas, Jerry L. Walls (Downers Grove, IL: InterVarsity Press, 2008), 23.

10 Paul M. Gould, *Cultural Apologetics: Renewing the Christian Voice, Conscience, and Imagination in a Disenchanted World* (Grand Rapids, MI: Zondervan, 2019), 31.

is a compelling case to be made for each of these and that each is crucial to the apologetics task.

3. *Without assuming the unbeliever subscribes to biblical authority.* It is, of course, possible to make a case for Christian faith that would not necessarily be an apologetic case. One might reason that God exists by appealing to Genesis 1:1, "In the beginning, God . . . ," and claiming, therefore, God exists. This is a case for the existence of God, but it rests on the Bible's authority without further argument. Is there anything wrong with quoting Scripture? Of course not! This is what we do as Christians in our Bible lessons, our sermons, and our own devotional studies. There is a sense in which pastors are making a case for Christianity each Sunday morning. But is the pastor doing apologetics if he quotes Scripture without developing an argument?

When we appeal to Scripture (or a Christian creed or some claim of Christian doctrine) to settle an issue, we are making a case, but it seems we are not making an apologetics case. I suggest that what distinguishes something as apologetics is that the case does not depend on already believing the Christian claims. That is, it is not question begging. Apologetics provides reasons and evidence for why we should believe the Christian claims. This is why in apologetics we often turn to philosophy, science, or history for making the case. So if we are making a case for the existence of God, we may appeal to the scientific fact that the universe began a finite time ago and with unbelievably precise conditions that are said to be fine-tuned for a life-permitting universe.[11] This is the consensus of contemporary science! But this is an exceedingly difficult fact to explain on the basis of atheism and gives us reason to believe that

---

11 See Stephen C. Meyer, *Return of the God Hypothesis: Three Scientific Discoveries That Reveal the Mind behind the Universe* (New York: HarperCollins, 2021).

a Creator God exists. We are, in effect, making a case for "In the beginning, God . . ."

The Distinct Roles of Apologetics

The fact that apologetics gives reasons and evidence in answer to objections makes it distinctly relevant to evangelism, which we will explore below. But what we should not miss is that apologetics plays a broader role than merely as a tool for the evangelist.

First and foremost, apologetics is a way for the Christian to love God with all of his or her mind. This is, by my lights, the very best way to get prepared to make a defense. Before we ever get out there on the field, as it were, to make a case for Christianity and address the questions of others, we should be asking the deep and difficult questions for ourselves. Sometimes well-intentioned Christians get some neat outlines and charts together to share with others without ever having wrestled with the questions. This can easily come across as dismissive and even inauthentic. Instead, I suggest taking time to really understand the deep questions and the problems that challenge us and wrestle with the best way forward. When we do this, we will have much more powerful answers to anyone who asks for a reason for the hope that is in us. This is what I call *devotional apologetics*.

Apologetics is also extremely relevant for discipleship. When people come to Christ, they of course do so without having it all figured out. And let us be honest, even if you have been a Christian for a very long time, you still do not have it *all* figured out. A normal part of Christian discipleship, then, is to ask the deep and difficult questions and grow in our knowledge of God, the Bible, the work of Christ, what is to come, and an endless list of other topics. In asking questions, Christians can sometimes experience doubts about the Christian answers to these questions.[12] When the questions are not about what we believe but why we should believe, here apologetics has significant value for discipleship. We of course need to know what the Bible says to grow in maturity, but we also need a growing knowledge of why we should believe the Bible. I call this *discipleship apologetics*.

We turn now to consider *evangelistic apologetics*.

The Aim of Apologetics in Evangelism

It should be clear at this point that, contrary to the views of some apologists, apologetics is not the same thing as evangelism. While apologetics is extremely relevant to evangelism, apologetics, as we have seen, plays a broader role in the life of the Christian, including both devotionally and in discipleship. If we are working on our own questions or we have mentored another Christian through a season of doubt, we of course would not call this evangelism. It is helpful, therefore, to think of these as distinct but overlapping disciplines and pursuits. Evangelistic apologetics is that part of apologetics that overlaps with evangelism and becomes quite indispensable when one is in a hostile context.

The aim of evangelistic apologetics, I suggest, is a soft heart—a heart that is open to the gospel. Let's be clear. The ultimate aim in evangelism is to faithfully proclaim the gospel and to invite the unbelieving person to place faith in Jesus. This is the ultimate aim, whether we are sharing the gospel or doing apologetics. But in the service of this ultimate aim, there is a more immediate goal in doing evangelistic apologetics: to break down resistance so that people can hear the gospel.

---

12 See Travis Dickinson, *Wandering toward God: Finding Faith amid Doubts and Big Questions* (Downers Grove, IL: InterVarsity Press, 2022).

A hard heart, as the Bible describes it, is a symptom of the lost person. For example, Paul describes the state of unbelieving Gentiles (for our purposes, those far from God) as "darkened in their understanding, alienated from the life of God because of the ignorance that is in them, due to their hardness of heart" (Eph. 4:18). Paul connects this intellectual problem to the unbeliever's resistance to the things of God.

Because apologetics can be used to soften this hardness, it is sometimes called "pre-evangelism." While this language can be helpful, I do not prefer the term, because it can drive a wedge between apologetics and evangelism. I prefer to think of evangelistic apologetics as an important part of the evangelistic task. We do not engage in our apologetics, our pre-evangelism, and then switch gears into evangelism proper. It is often more fluid than that. We may share the gospel first with someone and then find that the person has objections. We may answer the objections and then share the gospel again only to find more questions. If one is able to present an intellectually robust response that addresses objections and provides reasons to believe that Christianity is true, then God may use that to soften a person's heart.

A common objection is that Christianity is not good. People see the corruption of the church in history, in the news, and on social media. The Christian apologist can make a case for the many positive effects of the Christian church on the world, from health care to literacy to universal human rights, and so on. The apologist can also humbly confess that the church and everyone in it (as well as outside it) falls short, which is why we look to the person of Jesus as the one perfect person in history. He is the one we need precisely because of our sin and fallenness. This realism may help to soften a person's heart toward the goodness of Christianity.

Some may argue that even if Christianity is true and has some good effects on the world, it seems stifling, restrictive, and unattractive, given what must be sacrificed. If the Christian apologist makes a case for the stunning beauty and wonder of being reconciled and fulfilled in relationship to God, this may soften hearts to such an extent that they are open to the gospel of how that relationship is found in Jesus.

Arguing People into the Kingdom?

A common objection to the use of apologetics in evangelism is that it sounds like we are arguing people into the kingdom by our own efforts.

I agree that no one gets saved by an argument. Salvation only comes by the gospel (Rom. 1:16). But I do not agree that arguments and evidence play no role in someone's coming to Christ. Many people report having had no idea that such compelling evidence for Christianity exists. They were under the impression the Christian claims were just silly and delusional, similar to claims about fairies and believing in mythical creatures. But then someone took the time to make a case for Christianity that was robust and compelling. Did this case-making save them? Of course not, but it definitely played a role in opening them up to the gospel, perhaps for the first time. C. S. Lewis is a great example of this. By his own description, he was "the most dejected and reluctant convert in all of England."[13] For Lewis, the evidence for the truth, goodness, and beauty of Christianity played a major role in bringing him—"kicking, struggling, resentful, and darting his eyes in every direction for a chance of escape"—to a place of faith.[14]

13 C. S. Lewis, *Surprised by Joy* (1955; repr., San Diego: Harvest, 1984), 228.
14 Lewis, *Surprised by Joy*, 229.

Is all this just a matter of our human efforts? No! We are called to be faithful witnesses in whatever situations we find ourselves (Acts 1:8). The Holy Spirit alone makes our work effective. Not even the arguments and evidence of Christian apologetics are what soften hearts. The Holy Spirit does that work. It is entirely consistent to think that the whole of spiritual regeneration is solely of the Holy Spirit and that he uses both our feeble attempts at defending the truth, goodness, and beauty of Christianity to soften hearts and our feeble attempts to spell out what Jesus did for us on the cross to bring people to saving faith. Both in apologetics and in sharing the gospel, we should make a careful and passionate attempt to be faithful witnesses, but it is God who accomplishes the work. The Holy Spirit may use our efforts, or he may not. But there is no conflict in principle to faithfully bearing witness while using the apologetic evidence of Christianity.

Reformed theologian J. Gresham Machen makes a powerful point in this regard:

> It is true that the decisive thing is the regenerative power of God. That can overcome all lack of preparation, and the absence of that makes even the best preparation useless. But as a matter of fact God usually exerts that power in connection with certain prior conditions of the human mind, and it should be ours to create, so far as we can, with the help of God, those favorable conditions for the reception of the gospel. False ideas are the greatest obstacles to the reception of the gospel.[15]

---

15 Address delivered on September 20, 1912, at the opening of the 101st session of Princeton Theological Seminary, reprinted in J. Gresham Machen, *What Is Christianity?* (Grand Rapids, MI: Eerdmans, 1951), 162.

When someone is convinced that the Bible is riddled with contradictions and claims that are counter to scientific fact, or when people are unsure that Jesus even existed, much less that he walked on water or was raised from the dead, these false ideas present significant obstacles to hearing the gospel. Machen goes on to say, "We may preach with all the fervor of a reformer and yet succeed only in winning a straggler here and there."[16] If someone thinks our whole message is on the level of a fairy tale and all we do is lay out the basic claims of the gospel, even if we do it with great passion, God certainly could move in that person's heart, but the message is likely to be dismissed. And we need to realize that this is precisely how Christianity is perceived in many parts of our world today.

Christian apologetics indeed has a role to play in our evangelistic efforts. As we love God with all of our minds and reflect on the reasons for the hope within us, we become thereby ready to make a case to others. In our hostile world, questions and objections are going to come our way. Our aim is to soften hearts of people toward the gospel, that they may be saved by the power of God and for his glory.

Questions for Reflection

1. Are faith and reason necessarily at odds?

2. What is Christian apologetics?

3. What is the distinction between devotional, discipleship, and evangelistic apologetics?

---

16 Machen, *What Is Christianity*, 162.

4. How does Christian apologetics serve the ultimate aim of evangelism?

5. Does apologetics mean we are arguing someone into the kingdom by our own efforts? Why or why not?

Resources for Further Study

Beilby, James K. *Thinking about Christian Apologetics: What It Is and Why We Do It.* Downers Grove, IL: InterVarsity Press, 2011.

Chatraw, Joshua D., and Mark D. Allen. *Apologetics at the Cross.* Grand Rapids, MI: Zondervan, 2018.

Gould, Paul M., Travis Dickinson, and Keith Loftin. *Stand Firm: Apologetics and the Brilliance of the Gospel.* Nashville: B&H, 2018.

Moreland, J. P. *Love Your God with All Your Mind: The Role of Reason in the Life of the Soul.* Rev. ed. Colorado Springs: NavPress, 2012.

9

Learning from C. S. Lewis

Apologetic Approaches for Various Contexts

Harry Lee Poe

C. S. LEWIS never set out to write apologetics.[1] He did not aspire to become the most effective Christian apologist of the twentieth century. Nonetheless, sixty years after his death, his apologetics continue to have a compelling force that separates them from all other apologetics of the twentieth century and makes them almost unique in Christian history. Part of the success of the apologetics of Lewis comes from the fact that he did not have a single apologetic approach but used at least five approaches, each of which spoke to a different dimension of life.

Like Augustine, Lewis was a man of his times whose apologetics emerged from his own life experience. Augustine's *Confessions*

---

1 This chapter was originally presented as part of the inaugural Knickerbocker C. S. Lewis and Friends Lectureship at the Memphis Theological Seminary on April 8, 2008.

offers insight into why he would later write *The City of God*. In *Surprised by Joy*, Lewis explained why he had several different approaches to apologetics, represented by such diverse works as *Out of the Silent Planet, Miracles, A Grief Observed, Reflections on the Psalms*, and *A Preface to Paradise Lost*. In *The Personal Heresy*, Lewis warned against the problem of reading a book as though it were about its author. Such a reading depends on a pseudo-psychological analysis of the author by a literary critic unqualified and untrained in psychoanalysis. In the case of Augustine's *Confessions* and Lewis's *Surprised by Joy*, however, these books really are about the authors and do not require a clairvoyant's skill at reading between the lines.

Even in these books, however, Augustine and Lewis write to point beyond themselves. Dr. R. E. "Humphrey" Havard, physician to Lewis and member of his Inklings literary circle, once quipped that *Surprised by Joy* might more aptly have been named *Suppressed by Jack* because of how little Lewis actually reveals in it about himself.[2] Lewis told us much more about himself in his first autobiography, *The Pilgrim's Regress*, but since it was written as allegory, few modern readers understand the extent to which he poured out his innermost thoughts and feelings. He wrote *The Pilgrim's Regress* during a fortnight visit to Northern Ireland in 1932 while he was engaged in finishing his first important scholarly work, *The Allegory of Love*. In *The Pilgrim's Regress*, Lewis describes his plight as a modern man pulled in a variety of directions by competing ideas, emotions, and experiences. In *The Allegory of Love*, he explores the medieval allegorical love poetry tradition, its

2 George Sayer, *Jack: C. S. Lewis and His Times* (San Francisco: Harper & Row, 1988), 198. Havard made this remark in a letter to Sayer, one of Lewis's earlier pupils, who became a close friend and later wrote the best biography of Lewis.

treatment of the *bellum intestinum* (the internal war), and the ideal of being a whole person.

The value of wholeness permeates the Bible. In Hebrew, *shalom* is the word for wholeness, which is traditionally translated "peace," because peace is the practical result of wholeness. A person who experiences internal conflict between emotions, decisions, ideas, and values lacks peace. The biblical view of a whole person as a living soul involves both the physical body and the spiritual nature that are made in the image of God. Because of sin, however, people are not whole. Sin did not begin with the modern world, but the modern world has learned new ways to be torn into bits. Lewis laid a great deal of the modern problem at the feet of Aristotle, who provided a rationale for division and fragmentation. In *The Allegory of Love*, Lewis observed:

> Aristotle is, before all, the philosopher of divisions. His effect on his greatest disciple [Thomas Aquinas], as M. Gilson has traced it, was to dig new chasms between God and the world, between human knowledge and reality, between faith and reason. Heaven began, under this dispensation, to seem far off. The danger of Pantheism grew less: the danger of mechanical Deism came a step nearer. It is almost as if the first, faint shadow of Descartes, or even of "our present discontents" had fallen across the scene.[3]

Descartes introduced the ultimate modern division in the seventeenth century by separating mind and body as two distinct, virtually independent realms. The modern fragmentation of knowledge

3   C. S. Lewis, *The Allegory of Love* (New York: Galaxy, 1958), 88.

and the fragmentation of the person proceed from Descartes's dichotomy between the physical and the spiritual.

The Formation of an Apologist

Into the modern world of fragmentation and division at the height of British imperial power and prestige, C. S. Lewis was born on November 29, 1898. In time he would grow to love things medieval and ancient, but only after an adolescence and young adulthood in which he drank deeply of things Freudian and Darwinian. If Descartes had constructed an impenetrable barrier between the physical and the spiritual, the intellectual giants of the nineteenth century eliminated the spiritual altogether by reducing everything to the physical. Young Lewis studied logic with William T. Kirkpatrick, a fanatical disciple of the new way of thinking, who taught Lewis how to think and argue. Even as he was educated as a "modern man" while reading the classics, Lewis had lingering flights of fancy into the world of myth. Imagination posed a serious threat to the comfortable world of materialism Lewis had learned to inhabit, for imagination pointed beyond the physical to something else.[4]

As he grew from childhood to young adulthood, Lewis experienced firsthand the meaning of pain and suffering at several levels. He witnessed his mother's slow death to cancer. He experienced the bullying of the English public-school system. He experienced the horrors of total war in the trenches of France, where he was wounded, where his brother became a hopeless alcoholic, and where his friend Paddy Moore died. He experienced the problem

---

4 For a full account of Lewis's years of study with W. T. Kirkpatrick, his pleasure reading of literary classics, and his spiritual experience growing up, see Harry Lee Poe, *Becoming C. S. Lewis: A Biography of Young Jack Lewis, 1898–1918* (Wheaton, IL: Crossway, 2019).

of human alienation with his own father. He experienced sex, guilt, gallantry, and manipulation. Both emotionally and intellectually, he had amassed a varied collection of reasons not to believe in God. He accepted pain and suffering as the norm in Darwin's world, in which each member of the species competes for advantage against every other member. He learned to dismiss guilt, as Freud taught, since it was only the result of social conditioning and not a response to an objective moral order behind the universe. Like Kenneth Grahame's Mr. Toad, he flitted from one fashionable thing to the next in search of the reductionist's dream: the real thing. Like the preacher of Ecclesiastes, he tried everything from scholarship to aesthetics. Though he hoped to find the physical locus of everything, everything kept pointing beyond, to an ultimate spiritual reality.

After World War I, Lewis went back to Oxford, where he had completed only one partial term before enlisting in the Officer Training Corps. He completed a course of study in classics and philosophy, and then a second course of study in English literature. He hoped to make his mark as a great poet while earning his living as an academic. Lewis was surprised that the most interesting people he met after the war were all Christians. Throughout the 1920s he enjoyed the friendship of J. R. R. Tolkien, Nevill Coghill, and Hugo Dyson, who seemed perfectly sane except for their belief not only in God but also in the reality of the story of God taking on flesh, dying, and rising. By 1930 Lewis admitted that God was God, but he was not yet prepared to admit that Jesus was also God until a late-night stroll in the grounds of Magdalen College with Tolkien and Dyson on September 19, 1931.

In the course of their walk Lewis expressed the view that Christianity seemed like just another one of the myths about a dying and rising god. Tolkien agreed and said that the only thing different about Christianity was that it was the myth that actually happened. This comment had an enormous impact on Lewis, who mulled it over for almost two weeks before he realized, after a motorcycle ride to the Whipsnade Zoo, that he also believed that Jesus Christ was the Son of God.[5] The idea of the myth that actually happened also settled an enormous problem for Lewis as a student of literature. He knew the stories of the dying and rising god from all the major world cultures that have left written records. The presence of this story in cultures that had no contact with each other poses the problem of why such a universal story should exist. God solved this problem for Lewis, and this solution deepened his understanding of the power of stories and their transcendent nature.

His conversion experience would continue to inform his scholarship and his apologetics. In his second series of broadcast talks for the BBC during World War II, Lewis remarked that God had sent the human race "good dreams," by which he meant, "those queer stories scattered all through the heathen religions about a god who dies and comes to life again and, by his death, has somehow given new life to men."[6]

Because of the course his life took, Lewis understood both intellectually and experientially what difference Jesus Christ makes. Once he came to faith, Lewis had the background to talk to people who were curious, skeptical, undecided, or otherwise willing to examine the claims of Jesus Christ.

---

5 For the full story of Lewis's conversion, see Harry Lee Poe, *The Making of C. S. Lewis: From Atheist to Apologist, 1918–1945* (Wheaton, IL: Crossway, 2021).

6 C. S. Lewis, *Mere Christianity* (1952; repr., New York: HarperSanFrancisco, 2001), 50. Lewis made this remark in the chapter entitled "The Shocking Alternative."

The Preparation of an Apologist

Some people actually set out with the vocational goal of becoming Christian apologists. Theological seminaries and Christian colleges teach courses on apologetics. Some schools have full academic programs on apologetics. C. S. Lewis had no such vocational goal, nor any certified training in how to become an apologist. On the other hand, his academic training in philosophy and literature provided invaluable preparation for an avocational career he did not plan but accepted reluctantly.

Lewis was not the only Christian apologist of his generation. The apologists of his age tended to have training as philosophers or philosophical theologians. They tended to write for other philosophers and theologians rather than for the average person. Apologetics became an intellectual exercise within the academic world. In the English-speaking world since the eighteenth century, apologetics tended to be equated with natural theology and various proofs for the existence of God from nature. Charles Darwin dampened interest in this stream of thought by the last quarter of the nineteenth century. Karl Barth virtually killed off any remaining interest in the subject by the second quarter of the twentieth century, when Lewis began writing as a Christian. One of the great men of the worldwide Anglican communion of the twentieth century was Bishop Stephen Neill, an Englishman who served as a missionary to India and became the bishop of the Church of South India before returning to England as assistant to the archbishop of Canterbury. I had the privilege of studying with Bishop Neill in January 1976 when he taught a month-long course at my seminary titled "Christianity in the Twentieth Century." He understood almost everything, but he could not understand why Americans were so taken with C. S. Lewis. He preferred William Temple. His reasons for preferring Temple were the same reasons Americans were so taken with Lewis. Lewis spoke to them. Lewis understood that the audience for apologetics is the person who has the questions, not the expert who has the answers.

Lewis was the only show in town when many people with excellent academic preparation had no word for the *hoi polloi*. In perhaps his most heated response to a critic from the theological world, Lewis answered Norman Pittenger's critique of him that had appeared in the *Christian Century*.[7] Pittenger had criticized Lewis for using the modern word *miracle* rather than one of the Greek words found in the New Testament. Lewis replied that he was "writing for people who wanted to know whether the things could have happened rather than what they should be called."[8] After answering Pittenger's criticisms blow for blow, Lewis moved to his conclusion by laying out the problem with Pittenger's approach to criticism. Here we must recall that literary criticism was Lewis's area of international reputation at the highest level:

> He judges my books *in vacuo*, with no consideration of the audience to whom they were addressed or of the prevalent errors they were trying to combat. The Naturalist becomes a straw man [to Pittenger] because he is not found among "first-rate scientists" and readers of Einstein. But I was writing *ad populum*, not *ad clerum*. This is relevant to my manner as well as my matter.[9]

7 See W. Norman Pittenger, "Apologist versus Apologist: A Critique of C. S. Lewis," *Christian Century* 75 (October 1958): 1104–7.

8 C. S. Lewis, "Rejoinder to Dr Pittenger," in *God in the Dock: Essays on Theology and Ethics*, ed. Walter Hooper (Grand Rapids, MI: Eerdmans, 1979), 179.

9 Lewis, "Rejoinder to Dr Pittenger," 182.

The originality of Lewis lies not so much with what he had to say as with how he said it. He shrank from the idea of saying something original or innovative about the faith. He embraced the challenge of expressing the faith in a way that people could understand. He believed that both the revivalists and the cultured clergy, who became the conventional alternatives for Christian exposition during Lewis's time, failed equally at their real task. It was in the face of this massive failure in England that Lewis accepted the mantle put before him.

> My task was therefore simply that of a *translator*—one turning Christian doctrine, or what he believed to be such, into the vernacular, into language that unscholarly people would attend to and could understand. For this purpose a style more guarded, more *nuancé*, finelier shaded, much more rich in fruitful ambiguities—in fact, a style more like Dr Pittenger's own—would have been worse than useless. It would not only have failed to enlighten the common reader's understanding; it would have aroused his suspicion.[10]

Lewis not only had an interest in dispensing truth; he had a passionate desire that truth be understood.

Until his conversion, Lewis did not have the same skill or apparent desire for making himself understood. The two books of poetry he published in the 1920s do not lend themselves to the mass market. Lewis's gentlest critic, his brother, Warren, noted in his diary that *Dymer*, the book-length narrative poem from 1926, had failed with the public because it was simply "philosophy disguised as

---

10 Lewis, "Rejoinder to Dr Pittenger," 183 (emphasis original).

poetry."[11] Warren Lewis thought his brother's fling with philosophy, as reflected in Jack's diary entries, made him rather self-centered and a member of a superior class.[12] In *Mere Christianity*, C. S. Lewis acknowledged the accuracy of Warren's assessment when he set pride or self-conceit as the great sin.[13]

His first book after his conversion, *The Pilgrim's Regress*, suffers from obscurity, simply because so few modern people understand how to read allegory, but it does not suffer from the same sort of self-centeredness, even though it is about Lewis. He wanted the reader to understand the variety of forms his own self-conceit and pride had taken. The second book he wrote after his conversion, *The Allegory of Love*, presents a highly accessible window on the medieval world. To the reader of the twenty-first century, it may seem a bit pedantic for its regular citation of passages of Latin, for which Lewis provided no translation. In 1936, when the book was first published, however, Lewis would have reasonably assumed that his audience read Latin with the same ease that they read English. Thus, he left behind the arrogance of writing, along with the rest of his fallen nature, when he experienced the grace of Jesus Christ in 1931.

His desire to be understood answers for the *manner* of his apologetics, but that still leaves the *matter* of his apologetics. Lewis had something to say that he wanted the average person to easily understand, but what he said involved some of the most complicated theological and philosophical ideas of the last two and a half

11 Clyde S. Kilby and Marjorie Lamp Mead, *Brothers and Friends: The Diaries of Major Warren Hamilton Lewis* (New York: Harper & Row, 1982), 161.

12 C. S. Lewis kept a diary from 1922 until 1927 for the purpose of analyzing himself in the fashion of the Freudians of his day in Oxford. See Walter Hooper, ed., *All My Road before Me: The Diary of C. S. Lewis, 1922–1927* (New York: Harcourt Brace Jovanovich, 1991).

13 Lewis, *Mere Christianity*, 121. Lewis makes this assertion on the opening page of his chapter "The Great Sin."

millennia. A man who did not convert to Christianity until he was almost thirty-three had an amazing storehouse of theological knowledge for someone who had not trained as a theologian. How was this possible?

C. S. Lewis had accidentally studied the Christian faith for years while he read the ancient and medieval philosophical and literary texts of Europe. Faith and literature in medieval society stood in relationship to each other as hydrogen and oxygen do for water. He could not read and understand medieval allegorical courtly love poetry without understanding the Bible and all the theologians from the apostle Paul to Thomas Aquinas. As a good literary critic, he had to understand the worldview of the literature he studied. Lewis began work on *The Allegory of Love* long before his conversion, but in this book, which established his reputation as a major literary scholar, he reveals a profound knowledge of the content of Christian teaching. With Lewis we have the unusual situation of a person whose head was full of information before his heart was full of faith.

Lewis had a working knowledge of the church fathers who wrote between the apostolic period and the legalization of Christianity by Constantine in the fourth century. He had a much more detailed knowledge of Augustine and Boethius, whose combined influence set the agenda for Western theology from the fifth century until the high Middle Ages, when Aquinas gained the ascendency. One might even argue that the broad appeal of Lewis among Catholic, Protestant, and Orthodox Christians rests in part on his formative theology coming from a time before Rome split with Constantinople and before the Protestant churches split with Rome. Tolkien quipped about Lewis's "Ulsterior Motive," and Lewis acknowledged his self-conscious Protestantism. The very self-consciousness of his

Protestantism, however, contributed to the caution he took in his apologetics not to present the partisan peculiarities of the Church of England as normative Christianity.

By the time C. S. Lewis became a Christian, he had the intellectual tools in place to defend the faith as an apologist. In a relatively short time, he would have the inclination and motivation to do the work of an apologist. In terms of chronology, however, it is helpful to note that the apologetics of Lewis did not involve formal philosophical arguments.

The Five Paths

We have no reason to suppose that C. S. Lewis set out to utilize five distinct ways to present an apologetic for the Christian faith, but before he died, he had done just that. The five approaches he utilized may be called works of fiction, the testimony of experience, philosophical argument, works of scholarship, and what Lewis once referred to as "little books about Christianity." In some cases, a single work of apologetics might involve two or more of these approaches; for instance, *The Pilgrim's Regress* is a work of fiction that also testifies to personal experience. While all of his apologetics contain philosophical ideas, they do not necessarily involve formal philosophical arguments.

Austin Farrer, arguably the greatest theologian and philosopher within the Church of England in the twentieth century and a great friend of Lewis, gave a brief analysis of the apologetics of C. S. Lewis. He distinguished between the formal apologetics of Lewis and his other writings. Nonetheless, Farrer admitted that these other writings had an "apologetic effect."[14] In grouping the

14 Austin Farrer, "The Christian Apologist," in *Light on C. S. Lewis*, ed. Jocelyn Gibb (London: Bles, 1965), 31.

writings, he said that *The Screwtape Letters* and *The Great Divorce* do not repel any attacks on Christianity or resolve any difficulties, that *The Pilgrim's Regress* and *Surprised by Joy* "contain the intellectual history of conversion rather than straight apology," and that *Miracles* and *The Problem of Pain* are the best examples of Lewis's actual apologetic writing.[15] Farrer the philosopher focused on the formal arguments of philosophical apologetics for which Lewis became famous in Oxford in his verbal duels as president of the Socratic Club, in which Farrer frequently participated. Farrer began his essay by describing apologetics in terms of answering an attack, and Lewis's famous lecture on apologetics, given to youth ministers in 1945, primarily focuses on the public lecture as a defense of basic Christian doctrine.

Lewis rarely discussed his apologetic method in print, but in this lecture on apologetics he digressed from his general discussion of apologetic principles to explain his approach:

The difficulty we are up against is this. We can make people (often) attend to the Christian point of view for half an hour or so; but the moment they have gone away from our lecture or laid down our article, they are plunged back into a world where the opposite position is taken for granted. As long as that situation exists, widespread success is simply impossible. We must attack the enemy's line of communication. What we want is not more little books about Christianity, but more little books on other subjects—with their Christianity *latent*. You can see this most easily if you look at it the other way round. Our Faith is not likely to be shaken by any book on Hinduism. But if whenever

15 Farrer, "Christian Apologist," 31.

we read an elementary book on Geology, Botany, Politics, or
Astronomy, we found that its implications were Hindu, that
would shake us. It is not the books written in direct defense of
Materialism that make the modern man a materialist; it is the
materialistic assumptions in all the other books. In the same way,
it is not books on Christianity that will really trouble him. But
he would be troubled if, whenever he wanted a cheap popular
introduction to some science, the best work on the market was
always by a Christian. The first step to the re-conversion of
this country is a series, produced by Christians, which can beat
the *Penguin* and the *Thinkers Library* on their own ground. Its
Christianity would have to be latent, not explicit: and *of course*
its science perfectly honest. Science *twisted* in the interests of
apologetics would be sin and folly.[16]

Lewis used the example of science, but every other area of human
interest applies just as well. Alongside his books in which he laid out
formal arguments, Lewis produced works in which the Christian
assumptions remained latent.

Works of Fiction

The first approach to apologetics that Lewis employed was a work
of allegorical fiction written in 1932, less than a year after his conversion. In fact, he had made his first attempt at this work as an
allegorical poem in January 1932. *The Pilgrim's Regress* sorts out false
forms of Christianity and sets Christianity against rival emotional
and intellectual claims upon a person. It is a subjective work based
on the rival beliefs to which Lewis had attached himself along the

16 C. S. Lewis, "Christian Apologetics," in Hooper, ed., *God in the Dock*, 93 (emphasis original).

way to his own conversion. Having spent the greater part of a decade immersed in the medieval culture of allegory, he did not find it unusual to choose allegory as his medium. He intentionally modeled his allegory on Bunyan's *The Pilgrim's Progress*. Whereas Bunyan's Pilgrim journeyed from the City of Destruction to the Heavenly City, Lewis's Pilgrim journeyed through this world to Christ and then returned to live in this world. The subtitle makes clear that Lewis understood what path he had undertaken: *An Allegorical Apology for Christianity, Reason, and Romanticism*. The obscurity of *The Pilgrim's Regress* is not surprising for a modern audience. What is surprising is that it has gone through several editions and can still be bought.

Several years passed before Lewis wrote another work of fiction. This time he tried his hand at science fiction on a bet with Tolkien. Lewis would write a tale of space travel, and Tolkien would write a tale of time travel. Tolkien was too bogged down in elves, hobbits, and orcs at the time to write his story, but Lewis wrote *Out of the Silent Planet* in 1937 as Hitler's international politics grew more ominous. In a letter to Ruth Pitter ten years later, Lewis remarked that the great value of fictional journeys to other planets lay in their power to convey "*spiritual* adventures."[17] Lewis began a second abortive science-fiction novel that has survived in fragment form as *The Dark Tower*, but he did not complete another science-fiction work until 1942 with *Perelandra*, a continuation of the characters from *Out of the Silent Planet*. He wrote a third volume of science fiction, *That Hideous Strength*, in which the action takes place on earth in the midst of academic politics and what today might be called genetic engineering.

Before he finished his science-fiction trilogy, however, Lewis tried a satirical treatment of sin, Satan, and hell, with special attention to

---

17 C. S. Lewis, *The Collected Letters of C. S. Lewis*, ed. Walter Hooper, 3 vols. (New York: HarperSanFrancisco, 2004), 2:753 (emphasis original).

the objections that "good" people might have to the Christian teaching on these subjects. In *The Screwtape Letters*, Lewis explores the nature of sin and temptation through a glimpse at the grand demonic bureaucracy. Originally published as a series of short articles in *The Guardian* between May and November of 1941, the letters were collected as a book in 1942. This witty book made Lewis famous.[18] He followed this demonic exposé with *The Great Divorce*, which was also published in installments in *The Guardian* between November 1944 and April 1945. It then appeared as a book in 1946. The book explores how a good God can condemn people to eternity in hell.

Lewis did not set out to write The Chronicles of Narnia in order to teach Christian doctrine. He wrote the seven books as children's stories in an experiment to see if he could not do better than the current crop of children's stories in Britain. When he began *The Lion, the Witch and the Wardrobe*, Lewis did not even have the character of Aslan in his mind, nor did he plan to write more than one story. Even when Aslan entered the story, Lewis did not foresee what Aslan would ultimately do.[19] In Lewis's telling the stories, however, his Christianity lies latent but ever present. In the course of the seven books, the stories make clear the reasonableness of basic Christian ideas. In response to one of his many letters from children about the stories, Lewis said:

The whole series works out like this:
The Magician's Nephew tells the story of creation and how evil entered Narnia.

18 At the Christianity in the Academy Conference in Memphis on April 4, 2008, I met a professor emeritus of English at the University of California. When I told him I would deliver the lectures of which this chapter forms a part, he remarked that he owed his conversion to *Screwtape*.
19 Lewis, *Collected Letters*, 3:1113.

The Lion—the Crucifixion and Resurrection

Prince Caspian—restoration of the true religion after a corruption

The Horse and His Boy—the calling and conversion of a heathen

The Voyage of the Dawn Treader—the spiritual life (especially in Reepicheep)

The Silver Chair—the continued war against the powers of darkness

The Last Battle—the coming of Antichrist (the Ape). The end of the world, and the Last Judgement[20]

In *Till We Have Faces*, a novel that he tried to write on three separate occasions over a period of almost thirty years, Lewis achieved a quality of prose fiction he had never before reached. He considered it his best novel. The novel explores the problem of obsessive, possessive "love," which he had also treated in lighter fashion in *Screwtape* and *The Great Divorce*. The story presents the reasonableness of sacrifice as the true path of love.

Works of fiction fail as apologetics when they try to serve an instructional or argumentative role. Their great value lies in their ability to involve the reader in a story that becomes theirs. Nathan the prophet understood this principle when he told King David a story rather than giving him a lecture (2 Sam. 12:1–7). Fiction does not prove; it explains. It aims not at winning a debate but at answering a question. A successful story makes sense whether one likes what happens in it or not. Lewis had a high regard for Dorothy L. Sayers's dramatic works, which he thought did a "great deal of good," especially the BBC broadcast of *The Man Born to Be King*. He thought that drama provided an excellent

20 Lewis, *Collected Letters*, 3:1245.

medium for apologetic work, but he believed that he had no talent for writing drama.[21]

The Testimony of Experience

The personal stories that Lewis wrote of his own experience are rare. The most direct examples are *Surprised by Joy*, which tells of his conversion, and *A Grief Observed*, which tells of his grief after the death of his wife. To these, however, we must add *The Pilgrim's Regress*, which also tells the story of his conversion, but in an imaginative, allegorical form. He also adds brief words of personal experience in *The Problem of Pain* and *Mere Christianity*.

The power of personal testimony has lost much of its luster to the modern church at a time when personal testimony has more sway with the popular culture than in any time during the modern era. We live in a subjective age in which people are fascinated by the stories of ordinary people. Oprah Winfrey became the wealthiest woman in show business by inviting ordinary people to sit in her studio and tell their personal stories to millions of viewers. People will attend to another person's story. It does not feel like an attack, as Austin Farrer's version of formal apologetics does. On the contrary, it requires a vulnerability on the part of the one who discloses his or her story.

In the course of telling of his own life experiences, Lewis lays out many of the modern obstacles to faith and why he changed his mind. He aims the argument not at the reader but at himself. His method is descriptive rather than belligerent. In his personal testimony, he deals with major apologetic questions of the existence of God, the problem of pain, and the necessity of the death of Christ.

21 Lewis, *Collected Letters*, 3:1114.

Philosophical Argument

Though many people associate C. S. Lewis with the formal philosophical apologetic arguments that Farrer has suggested, this approach accounts for very little of his written corpus. Farrer noted only two works that fit this bill: *Miracles* and *The Problem of Pain*. He did not even consider *Mere Christianity* as apologetics by his strict definition. Instead, he considered the collection of radio broadcast talks as "plain exposition or imaginative realizations of doctrine; above all, moral analysis displaying the force of Christian ideas."[22] In his estimation of apologetics, Farrer falls within the realm of the technical professional of the academy who is most concerned for formal philosophical argument. The casual tone of *Mere Christianity* did not conform to his expectation of proper apologetics. Ironically, the little collection of radio talks remains Lewis's most effective and successful single apologetic effort. It would be difficult to estimate the number of people for whom *Mere Christianity* settled the intellectual obstacles that had prevented them from considering the truth of the gospel. The number may reasonably reach into the millions. I hold an endowed chair named for one such man, Charles Colson.

The first book Lewis wrote with a formal apologetic argument came in 1939 at the outbreak of World War II, when Ashley Sampson, founder of the Centenary Press and an editor with Geoffrey Bles, invited Lewis to write a book in The Christian Challenge series, which Sampson edited. The invitation came after Sampson had read *The Pilgrim's Regress*. Sampson asked Lewis to write on pain and suffering, a problem that Britain would face in earnest once the bombs began to fall on its cities. Lewis did not seek to

22 Farrer, "Christian Apologist," 31.

publish this kind of book; the editor sought him. The book was published in fall 1940 as *The Problem of Pain.*

The same was true of the series of radio talks that became *Mere Christianity*. Lewis did not decide to launch himself into this kind of apologetic; he did it as the result of an invitation. James Welch, director of religious broadcasting for BBC, asked Lewis to speak to the nation in a series of radio talks because *The Problem of Pain* had been such a help to Welch. Beginning in August 1941 Lewis spoke on the natural law as a pointer to God. Because of the success of that first series of talks, Lewis was asked to present a second series that focused on the incarnation of Christ. The talks were published in 1942 as *Broadcast Talks,* and they were combined with two later series of talks to form *Mere Christianity,* which he published in 1952. One might argue that Lewis only initiated one venture himself into the world of formal apologetics, when he began writing *Miracles* in 1943, a book that was not published until 1947. Even this book, however, came at the urging of Dorothy L. Sayers, who thought it needed to be written.[23]

Works of Scholarship

Austin Farrer did not mention any of Lewis's scholarly works in connection with apologetics, and few would do so. Yet in his address to youth ministers on the subject of apologetics, Lewis had stressed that the most effective apologetics comes in books on subjects other than Christianity in which the Christianity is latent. The scholarship of C. S. Lewis demonstrates how a Christian thinks about literature. Concerning this aspect of Lewis's writing, Farrer insisted that "we can step into a Christian world by opening Lewis."[24]

---

23 Sayers had written to Lewis on May 13, 1943, complaining about the lack of an up-to-date book on miracles. Lewis replied on May 17 that he was starting one. See Lewis, *Collected Letters,* 2:573.
24 Farrer, "Christian Apologist," 27.

The Allegory of Love, his first great piece of scholarship published in 1936, exemplifies what Lewis would later describe as an introductory work on any subject with its Christianity latent. He repeated the feat when he wrote *A Preface to Paradise Lost*, published in 1942. Both works were quickly recognized as major intellectual achievements and remain seminal works in the field with which scholars must engage when dealing with their subjects. In *The Abolition of Man*, published in 1943, Lewis demonstrated how philosophical ideas that have nothing to do with literary criticism can be imported into the discipline without anyone noticing until the alien ideas have become accepted. In 1954 he published *English Literature in the Sixteenth Century* as one of the volumes in the Oxford History of English Literature series. These major works were followed by smaller scholarly works that included *Studies in Words* (1960), *An Experiment in Criticism* (1961), and *The Discarded Image* (1964).

Perhaps Lewis's greatest legacy to the academic community is his body of scholarly work that demonstrates how a Christian thinks about a scholarly discipline. He does not import Christian ideas or themes into his work. In fact, his pupils have remarked that Lewis would never discuss Christianity in tutorials unless it arose within the text.[25] His scholarly works illustrate how his faith affected his approach to literary criticism. In his many scholarly battles over how one should undertake the task of literary criticism, his arguments rest on a set of assumptions about the nature of reality that emerge from his faith and that challenge alternative belief systems current in the academy of his day.

25 See the essay by W. Brown Patterson in Harry Lee Poe and Rebecca Whitten Poe, eds., *C. S. Lewis Remembered: Collected Reflections of Students, Friends and Colleagues* (Grand Rapids, MI: Zondervan, 2006), 92.

Little Books about Christianity

In the last decade of his life, Lewis wrote *The Four Loves, Reflections on the Psalms,* and *Letters to Malcolm Chiefly on Prayer.* *The Four Loves* is the book version of a series of recorded talks he delivered for the Episcopal Radio-TV Foundation. He prepared it and *Reflections on the Psalms* while his wife, Joy, was dying of cancer. He wrote *Letters to Malcolm* after Joy's death and after he had labored through *A Grief Observed.* This book on prayer is his last word on the subject and was published after his death in 1964. In 1949, Mary Van Deusen had written to Lewis suggesting that he write a book on prayer. He replied, "I don't feel I could write a book on Prayer: I think it would be rather 'cheek' of my part."[26] Not until he experienced the grief of Joy's death did Lewis know prayer well enough to write about it.

These little books about Christianity would certainly have a reading within the church, but Lewis wrote all of them in such a way that they might appeal to the non-Christian who reads over the shoulder of the church. In these books he deals with the hard parts of love, prayer, and the Bible. They certainly offer strength and encouragement to believers, but they offer non-Christians a new way of looking at the same old things they thought they understood but had actually misunderstood.

In his apologetics, Lewis did not limit his appeal to rational argument. All of his apologetics had a rational dimension, but he also addressed the imaginative and the emotional dimensions of life.

26 Lewis, *Collected Letters,* 2:965.

Having become a whole person, Lewis understood that people have questions, fears, misunderstandings, false assumptions, and a variety of other internal obstacles to faith that require attention in more than one mode. His apologetic works still speak powerfully in a postmodern generation because he saw and prophesied the coming of this age in *The Abolition of Man*. In anticipation of this age, he left a literary legacy that continues to speak.

Questions for Reflection

1. How did C. S. Lewis use rational arguments in his approach to apologetics?

2. How did Lewis use the imagination in his approach to apologetics?

3. What other approaches did Lewis employ in his apologetic work?

4. What can we learn from C. S. Lewis for our work of apologetics and evangelism in the third decade of the twenty-first century?

Resources for Further Study

Lewis, C. S. *God in the Dock: Essays on Theology and Ethics*. Edited by Walter Hooper. Grand Rapids, MI: Eerdmans, 1970.
Lewis, C. S. *Mere Christianity*. 1952. Repr., New York: Harper San Francisco, 2001.
Poe, Harry Lee. *The Making of C. S. Lewis: From Atheist to Apologist, 1918–1945*. Wheaton, IL: Crossway, 2021.
Sayer, George. *Jack: C. S. Lewis and His Times*. San Francisco: Harper & Row, 1988.

10

Evangelism for All Peoples

*A Global Commission with Implications
for the Global Church and Global
Christian Higher Education*

Anna Daub

AFTER HIS RESURRECTION and before his ascension, Jesus gave his disciples instructions, often called "the Great Commission." These are some of his last, weighty words filled with mission and purpose, giving Christians across the centuries their marching orders.[1] Found at the end of each Gospel and the beginning of Acts are passages describing the global God's global mission for his global church. This chapter will first introduce these three critical components of the Great Commission—the global God,

---

1   Akin, Merkle, and Robinson use this phrase and cite others who use it in Daniel Akin, Benjamin Merkle, and George Robinson, *40 Questions about the Great Commission* (Grand Rapids, MI: Kregel, 2020).

the global church, and the global mission—and then provide practical implications for students, faculty, and administration as they consider their roles in God's Great Commission.

The Global God and His Global Mission

Though some Christians think of the Great Commission as a New Testament phenomenon, it merely spotlights what God already revealed about himself. The entire Bible tells the story of God's mission. From his command to "be fruitful and multiply" (Gen. 1:28), through the utterance of the protevangelium (Gen. 3:15), the call of Abraham (Gen. 12:1–3), the unique priestly position of Israel, the songs of the Psalter, and the prophecies foretelling a coming suffering servant and the mountain of God, God illustrated in the Old Testament that he is a global God with a global message.

In the New Testament, God's global mission continues. God the Father sent God the Son, Jesus, to earth to accomplish a specific mission. He came to seek and save that which was lost (Luke 19:10), to make the dead ones live (John 11:25), to bring sight to the blind (Luke 4:18), to inaugurate his kingdom (Matt. 4:17), and to save his people from their sins (Matt. 1:21). His mission was unique; only God the Son, fully human and fully divine, could complete such an enterprise. He was conceived by the Holy Spirit, lived a sinless life, and offered himself as the sacrifice for a depraved and wayward world. He declared on the cross, "It is finished" (John 19:30), signifying that he had completed what he came to do. Then he rose again, defeating death as the firstfruits of the resurrection (1 Cor. 15:20–22).[2]

---

2 This section has been further expounded in Anna P. Daub, "Theology and Missions," in *All Our Minds: Why Women Should Study Theology*, ed. Rhonda Smith (Athens, GA: College and Clayton, 2021), 7–30.

The resurrected Jesus finished his mission and then gave his disciples theirs, a command that many Christians now call "the Great Commission."[3] Though historically many Christians have labelled the Matthew passage "the Great Commission," there are five Great Commission passages that add depth and nuance to Christ's final command. In Matthew 28:18–20, Jesus commands his followers to "make disciples." To do so, they go, baptize, and teach others to obey, recognizing that their authority to do so comes from Christ himself, who promises to be with them always.[4] In Mark 16:15, Jesus orders his disciples to go and "preach the gospel to all creation."[5] He utters the half-fulfilled prophecy-promise in Luke 24:46–47, pointing to his finished death and resurrection as the hope that "repentance for the forgiveness of sins should be proclaimed in his name to all nations" (v. 47). The resurrected Son, sent by the Father, states in John 20:21, "As the Father has sent me, even so I am sending you." Before his ascension, Jesus encourages his disciples to be about God's work, calling them to "be [his] witnesses in Jerusalem and

---

3   Andreas Köstenberger points out this distinction between Christ's mission and the church's mission when he describes the difference between incarnational and representational models in Andreas J. Köstenberger, *The Missions of Jesus and the Disciples according to the Fourth Gospel: With Implications for the Fourth Gospel's Purpose and the Mission of the Contemporary Church* (Grand Rapids, MI: Eerdmans, 1998), 212–17.

4   Christopher Wright includes this authoritative claim as one of the famous indicative-imperative combinations. He states, "Biblical imperatives are characteristically founded on biblical indicatives." Christopher J. H. Wright, *The Mission of God: Unlocking the Bible's Grand Narrative* (Downers Grove, IL: InterVarsity Press, 2006), 59. He continues, "The identity and the authority of Jesus of Nazareth, crucified and risen, is the cosmic indicative on which the mission imperative stands authorized" (60).

5   Akin, Merkle, and Robinson point to Mark 13:10 instead of the traditional Mark 16:15 passage because "the passage typically labeled in Mark as the Great Commission, Mark 16:15–20, is a part of the longer ending to Mark's Gospel (Mark 16:9–20), which scholars almost unanimously agree is a later addition to the book." Akin, Merkle, and Robinson, *40 Questions about the Great Commission*, Kindle, chap. 1, n. 24.

in all Judea and Samaria, and to the ends of the earth" through the power of the Holy Spirit (Acts 1:8).

In these Great Commission passages, Jesus calls his disciples to lift their gaze to the great harvest God is preparing beyond the borders of Israel. As the Old Testament prophet Isaiah says,

> It is too light a thing that you should be my servant
>> to raise up the tribes of Jacob
>> and to bring back the preserved of Israel;
> I will make you as a light for the nations,
>> that my salvation may reach to the end of the earth. (Isa. 49:6)

The global God calls his followers to a global mission.

To complete this global mission, Christians need to understand what it entails. Evangelism is vital to the Great Commission because "making disciples" intrinsically includes gospel proclamation.[6] Gospel authors use the verb "proclaim" in two Great Commission passages (Mark 16:15; Luke 24:46–47). The Matthew passage, which calls Christians to "make disciples," commands them to "teach" disciples to obey. Acts 1:8 calls Christians to "be . . . witnesses," which includes testifying. As Romans 10:14 states: "How are they to believe in him of whom they have never heard? And how are they to hear without someone preaching?" While making disciples is often more than the intentional proclamation of the gospel, it is never less.[7] To complete God's global mission, Christians must be intentional in their evangelistic efforts.

---

6 Since this entire book has discussed evangelism, this section will not discuss it in detail. To minimize any confusion, though, this section assumes that evangelism is the intentional proclamation of the gospel, which includes the life, death, burial, and resurrection of Jesus, why it matters, and what to do about it.

7 Missiologists debate the importance of evangelism in mission(s). An overview of these views is outside the scope of this chapter, but David Hesselgrave provides a helpful overview in

The Global Church

The global God tasks his global church to fulfill his global mission. While some Christians from the West can be tempted to view this global mandate as theirs alone, God has prepared his global church to do this work together. This calls for an appreciation of the global church and how it came to be.

What Is the Global Church?

The global church includes contextual churches distributed across geographic boundaries. Its existence proves that Christianity truly is a worldwide religion. For centuries, the majority of Christians resided in the West—primarily in Europe and North America. Textbooks describing significant events in Christian history and theology traditionally focused on these Western contexts. Christian intellectual thought predominantly flowed from Western institutions. These and other factors caused many Western Christians to assume they were the center of Christianity. But the world has shifted. Christians from Latin America, Africa, and Asia write theology textbooks, teach the history of Christianity in their own areas, contextualize the faith, and send their own missionaries. The global church has awakened.

Statistics illustrate this movement. Gina Zurlo observes: "In 1900, 82% of Christians lived in the North. By 2020 this figure had dropped dramatically to just 33%. . . . By the year 2050,

---

David J. Hesselgrave, "Holism and Prioritism," in *Paradigms in Conflict: 10 Key Questions in Christian Missions Today* (Grand Rapids, MI: Kregel, 2005). He concludes, "We can affirm that, at its heart, Christian mission (Great Commission mission, primary mission, essential mission) has to do with making the true and good gospel of Christ known to those who are most separated geographically, ethnically, and religiously from centers of gospel knowledge and influence" (120).

an estimated 77% of Christians will live in the global South."[8] Douglas Jacobsen describes the shift:

> Europeans and their new world descendants thus accounted for more than 90 percent of all the Christians in the world. Over the last hundred years, Europe's share of the world's Christian population has collapsed from about 65 percent to 25 percent, and it is still falling. Meanwhile, the number of Christians in Africa, Asia, and Latin America has exploded. Today, roughly a quarter of the world's Christians are African, another quarter live in Latin America, and about 15 percent reside in Asia.[9]

The landscape of global Christianity is constantly in flux, but Jesus continues to build his church (Matt. 16:18).[10]

In the twentieth century, Christianity flourished in unexpected corners of the globe. Believers within national borders of traditionally non-Christian countries gathered in churches, developed leaders, and began to work out the intricacies of what Christian faith and life might look like in these new contexts. These churches began to partner together, forming conventions, mission boards, and theological education entities like seminaries or Bible colleges.

---

8 Gina A. Zurlo, *Global Christianity: A Guide to the World's Largest Religion from Afghanistan to Zimbabwe* (Grand Rapids, MI: Zondervan, 2022), 3.

9 Douglas Jacobsen, *Global Gospel: An Introduction to Christianity on Five Continents* (Grand Rapids, MI: Baker, 2015), 8.

10 For more information about current statistics, see the most recent edition of the *World Christian Encyclopedia* (at the time of publication, the most recent edition is Todd M. Johnson, Gina A. Zurlo, and Becky Yang Hsu, *World Christian Encyclopedia*, 3rd ed. [Edinburgh: Edinburgh University Press, 2020]), or "Annual Statistics," Gordon Conwell Theological Seminary (website), accessed March 4, 2023, https://www.gordonconwell.edu/center-for-global-christianity/resources/status-of-global-christianity/.

Christians around the world are poised and ready for their roles in God's mission.

The Road to a Global Church

Many factors led to the rise of the global church. Christianity had existed outside the West for centuries, but this exponential worldwide growth was new. Through missionary activity fueled by revival, the gospel crossed cultural boundaries and took root in unprecedented ways.[11] During what became known as the Great Missionary Century (1792–1910), volunteer missionaries poured into Latin America, Africa, and Asia.[12] These men and women took the gospel to the known world, often following the paths of traders and empires. Many of them, like David Livingstone in Africa or Hudson Taylor in China, were unsatisfied with border stations and longed to take the gospel inland to areas with little or no gospel impact.

College students played an important role in missions in the late 1800s and early 1900s. Officially known as the Student Volunteer

11 In the 1700 and 1800s, two Great Awakenings had swept through the centers of Christianity, bringing a revitalized faith and a passion for the Great Commission. Ruth Tucker explains: "The eighteenth-century evangelical revivals . . . played an important role in awakening Christian leaders and laypeople to the responsibility for evangelism worldwide. . . . Evangelism was the responsibility of the church and its leaders, and it was this once again rediscovered truth that launched the modern missionary movement." Ruth A. Tucker, *From Jerusalem to Irian Jaya: A Biographical History of Christian Missions*, 2nd ed. (Grand Rapids, MI: Zondervan, 2004), 118.

12 There is some debate about these dates, with some scholars, like Ed Smither and Ruth Tucker, preferring clean century dates (1800–1900). See Edward L. Smither, *Christian Mission: A Concise Global History* (Bellingham, WA: Lexham, 2019), 103; Tucker, *From Jerusalem to Irian Jaya*, 117, 121. Other authors like Mark Noll and Timothy Tennent bookend the century using two milestones in missions—the preaching of William Carey's famous sermon "Expect Great Things from God, Attempt Great Things for God" (1792) and the Edinburgh 1910 conference. Mark A. Noll, *The New Shape of World Christianity: How American Experience Reflects Global Faith* (Downers Grove, IL: InterVarsity Press, 2009), 39; Timothy C. Tennent, *Invitation to World Missions: A Trinitarian Missiology for the Twenty-First Century* (Grand Rapids, MI: Kregel, 2010), 255–83.

Movement (SVM), numerous college students answered the call of the Lord to forsake promising professions and serve the Lord in difficult places. Ruth Tucker suggests, "During the early twentieth century it is estimated that student volunteers constituted half of the total Protestant overseas missionary force."[13] For around fifty years, droves of college students added their names to missionary rosters, dedicating their lives for the sake of the Great Commission.

These Western missionaries did not work alone. National believers in these countries also carried the gospel to their people or went as missionaries to other areas. National Christians like Ko Tha Byu, who worked with George and Sarah Boardman, and Adoniram Judson in Burma, often played essential roles in the work of the mission.[14] Through the work of both Western and indigenous missionaries, people who had previously been unreached had opportunities to hear and respond to the message of salvation.

The center of Christianity, which had initially started in Jerusalem and moved westward, began to advance southward and eastward into places across Africa, Asia, and Latin America.[15] The ebbing of one Western center accompanied the blossoming of multiple centers around the world.[16] Timothy Tennent describes

---

13 Tucker, *From Jerusalem to Irian Jaya*, 312.

14 To learn more about Ko Tha Byu, see Samuel Hugh Moffett, *A History of Christianity in Asia, 1500–1900*, 2 vols. (Maryknoll, NY: Orbis, 2007), 2:327–29.

15 For authors who discuss this demographic shift, see Andrew F. Walls, *The Missionary Movement in Christian History: Studies in the Transmission of Faith* (Maryknoll, NY: Orbis, 1996); Philip Jenkins, *The Next Christendom: The Coming of Global Christianity* (Oxford: Oxford University Press, 2002); Noll, *The New Shape of World Christianity*; Todd Johnson and Kenneth Ross, eds., *Atlas of Global Christianity: 1910–2010* (Edinburgh: Edinburgh University Press, 2009); Allen Yeh, *Polycentric Missiology: 21st-Century Mission from Everyone to Everywhere* (Downers Grove, IL: InterVarsity Press, 2016).

16 Kenneth Scott Latourette uses this imagery throughout his comprehensive seven-volume *History of the Expansion of Christianity*. For example, in vol. 3, he states: "Occasionally, as we have seen, there have been ebbs in the onward flow of Christianity. After each ebb, however,

the shift this way: "The major point to recognize, however, is that never before has the church had so many dramatic and *simultaneous* advances into *multiple* new cultural centers. . . . We now have the collapse of the old center and the simultaneous emergence of multiple new centers."[17] Christianity became a truly global phenomenon.

The Edinburgh 1910 Missionary Conference was a significant marker in the rise of the global church. This conference represents a turning point in global Christianity.[18] An initial overview of this conference might leave observers scratching their heads about how it could possibly be significant in this arena. Its overwhelming Western triumphalism and lack of non-Western representation make it seem like a poor candidate for such a title.[19] The non-Western voices, however, called for change. One example, an Indian missionary named V. S. Azariah, gave a speech in which he called for a new relationship between Western missionaries and non-Western Christians.[20] He said: "Through all the ages to come the Indian Church will rise up in gratitude to attest the heroism and self-denying labours of the missionary body. You have given your goods to feed the poor. You have given your bodies to be burned.

---

the tide has come back and has gone on to new heights." Kenneth Scott Latourette, *Three Centuries of Advance, A.D. 1500–A.D. 1800*, vol. 3 of *A History of the Expansion of Christianity* (New York: Harper & Brothers, 1939), 9.

17 Tennent, *Invitation to World Missions*, 37 (emphasis original).

18 For a concise argument for Edinburgh as a turning point in World Christianity, see Dana L. Robert, *Christian Mission: How Christianity Became a World Religion* (Chichester, UK: Wiley-Blackwell, 2009), 54.

19 For a further description of the importance of this conference, see Anna Daub, "Vern Poythress's Perspectivalism in a Global Context: A Symphony of Contextual Theologies Seeking Harmony" (PhD diss., Southeastern Baptist Theological Seminary, 2021), 38–43.

20 V. S. Azariah, "The Problem of Co-Operation between Foreign and Native Workers, Part 3," in *The History and Records of the Conference: Together with Addresses Delivered at the Evening Meetings*, vol. 9 (Edinburgh: Oliphant, Anderson, and Ferrier, 1910), 306–15.

We also ask for *love*. Give us friends!"[21] Non-Western Christians called for their Western colleagues to recognize their place in God's mission, and some Westerners listened and changed.

The presence and message of the non-Western delegates at the conference provided some missionaries with a vision for global Christianity. Dana Robert states, "The World Missionary Conference . . . stands as an apt symbol for the dawning of a new era— that of Christian mission as a multi-cultural, multi-directional network."[22] For the next century, missionaries and agencies worked toward multicultural approaches, recognizing that one culture or country alone could not fulfill the Great Commission. Instead, a symphony of Christian voices from every nation needed to proclaim the gospel of Jesus in contextually appropriate ways, bidding people from all kinds of contexts to follow King Jesus.

As more and more people in far-off lands decided to follow Jesus, missionaries had to make plans for leadership development. What would be the relationship between the missionaries and the fledgling churches? Who would lead? In the nineteenth century, missionaries like Rufus Anderson and Henry Venn called for indigenous churches to be self-governing, self-supporting, and self-propagating.[23] These three selves required missionaries and sending churches to relinquish authority and pass the torch to indigenous leadership. In the twentieth century, missionaries like Paul Hiebert built on the work of Venn and Anderson, calling for further focus on developing indigenous leadership. Hiebert called for a fourth

21 Azariah, "The Problem of Co-Operation," 315 (emphasis original).

22 Robert, *Christian Mission*, 56.

23 See Anderson's and Venn's works in Rufus Anderson, *To Advance the Gospel: Selections from the Writings of Rufus Anderson*, ed. R. Pierce Beaver (New York: Random House, 1967); Henry Venn, *The Life and a Selection from the Letters of Henry Venn* (New York: HardPress, 2019).

self—self-theologizing—recognizing the need for Christian leaders to know how to handle the word of God in such a way that made them faithful to the Scriptures and able to apply the Bible to differing cultural contexts.[24] As a result, churches developed indigenous leaders who contextualized the faith. Multiple cultural expressions of Christianity flourished.

The Global Mission of the Global Church

The Great Commission is a global mission for a global church. Believers across time and geography have picked up the mantle of this call and taken the gospel across cultural barriers. Jesus's last words call disciples from every nation to take the gospel message to every nation.[25]

As the global church continues to grow, its members also seek to follow Christ's final command. People once trapped in darkness have seen a great light (Matt. 4:16), and now they share that light with others. Christians from nations once considered the target of the Great Commission now recognize that they, too, are responsible for the King's charge. In the *African Bible Commentary*, Joe Kapolyo states::

> For too long we [the African church] have been recipients of the benefits of the gospel, and with few exceptions most of our church communities do not anticipate, let alone participate in, mission. We do not see it as our duty to go and spread the good news to people within our own countries, or to people beyond

24 Paul G. Hiebert, *Anthropological Insights for Missionaries* (Grand Rapids, MI: Baker, 1985), 195.
25 Samuel Escobar and Allen Yeh both describe this new polycentric mission reality similarly. Escobar calls it "the gospel from everywhere to everyone," and Yeh calls the polycentric nature of the mission, "mission from everyone to everywhere." Samuel Escobar, *The New Global Mission: The Gospel from Everywhere to Everyone* (Downers Grove, IL: InterVarsity Press, 2003); Yeh, *Polycentric Missiology*.

the borders of our own countries. . . . We must repent of this sin and take up [Jesus's] call to make disciples of all nations.[26]

The global church is the result of faithful missionaries and national Christians fulfilling the Great Commission around the world. Now the global church continues this mission, sending missionaries from Korea, Brazil, China, India, Iran, the Philippines, various countries in Africa, and many other unexpected nations around the world in Jesus's name. The global church goes to the ends of the earth for the sake of the global God and his global mission!

Implications for Global Christian Higher Education

Thus far this chapter has described a global God with a global mission and provided a glimpse of the global church and the polycentric nature of Great Commission fulfillment today. This global church, with its global mission, is a reason to celebrate! God is on the move. Yet people can easily read about the global church, breathe a prayer of thanks, feel a twinge of hope, and still dismiss it as something far away and "out there." So, what impact does this global church and global mission have on the college experience? This section provides practical ways Christians can leverage the college experience and education in general for the good of the global church and the goal of the Great Commission.

Opportunities for Students

Students from both the West and the majority world have meaningful opportunities to participate in this global Great Commission during their time at a university or college. This section

---

26 Joe Kapolyo, "Matthew 28:16–20," in *Africa Bible Commentary: A One-Volume Commentary Written by 70 African Scholars* (Grand Rapids, MI: Zondervan, 2010), 1196.

suggests a few, including praying for the nations, pursuing intentional relationships with people from different cultures, leveraging study-abroad options for God's mission, and considering the nations after college. By implementing these and other practices, Christians can take part in God's global mission through his global church.

1. *Pray for the nations.* Prayer is foundational to Great Commission fulfillment. College students can pray for the global fulfillment of the Great Commission in many ways. First, students should develop the habit of praying for the nations. They can commit to praying weekly or daily and even find friends to pray with them. Missions agencies and research organizations like Joshua Project, Operation World, and the International Mission Board provide easy-to-access resources to help guide missional prayers.[27]

Second, college students can pray for the global church, thanking God for his work among the nations and asking for boldness, wisdom, and faithfulness as these Christians navigate issues like poverty, war, persecution, and being minorities among other world religions. Christian college students can also intercede intentionally for students from the global church. These fellow students are in similar stages of life but often very different contexts. Pray for them as they navigate college life, cultures, and faithful obedience to the Great Commission.

Next, students can pray for the nations at their doorstep. Global migration has resulted in a kaleidoscope of ethnicities and cultures in many places. Students can pray for both Christians

27 Online information about these resources can be found at Joshua Project, https://joshua project.net/; Operation World, https://operationworld.org/; IMB (International Mission Board), https://www.imb.org/.

and non-Christians, asking that they might have opportunities to hear and embrace the gospel, participate in healthy churches, share the Christian faith, disciple others, and be discipled by others.

Finally, college students can pray for themselves. They can ask God to give them hearts that reflect his own love for the nations. Like the apostle Paul, they should pray that God will give boldness to proclaim the word of God (Eph. 6:19).

2. *Evangelize, disciple, and be discipled by people from other cultures.* The nations are moving to receive education. This migration allows students to evangelize, disciple, and be discipled by people from other cultures. In 2022, the *Washington Post* reported on "nearly a million [international] students, coming from more than 200 countries" in the USA.[28] Nations across the globe provide student visas to temporary immigrants moving for their studies. Universities have often become diverse hubs where students from different cultures gather for education.

Both Western and majority-world students can leverage their college years for God and his mission by building strong cross-cultural relationships. Meeting people from other nations does not require boarding an airplane. Instead, students can engage in cross-cultural evangelism in their dorms and gather at the cafeteria for multiethnic discipleship.

Students should also look for opportunities to be discipled by people from other nations. They can miss out on a wealth of knowledge and experience if they only view themselves as the disciplers and are not open to being discipled. When willing to humble themselves and learn from Christians from other

---

28 Susan Svrluga, "International College Enrollment Ticks Back Up after Pandemic," *Washington Post*, November 14, 2022, https://www.washingtonpost.com/.

cultural contexts, students often find unexpected blessings and experiences.

3. *Leverage opportunities for studying abroad and college breaks for God's mission.* For many students, the college experience offers unique opportunities for global travel. Some students travel abroad for study programs. Others seek out adventures during their breaks. Either way, this season of life often has space for international travel that many people never experience again. Christian college students can leverage these experiences for God's global mission! If students go on a trip to study abroad, they can connect with an area church or missionaries to find ways to make Jesus known. When they have a break week, they can consider going on a volunteer mission trip with their church, campus ministry, or a missions agency. They can spend their summer break in a different country for the gospel's sake. This time in college can provide once-in-a-lifetime opportunities for students to participate in God's mission and to work with long-term missionaries.

4. *Consider the nations after college.* After college, Christians have a plethora of options before them. As they plan for their future, they should consider opportunities that put them in direct contact with the nations. Missions organizations like the Southern Baptist Convention's International Mission Board offer two-year programs specifically catered to young men and women who have just finished college.[29] Some businesses provide opportunities to work in other countries or culturally diverse cities worldwide. Other jobs have remote options, allowing employees to work from anywhere. Christian students can utilize these or other creative opportunities to get to the nations for the sake of the name of Jesus.

---

29 For information about this program, see "Journeyman," IMB, accessed March 16, 2023, https://www.imb.org/go/options/journeyman/.

A Note for Students in and from the Global Church

Students in and from the non-Western global church might assume that a chapter like this does not apply to them. However, the Great Commission is not just for the Western church. Therefore, students in and from the rest of the global church can embrace this global Great Commission in many of the ways mentioned above. They can pray for the nations. They should seek to evangelize, disciple, and be discipled by people from other countries. They can leverage opportunities to study abroad and consider where they might serve the Lord after college. They should not shy away from these opportunities because they are not from the West. Instead, they recognize that the global church needs Christians from all nations to join together for his mission. The nations are calling—sometimes from across the student center, the dorm, or the street, and at other times, from across the world. God's global church must answer.

A Note for Faculty and Administration

Students are not the only ones who need to consider the implications of God's global Great Commission. Faculty and administration can also recognize that Jesus's mandate should significantly impact how they think about education. This Great Commission reframes the opportunities in front of them. Whether American, Peruvian, or Nigerian, professors can play unique roles in mobilizing the global church. First, they can cast a vision for their students to consider and go to the nations. Second, they can invest intentionally in international students, encouraging and discipling future leaders from other countries. Finally, they can consider the nations themselves. Professors can go on short-term trips, partnering with colleges and seminaries in other countries to train Christians who cannot travel for education because of cultural or economic barriers. They can also move to new places, committing to long-term service and using their knowledge, expertise, and teaching skills to access hard places for the gospel's sake.

———

The Great Commission describes the global God's global mission for his global church. As we have seen, the global God has always had a heart for the nations. The church's global mission, alluded to in all Scripture, is explicitly stated in the Great Commission passages. Several key historical markers have led to the new reality of a global church that is now actively participating in God's mission together. Finally, we have seen practical ways in which students, faculty, and administration can join in the global God's global mission for his global church.

The global church has awakened. Its growth can be compared to the roots of a tree. "Some days we can see growth as we watch people descend into the water on a baptism Sunday or celebrate a new church plant. Other times, the growth is hidden, spreading like roots of a tree, often unseen, winding and inching along and exploding to the surface periodically."[30] God is building his global church, and the Great Commission carries implications for both the global church and global higher education, inviting people from various languages, tribes, and nations to participate with him as he does.

Questions for Reflection

1. How does the idea of God as a global God change the way you think about the Great Commission?

30 Anna Daub, "The Hope of the Global Church," in *Because of Hope: Reflection of Faith* (Birmingham, AL: Women's Missionary Union, 2022), 139.

2. How does the reality of the global church change the way you think about the Great Commission?

3. Consider the suggestions given under the heading "Implications for Global Christian Higher Education" (p. 180). Do any opportunities described there interest you? What barriers might stop you from leveraging your college years for the sake of God's mission?

Resources for Further Study

Akin, Daniel, Benjamin Merkle, and George Robinson. *40 Questions about the Great Commission.* Grand Rapids, MI: Kregel, 2020.

Jenkins, Philip. *The Next Christendom: The Coming of Global Christianity.* Oxford: Oxford University Press, 2002.

Robert, Dana L. *Christian Mission: How Christianity Became a World Religion.* Chichester, UK: Wiley-Blackwell, 2009.

Walls, Andrew F. *The Missionary Movement in Christian History: Studies in the Transmission of Faith.* Maryknoll, NY: Orbis, 1996.

Young, F. Lionel, III. *World Christianity and the Unfinished Task: A Very Short Introduction.* Eugene, OR: Cascade, 2021.

11

Cultivating, Planting, and Reaping in Evangelism

Tim McKnight

MY FATHER comes from a farming family in Eastern Kentucky. His dad purchased bottomland near London, Kentucky, to start his farm. If you are familiar with Eastern Kentucky, you know that the land is fertile, but farmers must often remove boulders and trees to make it conducive to farming. In addition to clearing the ground, my grandfather would use a disc harrow to cultivate the soil in preparation for planting. This device breaks up the soil into rows so farmers can plant seeds. The seeds will not take root and grow if the ground is too hard. He would add nutrients or fertilizer to the soil to create optimum conditions for seed growth. Such cultivation of the earth is critical to the process of producing a good crop.

The next thing my grandfather would do was plant the seed. He would pull a planter filled with seeds behind his tractor. This device drops the seeds into the rows created by the disc harrow. My grandfather would use every square inch of the cultivated land, planting seeds throughout his fields. This indiscriminate and thorough planting of the seeds increased the potential of a larger harvest once the plants matured.

Grandpa did not have an irrigation system, so his next step would be to wait for rain. He depended on rain to provide the necessary water for the plants to grow to maturity. Without rain, the seeds would not grow, and there would be no harvest. He was dependent on the Lord for the harvest.

When the fields experienced rain over time, they produced a bumper crop of corn or tobacco. Then it was time for my dad and his siblings to go into the fields and harvest the plants. They would work hard reaping the corn and tobacco produced by the fields. This work was both challenging and rewarding.

As you can see, my family's farming life involved cultivating, planting, and reaping.

Scripture frequently uses the language of farming when referring to evangelism. The Bible indicates that, like farming, evangelism involves cultivating, planting, and reaping. Referring to this process in his letter to the church in Corinth, the apostle Paul wrote:

> What then is Apollos? What is Paul? Servants through whom you believed, as the Lord assigned to each. I planted, Apollos watered, but God gave the growth. So neither he who plants nor he who waters is anything, but only God who gives the growth. He who plants and he who waters are one, and each will receive his wages according to his labor. For we are God's fellow workers. You are God's field, God's building. (1 Cor. 3:5–9)

Jesus spoke about the condition of the soil, the work of planting seeds, and the fields yielding harvest in his parable of the sower (Matt. 13:1–23; Mark 4:1–20; Luke 8:4–15). Regarding the harvest, he admonished the disciples:

> Do you not say, "There are yet four months, then comes the harvest"? Look, I tell you, lift up your eyes, and see that the fields are white for harvest. Already the one who reaps is receiving wages and gathering fruit for eternal life, so that sower and reaper may rejoice together. For here the saying holds true, "One sows and another reaps." I sent you to reap that for which you did not labor. Others have labored, and you have entered into their labor. (John 4:35–38)

These are just a few of the instances in Scripture that refer to aspects of evangelism using the language of farming.

In the following pages, I will examine this biblical process of cultivating, planting, and harvesting related to evangelism. We will consider how to prepare people to hear the gospel. The second section of this chapter will focus on planting the seed of the gospel in evangelism. Finally, we will examine how God can use us as harvesters in the evangelism process.

Without further ado, off to the fields!

Cultivating in Evangelism

Like farming, evangelism involves cultivating before planting the seeds of the gospel. Salvation consists of the Holy Spirit opening people's minds and hearts to receive the gospel through repentance and faith. He uses believers who evangelize to help in this process. Some people have questions about the gospel for which they need answers. Others need to build trust in a believer before they open themselves to the good news of Jesus Christ. A few others might be openly hostile toward the gospel and need their walls of hostility broken down over time. Whatever the case, this section will focus on how you, as an evangelist, can cultivate the soil of the lost person with whom you share the gospel.

Prayer

Prayer is connected with evangelism throughout the New Testament. Jesus commanded the disciples to pray for field workers as they shared the gospel (Matt. 9:35–38). Prayer was pivotal in spreading the gospel in the book of Acts. We see the early church gathering for prayer and the Holy Spirit empowering them to go out and witness boldly (Acts 1:14; 4:31). The apostle Paul asked early believers to pray for him in his efforts to share the gospel (Rom. 15:30–32; Eph. 6:19; Col. 4:2–4). He offered prayers for unbelievers' salvation. In Romans 10:1, Paul wrote of the Jews, "Brothers, my heart's desire and prayer to God for them is that they may be saved." These examples of the relationship between prayer and evangelism in Scripture should guide our efforts in the soil of souls with whom we share the gospel.

So how should you pray? Pray that God will grant you wisdom and discernment as you interact with people who do not know Jesus. Pray that the Holy Spirit will open their minds and hearts to the gospel. Pray that God will grant them repentance and faith in Jesus Christ. Pray that the Lord will protect you from error in sharing the gospel. Pray that he will embolden and protect you as you share.

We are dependent upon the Lord in our evangelistic work. Prayer is an admission of this dependence. Tim Beougher, professor of evangelism at the Southern Baptist Theological Seminary, offers this insight into this relationship between prayer and reliance on the

Lord in evangelism: "God alone can save. God alone can change a sinner's heart. But God has ordained that our prayers are part of the means he uses to accomplish his ends. When we pray, we are joining our frail hands of clay with God's mighty omnipotent hands."[1] Prayer is our connection to God's omnipotent power in evangelism and is necessary for our cultivation work.

Love, Grace, and Respect

The love of Christ that we display in our actions and words is another powerful means of cultivating an unbeliever to receive the seed of the gospel. Scripture affirms that people will know that we are followers of Jesus because of the love they see in us (John 13:34–35; 1 John 3:11–18; 4:7–8). Our love for God and for people who do not know him should motivate us to engage lost people with the gospel. Regarding the motivation for his missionary efforts, Paul wrote, "The love of Christ controls us, because we have concluded this: that one has died for all, therefore all have died; and he died for all, that those who live might no longer live for themselves but for him who for their sake died and was raised" (2 Cor. 5:14–15). Our love is a powerful witness with great potential to cultivate in unbelievers an openness to hearing us share the gospel.

The Bible also guides believers in how they should show the grace and love of Christ in their interactions with people in the world. Paul encouraged believers in Colossae: "Walk in wisdom toward outsiders, making the best use of the time. Let your speech always be gracious, seasoned with salt, so that you may know how you ought to answer each person" (Col. 4:5–6). We must use gracious words when interacting with people, especially men and women

---

1 Timothy K. Beougher, *Invitation to Evangelism: Sharing the Gospel with Compassion and Conviction* (Grand Rapids, MI: Kregel, 2021), 158.

who do not know Jesus Christ as Lord and Savior. In addition, Christ followers should also display the humility of Christ when interacting with unbelievers. Peter admonished the early church:

> But even if you should suffer for righteousness' sake, you will be blessed. Have no fear of them, nor be troubled, but in your hearts honor Christ the Lord as holy, always being prepared to make a defense to anyone who asks you for a reason for the hope that is in you; yet do it with gentleness and respect, having a good conscience, so that, when you are slandered, those who revile your good behavior in Christ may be put to shame. For it is better to suffer for doing good, if that should be God's will, than for doing evil. (1 Pet. 3:14–17)

Although we must prepare ourselves to give an apologetic, a defense or reason for our faith in Christ Jesus, we will not gain a hearing of the gospel by arguing with people. In my evangelistic conversations with people from various worldviews, I have never clashed over the real differences between my faith and theirs. I have gained a hearing by showing them respect and trying to be a gracious listener. I agree with Scott Hildreth and Steven McKinion's assertion:

> Evangelism is not about winning a debate; evangelism is about helping people understand the means by which they can be saved. The goal is not to show non-Christians they're wrong about everything—about God, Jesus, the Bible, sin or anything else. Evangelism is the announcement of what God has done for all of us, and how each of us can enjoy the fruit of that work.[2]

2 D. Scott Hildreth and Steven A. McKinion, *Sharing Jesus without Freaking Out: Evangelism the Way You Were Born to Do It* (Nashville: B&H, 2020), 23.

Part of cultivation in evangelism is showing people the love, grace, and respect that the gospel calls for us to communicate to them.

Contextualization

Contextualization is another vital element in evangelism for cultivating hearers to receive the gospel. In his letter to the church in Corinth, the apostle Paul referred to this process when he wrote:

> For though I am free from all, I have made myself a servant to all, that I might win more of them. To the Jews I became as a Jew, in order to win Jews. To those under the law I became as one under the law (though not being myself under the law) that I might win those under the law. To those outside the law I became as one outside the law (not being outside the law of God but under the law of Christ) that I might win those outside the law. To the weak I became weak, that I might win the weak. I have become all things to all people, that by all means I might save some. I do it all for the sake of the gospel, that I may share with them in its blessings. (1 Cor. 9:19–23)

In these words, Paul does not advocate changing the gospel's message but describes how he varied his methods of communicating the good news to help his hearers better understand it. He studied the culture in which he engaged people with the gospel to know how to convey the gospel more effectively. In so doing, he cultivated the soil upon which he planted the seeds of the gospel.

Paul's interaction with the Epicurean and Stoic philosophers on the Areopagus is an excellent example of contextualization (Acts 17:22–34). He knew enough about these Greek thinkers' culture, worship, and philosophy to use elements of their context to clarify his gospel presentation. Paul referred to their idolatry in order to introduce the God of Scripture to the Athenians (vv. 22–25). He also quoted the Greek philosopher and poet Aratus to help his hearers understand that God could not look like these idols of stone if we are his offspring (vv. 28–30). Paul then focused the conversation on the resurrection of Christ and their need for repentance in preparation for the coming judgment and resurrection of the dead (vv. 30–31). Throughout his discussion with these philosophers, Paul built cultural bridges over which the gospel message could travel to his hearers.

We should also utilize cultural reference points to help our hearers better understand the gospel. This process demands that we study the culture of the people we evangelize. What books do they read? What music do they enjoy? What sports do they watch? What are their values? By becoming familiar with the culture, we can better communicate the gospel within their contexts. As we do so, we must always protect the gospel message's integrity. The message never changes, but the means through which the message is communicated are constantly evolving. These contextualization efforts help cultivate the soil upon which the seed of the gospel is planted.

Final Thoughts on Cultivation

As you can see from the discussion in this section, cultivation involves our work and the work of the Holy Spirit in preparing the hearts of individuals to hear and receive the gospel. We prayerfully engage people we encounter, contextualizing the truth of God's word as we share it with love and respect. This process of cultivation might occur over a matter of minutes. Sometimes people are ready to hear the gospel in a single conversation, including total strangers we encounter. Most of the time, we must cultivate the soil of a person's heart to receive the seed of the gospel over a more extended period—usually weeks or months. In either case, through the power and work of the Holy Spirit, we prepare people for the seed of the gospel we plant in their lives as we evangelize.

Planting in Evangelism

It does not matter how much Christ followers cultivate the soil if they never plant the seeds of the gospel. Without sharing the gospel, there can be no harvest of people who give their lives to Jesus as Lord and Savior. Jesus calls us to make disciples of people from every tribe, tongue, and nation (Matt. 28:19–20). The Lord commanded the disciples to be his witnesses to people in Jerusalem, Judea, Samaria, and the farthest reaches of the world (Acts 1:8). This command applies to us as disciples today. Scripture is clear in calling followers of Jesus to share the gospel's good news with people we encounter as we live our lives every day. This section of our chapter will focus on how we can plant the seeds of the gospel well.

Planting Indiscriminately

In the parable of the sower, the Bible states that he planted the seed on all types of soil—a hardened path, rocky ground, thorny ground, and good soil (Matt. 13:1–23; Mark 4:1–20; Luke 8:4–15). In his commentary on Mark's account of this parable, James Brooks points out the differences between modern and ancient methods of cultivating and sowing. He writes:

> Unlike the modern method, the seed was sown first and then plowed under. The sower held it in an apron with one hand and broadcast it with the other. It was inevitable that some would fall

upon the hardened path through the field, some where the soil was too shallow, and some among thorns as well as on good ground.[3]

Planters in the first century sowed the seed wherever they walked, not focusing on a particular soil.

This example from Scripture encourages contemporary Christ followers also to sow the gospel indiscriminately. We do not know who will respond to the gospel. Sometimes people we least expect to give their lives to Christ surrender to him as Lord and Savior. Scripture states that the gospel call is for whoever is willing to come to Jesus (John 3:16; Rev. 22:17). Again, that invitation includes people from every tribe, tongue, and nation (Matt. 28:19–20; Rev. 5:7–10; 7:9–14). If people from every country are to hear the gospel, we must communicate it to them. Christ followers must share the gospel with all kinds of people they encounter in their communities as they live daily. The Bible teaches that we must plant the seeds of the gospel everywhere we go with everyone we meet.

Gospel Conversations versus Gospel Presentations

Sometimes in sharing the gospel, we focus more on the presentation than on the person with whom we are conversing. As mentioned above in the section on cultivation, our motive in planting the seeds of the gospel is love for the people with whom we are sharing. Because we love them, we want to get to know them and hear their stories. That said, I believe that Hildreth and McKinion are correct when they state: "People are much more likely to gain a real understanding of the gospel—the kind that draws them into a lifetime of genuine faith—through an ongoing relationship and

---

3 James A. Brooks, *Mark*, The New American Commentary (Nashville: Broadman, 1991), 79.

dialogue with a Christian rather than just through hearing a fifteen-minute presentation."[4] If we care about the people we are engaging with the gospel, we will want to have meaningful conversations with them focused on getting to know them and where they are in their spiritual journeys.

The foundation of having conversations with people is being good listeners. When we listen to people's stories, we hear where they are spiritually. We can also find what they consider most important in their lives. Such dialogue reveals their passions and their pain. They communicate what drives them and what experiences have caused them the most suffering.

Having gospel conversations also allows us to ask questions about the people we communicate with. These questions are very effective means of understanding where we can connect the gospel message with their lives. Our conversations should also allow the people we engage with the good news of Christ to ask their questions. I agree with Randy Newman's assertion that when we focus on such dialogue, "our evangelistic conversations will sound less content/persuasion driven and more relationship/understanding driven. They'll sound more like rabbinic dialogues than professional monologues."[5]

When we interact with lost individuals we encounter in conversations, they are more likely to offer questions and reveal aspects of their lives that will help us connect them to the gospel. We will understand more about their spiritual condition and learn how we can help lead them to Jesus. Such conversations also show Christlike love and respect for them.

4   Hildreth and McKinion, *Sharing Jesus*, 41.
5   Randy Newman, *Questioning Evangelism: Engaging People's Hearts the Way Jesus Did* (Grand Rapids, MI: Kregel, 2004), 15.

Sometimes it takes work to start a conversation focused on the story of Jesus. We often struggle to steer conversations toward the gospel. Practicing the habit of dialogue rather than monologue will help us in our efforts. In addition, we can use potential bridges to the gospel to introduce the good news of Christ, transitions into sharing the story of Jesus with the family members, friends, and acquaintances. Tim Beougher offers some helpful bridges to the gospel we might use in conversations.[6] We can ask people their opinion about spiritual matters. If we're talking with a sports fan, we might mention an athlete who is a Christ follower. People might respond to a question regarding their opinions about God or eternal life. These are just a few of Beougher's suggested bridges to a gospel conversation.

In addition to such transitions, our testimonies, or stories of how the gospel changed our lives, can serve as excellent bridges to the gospel. These accounts describe our lives before we came to Christ, how we gave our lives to Jesus, and what our lives look like now as Christ followers. When sharing our testimonies, we should make them under five minutes and focus on Jesus and not ourselves. Such stories might motivate our hearers to inquire about the gospel or ask further questions about how we started following Christ.

Engaging in such conversations rather than presentations will help us plant the seed of the gospel more effectively through grace-filled dialogues.

Planting Good Seed

Our bearing witness must involve a verbal proclamation of the gospel if we seek to fulfill our role as planters. The seed we plant must be good, including a declaration of the whole gospel of Scripture. We must not

6 Beougher, *Invitation to Evangelism*, 187–95.

add anything to the good news of Jesus, nor may we take anything away from it. There are eternal ramifications if we do not accurately share the gospel message. The apostle Paul admonished the Galatians: "Even if we or an angel from heaven should preach to you a gospel contrary to the one we preached to you, let him be accursed. As we have said before, so now I say again: If anyone is preaching to you a gospel contrary to the one you received, let him be accursed" (Gal. 1:8–9).

We must share the full content of the good news of Jesus Christ that we find in Scripture. Previous chapters of this book focus on the biblical content of the gospel. I refer you back to them; however, we might utilize several models to share this gospel message. The North American Mission Board offers a helpful description of the gospel in its "3 Circles" approach. You can learn this approach by utilizing their app, videos, and website.[7] Another method is the four-part metanarrative of the gospel—creation, fall, redemption, and future hope—which describes how the good news of Jesus involves the whole of Scripture, from the garden of Eden to the return of Christ.[8] Christ followers can also use the "Romans Road" method of sharing the gospel.[9] This approach takes listeners through crucial passages from the book of Romans related to the good news of Jesus. Although these examples do not exhaust the possible approaches you might use in sharing the gospel, they offer a few options. The best models are ones that are true to Scripture and ones that you use.

7 "3 Circles," North American Mission Board, accessed March 26, 2023, https://www.namb.net/evangelism/3circles/.

8 Christopher J. H. Wright, *The Mission of God: Unlocking the Bible's Grand Narrative* (Downers Grove, IL: InterVarsity Press, 2006), 63–64. In this book, Wright gives readers an excellent presentation of the story of redemption from the Old Testament to the New Testament. It is a tremendous aid in helping readers understand the gospel as a metanarrative.

9 "What Is the Romans Road to Salvation?" Got Questions, accessed March 27, 2023, https://www.gotquestions.org/.

Clarity and Questions

No model for sharing the gospel is effective if we do not communicate its content clearly. People must understand what we are saying. Most people we encounter do not speak the verbiage related to the church and Scripture that so many of us use. Speaking "churchese" might involve talking about being "saved," being "washed in the blood," "having repented of our sins," and being "born again." Modern listeners do not have a reference point to understand these terms. Only 6 percent of millennials and 4 percent of the members of Generation Z have a biblical worldview.[10] We must ensure that we use terms in presenting the gospel that our listeners can understand.

One way we can be sure that we communicate the gospel effectively is to ask: "Do you understand what I'm sharing with you? Do you have any questions?" As we invite our listeners to ask questions, they will point us to areas in the gospel conversation where they need more clarification. We want them to respond with questions or statements related to our discussion of the gospel. Failure to clarify our terms and allow questions will restrict our planting efforts.

Final Thoughts on Planting

Like the sowers in the New Testament, we must plant the seed of the gospel indiscriminately. We should share the gospel with as many people as we can, whenever we can. As we sow, we focus on the people we interact with, engaging them in conversations rather than focusing on our presentation. We share the good seed of the whole gospel with them, not omitting truths or adding to the message but being faithful to Scripture. Finally, we will avoid

---

10 Barna, *Gen Z: The Culture, Beliefs and Motivations Shaping the Next Generation* (Ventura, CA: Barna Group, 2018), 25.

"churchese," explain terms that might be foreign to our listeners, and offer them opportunities to ask questions for clarification.

Reaping in Evangelism

After we sow the seeds of the gospel, we need to focus on reaping where we have planted. We understand that God is the only one who can give life to the gospel seeds we plant. He is Lord of the harvest. As mentioned above, Paul wrote: "I planted, Apollos watered, but God gave the growth. So neither he who plants nor he who waters is anything, but only God who gives the growth" (1 Cor. 3:6–7). While God is the only one who can bring the harvest, he allows us to participate in the harvesting process related to evangelism. Jesus encouraged us to pray for such harvest workers when he said, "The harvest is plentiful, but the laborers are few; therefore pray earnestly to the Lord of the harvest to send out laborers into his harvest" (Matt. 9:37–38). As workers in the harvest, we have several responsibilities.

Invite Them to Respond

Whenever we share the gospel, we must allow our conversation partners to respond to its message. Failure to call for a response in evangelism is like fishing without drawing the net. The disciples used nets with weights to fish in deep water. When they pulled on a rope to draw the net, it would close the net around the fish and gather them. The disciples would never have landed any fish on the boat if they did not draw the net. We must call for a response in evangelism and pull the net.

Jesus drew the net in his preaching. He called for a response, declaring, "The time is fulfilled, and the kingdom of God is at hand; repent and believe in the gospel" (Mark 1:15). Following his example, we should call for the same response—repentance and belief.

Before people can respond to our invitation, they must first know its meaning. Good harvesters will explain the terms they use in their invitation. We must define what it means to repent. Repentance refers to turning away from ourselves, sin, and Satan and turning toward Christ to follow him. It involves the confession of our sin and our sins to God. Such repentance also includes a surrender to Christ as Lord. In responding to the gospel, we turn from ourselves to follow Christ as Lord. He has control over our lives.

We also call people to believe the gospel. This belief involves more than mere intellectual assent. When people believe the gospel, they trust in Christ for their salvation. They trust that Jesus is the Son of God, who lived a perfect life in their place that they could not have lived; that he took their sins upon himself and died a death they deserved, paying a ransom for their sin; that he was buried and rose from the dead on the third day, showing that he is the Son of God; that he ascended to the right hand of the Father; and that he will return to judge the dead at the final resurrection. When we call others to believe the gospel, we ask them to stake their lives upon these truths about Christ.

When people come to Christ through repentance and faith, they inherit eternal life through Christ. We must define for them what eternal life means. The best definition comes from Jesus himself. While praying to the Father, he said, "And this is eternal life, that they know you, the only true God, and Jesus Christ whom you have sent" (John 17:3). Eternal life is knowing God through a relationship with Jesus Christ. We enter into that relationship by repenting of our sins and trusting (believing) in Christ. We must communicate this result of repenting of our sins and believing in the gospel; however, people will not repent and believe unless we invite them.

Reaping and Next Steps

Once people surrender their lives to Christ through repentance and faith, we must help them become grounded in the faith. As a Baptist, I encourage people to be baptized as a next step. I believe baptism is a believer's public profession of faith in Christ. It is our first act of obedience as Christ followers.

In addition, I encourage new believers to share their faith in Christ with their family and friends. Those who have just come to Christ are powerful witnesses to the gospel. People close to them see their changed lives and wonder what happened. What an excellent opportunity for the new believer to give a reason for his or her hope in Christ by having gospel conversations. We need to encourage new disciples to share the gospel early in their faith. We must teach them how to cultivate, plant, and reap.

New believers must also learn to develop daily Bible reading and prayer time. We need to disciple them to begin to read God's word. I encourage new believers to start reading through the Gospel of John. We meet once a week to talk about what they are reading and to allow them to ask questions about the text.

These first steps begin a long journey of faith. New believers need us to walk with them after their conversion. Jesus's command to make disciples does not end with sharing the gospel. We must help them mature in their faith and in practicing spiritual disciplines in their lives.

———

My grandfather was very proficient at cultivating, planting, and reaping the fields of his Eastern Kentucky farm. His skill developed through repetition. I pray that you will practice the evangelistic steps described in this chapter by prayerfully cultivating the soil, indiscriminately planting the seeds of the gospel, and working as a reaper in the harvest fields, calling for people to respond to the gospel through repentance and faith. I pray that the Lord will allow you to reap a great harvest through the Holy Spirit's work in your efforts.

Questions for Reflection

1. If prayer is one of the steps to cultivating a believer for the seed of the gospel, how will you utilize prayer in your evangelistic efforts?

2. How can you show the love of Christ to people around you to prepare them to hear the gospel?

3. How can you hold out the truth of God's word with gentleness and respect toward people with whom you communicate in person and on social media?

4. What aspects of your culture can you use to build bridges of contextualization for the gospel? What dangers do you need to avoid in reaching people within your context?

5. How can you ensure that you are indiscriminately planting the seed of the gospel, engaging people from every tribe, tongue, and nation in your community?

6. What are the critical differences between having gospel conversations and making gospel presentations?

7. What are the essential elements of the gospel? What model will you use to share it?

8. What practices will you adopt to help people understand the gospel concepts you share?

9. How will you invite people to respond to the gospel? How will you explain repentance, belief, and eternal life?

10. What will you do to help someone take the next steps after he or she becomes a Christ follower?

Resources for Further Study

Beougher, Timothy K. *Invitation to Evangelism: Sharing the Gospel with Compassion and Conviction.* Grand Rapids, MI: Kregel, 2021.

Green, Michael. *Evangelism in the Early Church.* Rev. ed. Grand Rapids, MI: Eerdmans, 2004.

Hildreth, D. Scott, and Steven A. McKinion. *Sharing Jesus without Freaking Out: Evangelism the Way You Were Born to Do It.* Nashville: B&H, 2020.

Moreau, A. Scott. *Contextualization in World Missions: Mapping and Assessing Evangelical Models.* Grand Rapids, MI: Kregel, 2012.

Newman, Randy. *Questioning Evangelism: Engaging People's Hearts the Way Jesus Did.* Grand Rapids, MI: Kregel, 2004.

12

The Ministry of the Holy
Spirit and Prayer

Susan Booth

IMAGINE YOU WERE among the first disciples to hear Jesus's command "Go . . . and make disciples of all nations" (Matt. 28:19–20).[1] What would you have been thinking and feeling as the global nature of the Great Commission began to dawn on you? Maybe a combination of fear, excitement, surprise, inadequacy, or perhaps being overwhelmed. Who, me? How? The whole world? Where to begin? This isn't what I signed up for! Providentially, every record of the commission (cf. Luke 24:46–49; John 20:21–22; Acts 1:8) shows that Jesus anticipated and answered these concerns by supplying the one thing his disciples needed most: the promise of his power and presence through the indwelling Holy Spirit.

---

1 Scripture quotations in this chapter are from the Christian Standard Bible®, copyright © 2017 by Holman Bible Publishers. Used by permission. Christian Standard Bible® and CSB® are federally registered trademarks of Holman Bible Publishers.

The Ministry of the Holy Spirit and God's Mission in the Old Testament

Jesus's disciples would've had at least a rudimentary understanding of the ministry of the Holy Spirit from Hebrew Scripture. The Holy Spirit is the third person of the Trinity, and his ministry in the Old Testament foreshadows his missional role in the New Testament. As part of the Godhead, the Spirit imparts life through his breath (Job 33:4). The Spirit was present at creation, hovering over the waters that covered the earth (Gen. 1:2). Intriguingly, that imagery faintly foreshadows the mission of God.

> The earth will be filled
> with the knowledge of the Lord's glory
> as the water covers the sea. (Hab. 2:14)[2]

God's command to the first humans—"the first Great Commission"[3]— articulates the global nature of God's mission: "Be fruitful, multiply, fill the earth" with image bearers who extend God's rule and worship (Gen. 1:28). From the beginning, God intended that his sanctuary presence in Eden would expand to fill the entire earth so that all people in every place would worship the God of glory.

Genesis 3:8 contains the barest hint of intimate fellowship in the immediate presence of God, but even that description comes after the fall of the human race into sin. Humanity's rebellion grieved the Holy Spirit, who continually contended with them (Gen. 6:3; Isa. 63:10). Following the advent of sin, the mission of God shifted to

---

2 See Isa. 11:9.

3 G. K. Beale, *The Temple and the Church's Mission: A Biblical Theology of the Dwelling Place of God* (Downers Grove, IL: InterVarsity Press, 2004), 117.

a rescue mission. Even so, the means of the mission remained the same as its goal—the presence of God among his people.

The Old Testament shows that God's unfolding rescue plan involved the ministry of the Holy Spirit. Sometimes the Spirit filled certain individuals to fulfill specific tasks of leadership for God's advancing mission: for example, Moses and the seventy elders (Num. 11:17, 25–29), Joshua (Num. 27:18), several judges,[4] and Kings Saul and David.[5] Through the prophets, the Holy Spirit spoke warnings,[6] revealed visions and reasons for the Lord's discipline,[7] and inspired the Scriptures.[8]

Significantly, the Holy Spirit's ministry also provided for God's ongoing sanctuary presence among his people in physical sanctuaries. The Lord filled the artist Bezalel with his Spirit to oversee the construction of the tabernacle (Ex. 31:1–5), and the Spirit gave King David all the plans for the temple (1 Chron. 28:11–19). The Lord encouraged the returned exiles to rebuild the temple, saying: "Work! For I am with you. . . . And my Spirit is present among you" (Hag. 2:4–5). He also revealed the source of power for the temple's reconstruction: "Not by strength or by might, but by my Spirit" (Zech. 4:6). The prophet Isaiah, however, indicated that the locus of God's presence was shifting from the physical temple to the Spirit's presence going throughout the world.[9] Several verses

---

4 Othniel, Judg. 3:10; Gideon, Judg. 6:34; Jephthah, Judg. 11:29; and Samson, Judg. 13:25; 14:6, 19.

5 1 Sam. 10:6, 10; 16:13.

6 Neh. 9:30; Zech. 7:12. Cf. Elijah, 1 Kings 18:12; Azariah, 2 Chron. 15:1; Jehaziel, 2 Chron. 20:14; and Zechariah, 2 Chron. 24:20.

7 Ezek. 3:14; 8:3; 11:1, 5, 24.

8 1 Pet. 1:10–11; 2 Pet. 1:21; cf. Matt. 22:43; Acts 1:16; 4:25; 28:25.

9 Joseph R. Greene, "The Spirit in the Temple: Bridging the Gap between Old Testament Absence and New Testament Assumption," *Journal of the Evangelical Theological Society* 55, no. 4 (2012): 717–42.

in Isaiah that describe the Spirit as uniquely resting on the Messiah are set within a global context (Isa. 11:2; 42:1; 61:1).

There are also Old Testament hints that the Holy Spirit would ultimately rest not just on individual leaders but on a much wider population. For example, when the Lord placed his Spirit on the seventy elders, Moses declared, "If only *all* the LORD's people were prophets and the LORD would place his Spirit on them" (Num. 11:29). Speaking to those returning from exile, the Lord promised, "I will cleanse you. . . . and put a new spirit within you. . . . I will place my Spirit within you and cause you to follow my statutes" (Ezek. 36:25–27; cf. 37:14). His promises in Joel 2:28–29 are even more explicit: "I will pour out my Spirit on all humanity"—men and women, old and young, slave and free (cf. Isa. 44:3). The stage was set for the breathtaking developments in the ministry of the Holy Spirit witnessed by the earliest disciples in the New Testament—first, in life of Jesus and, second, in their own lives as part of the early church.

The Ministry of the Holy Spirit and Prayer in the Life of Jesus

Imagine the huge paradigm shift for Jesus's early disciples as these Jews came to understand that Jesus was the true sanctuary—the meeting place between God and humanity—that the tabernacle and temple had foreshadowed.[10] The early disciples had a front-row seat to the ministry of the Holy Spirit in the life of Jesus. Although he was the Son of God, Jesus displayed a striking dependence on the Spirit, from his miraculous conception to his final instructions to his disciples (Luke 1:35; Acts 1:2). The Holy Spirit revealed

---

10 See John 1:14; 2:19–22. This revelation came after Jesus's resurrection.

Jesus's identity as an infant to those who had longed and prayed for the Messiah's coming.[11] Coming out of the water at his baptism, Jesus prayed, and the Holy Spirit descended on him "like a dove"—authenticating his sonship (Luke 3:21–22). John the Baptist prophesied that Jesus would baptize "with the Holy Spirit and fire" (Luke 3:16). Full of the Spirit, Jesus was led by the Spirit into the wilderness, and he returned in the power of the Spirit (Luke 4:1, 14). Inaugurating his ministry, Jesus read Isaiah 61:1–2 and announced that he was the fulfillment of this Spirit-filled ministry of justice (Luke 4:16–21).

Luke's Gospel emphasizes that Jesus remained in the Spirit through continual prayer. Jesus prayed in public, in private, and all night before choosing his disciples (6:12; 9:16, 18). The Son of God rejoiced in the Holy Spirit and praised the Father (10:21). Jesus urged his disciples to pray for their enemies and for laborers to join the spiritual harvest (6:28; 10:2). Although his disciples had undoubtedly heard prayer their entire lives, they witnessed something extraordinary in Jesus's prayer life that prompted them to ask, "Lord, teach us to pray." Jesus responded by giving them a model for prayer, and he encouraged them to ask with persistence (11:1–4, 5–10; cf. 18:1–8). Significantly, Jesus assured his disciples that the Father would give the Holy Spirit to those who ask, and the Spirit would teach them what to say when they were brought before authorities (11:13; 12:12). Jesus also encouraged them to pray for strength to endure tribulation and for deliverance from temptation (21:36; 22:40). Jesus then demonstrated the power of such fervent prayer when he relinquished his own will to that of his Father the night before his crucifixion. After the Spirit made

11 Elizabeth, Luke 1:41; Zechariah, Luke 1:67; Simeon, Luke 2:25–28; Anna, Luke 2:37–38.

Jesus alive in the resurrection,[12] Jesus tied the disciples' global commission of proclaiming "repentance for forgiveness of sins" to one essential factor: they were to wait for the power of the Holy Spirit (24:47–49).

Jesus's teaching in the Gospel of John also expanded the disciples' understanding of the ministry of the Holy Spirit. Jesus chided Nicodemus for his lack of spiritual perception and explained that the kingdom of God is open only to those who are born again by the Spirit, who gives life (3:3, 5; cf. 6:63). On mission to find those who would worship the Father "in Spirit and in truth" (4:23–24), Jesus offered the Samaritan woman "living water"—i.e., the Holy Spirit (cf. 7:38–39)—that would spring up within her for eternal life (4:14). In the Farewell Discourse, Jesus explained that the Father would give the disciples "another Counselor"—one like himself—who would dwell in them and remain with them forever (14:16–17). This Helper would equip Jesus's disciples for ministry, instructing them and reminding them of Jesus's teachings (14:26). The Spirit convicts the world of sin, righteousness, and judgment; he guides disciples into truth (16:7–13). Significantly, the Spirit doesn't magnify himself; rather, he glorifies Jesus and testifies about him (15:26; 16:14–15). Jesus prayed that Spirit-filled believers sent out in every generation would display unity and glory that convince the world of God's love in sending him (17:21–23).[13]

---

12 1 Pet. 3:18.

13 Labeling the priestly prayer of John 17 a "missionary prayer," Lucien Legrand, *Unity and Plurality: Mission in the Bible* (Maryknoll, NY: Orbis, 1990), 141–42, observes that the sending focuses more on "*consecration* to truth" than on "*communication* of truth" (emphasis original): "The envoy remains before all else a 'disciple.' . . . To be sure, they are to proclaim the gospel; but more specifically, and more profoundly, they are called to be one with the truth of the Word: it is the Word that will have the initiative in the deepest heart of their mission."

The Ministry of the Holy Spirit and Prayer in the Early Church

Whatever hesitations the original disciples may have had about the Great Commission were dispelled by the events described in the opening chapters of Acts. The book begins with Jesus's final words before his ascension: the Father promised to baptize Jesus's followers with the Holy Spirit so they would have power to be witnesses in ever-expanding geographic circles (1:4–5, 8). Not surprisingly, the Spirit's coming was linked to continual, united prayer (1:14). The promised power was on display when the Spirit fell at Pentecost, giving believers the ability to speak in the heart languages of those who had traveled from all over the earth (2:4–11). Peter proclaimed that the experience was the fulfillment of Joel 2: the risen Lord Jesus was pouring out the Father's gift of the Spirit on all kinds of people (Acts 2:16–18, 33). Peter called each one to repent and be baptized in Jesus's name for forgiveness of sins, and they too would receive the gift of the Holy Spirit (Acts 2:38). The Spirit-filled church was devoted to prayer (Acts 2:42).

Although the narrative of the Holy Spirit's ministry in Acts is descriptive rather than prescriptive, tracing the activity of the Spirit in the life of the early church yields valuable insights for disciples committed to evangelism and discipleship. Throughout Acts, the Holy Spirit supplies witnesses with boldness (Peter, Acts 4:8; believers, 4:31; Stephen, 7:55) and the words to address opposition. His presence evoked fear, encouragement, and joy (5:1–11; 9:31; 13:52). The Spirit prompted divine encounters with those who were ready to respond to the gospel (Philip and the Ethiopian eunuch, 8:29, 39; Peter and Cornelius, Acts 10:19, 44), and he provided evidence of authentic conversion as the gospel crossed ethnic barriers

(Samaritans, 8:15–17; Gentiles, 10:44–45; 11:15–16). As the primary evangelist, the Spirit played the leading role in directing the church's advance among the Gentiles by sending out missionaries and guiding their work (13:2; 15:28; 16:6–7; 19:21).

The Ministry of the Holy Spirit in the Epistles

The Epistles reveal considerable theological reflection on the ministry of the Holy Spirit. The author of Hebrews notes that it was "through the eternal Spirit" that Christ offered himself as an unblemished sacrifice so that we might have "boldness to enter the [heavenly] sanctuary through the blood of Jesus" (Heb. 9:14; 10:19–21). Paul observes that not only are believers able to enter the sanctuary; they have *become* the sanctuary. This revelation is so stunning, he had to remind his readers repeatedly, "Don't you yourselves know that you are God's temple and that the Spirit of God lives in you?" (1 Cor. 3:16; cf. 6:19; 2 Cor. 6:16). Paul explains that Christ is the cornerstone, and every single believer—regardless of ethnicity—is being built into a "holy temple," where God dwells in the Spirit (Eph. 2:21–22). Peter likewise describes believers as "living stones, a spiritual house" (1 Pet. 2:5). This revelation— believers as sanctuary people—is a crucial development toward the fulfillment of God's original mission to make his home with humanity. Not only are they temple people; they are also family. The "Spirit of adoption" makes believers children of God (Rom. 8:14–17; cf. 2 Cor. 6:16–18; Gal. 4:6–7; Rev. 21:3, 7). In both Testaments, God's presence among his people is the goal *and* the means of God's mission.

The Epistles demonstrate that the ministry of the Holy Spirit is crucial in conversion—the entry point for faith in Christ. When witnesses shared the gospel "by the Holy Spirit sent from heaven"

(1 Pet. 1:12), their spoken message did not come through "persuasive words of [human] wisdom but with a demonstration of the Spirit's power" (1 Cor. 2:4; cf. 1 Thess. 1:5).[14] Those who responded "welcomed the message with joy from the Holy Spirit" (1 Thess. 1:6). The Spirit of truth testifies to the truth of the gospel, enabling a believer to declare "Jesus is Lord" and "Jesus Christ has come in the flesh" (1 Cor. 12:3; 1 John 4:2; 5:6–8). God saves people "through the washing of regeneration and renewal by the Holy Spirit," and he pours out his Spirit on them (Titus 3:5–6; cf. John 3:3–6). Receiving the Spirit by faith, all believers drink of one Spirit, and all are baptized by the Spirit into one body (Gal. 3:14; 1 Cor. 12:13). The Spirit, who seals believers in Christ (Eph. 1:13), indwells and gives life to every believer. "If anyone does not have the Spirit of Christ, he does not belong to him" (Rom. 8:9–10).[15] The "Spirit of adoption" assures believers that they are indeed God's children, and that Jesus remains in them (Rom. 8:15; 1 John 3:24). In summary, the Spirit of God washes, sanctifies, and justifies believers in the name of Jesus (1 Cor. 6:11).

Furthermore, the Epistles indicate that the work of the Holy Spirit is critical not only for initial conversion but also for ongoing, daily discipleship. Just as the Christian life begins with the power of the Spirit, so it continues by the power of the Spirit (Gal. 3:3). Prescriptive commands urge believers to "walk by the Spirit," "live by the Spirit," and "keep in step with the Spirit" (Gal. 5:16, 25).

---

14 Rev. 22:17 reflects the roles of the Spirit and human witness: "Both the Spirit and the bride say, 'Come!' "

15 Although the Spirit seals those who are in Christ, the New Testament contains sober warnings that there is no such thing as a believer whose life presents no evidence of the indwelling Spirit (Matt. 7:16–23; Luke 6:45–46; 2 Cor. 13:5; 1 Tim. 4:1; Heb. 6:4–8; 10:26–29). The evidence for faith is not pointing to a previous "decision," church membership, or even baptism; it is the fruit of the indwelling Holy Spirit (Gal. 5:22–23).

Because the Holy Spirit resides in them, sanctuary people must be holy. By setting their minds on the things of the Spirit, they are to put to death the deeds of the flesh (Rom. 8:5, 13; cf. Gal. 5:16). They take up "the sword of the Spirit—which is the word of God" (Eph. 6:17). They must not grieve or stifle the Spirit (Eph. 4:30; 1 Thess. 5:19); instead, they should continually "be filled by the Spirit" (Eph. 5:18).

The presence of the indwelling Spirit should characterize the lives of believers. He produces an abundance of righteous fruit in the lives of those who remain in him: "love, joy, peace, patience, kindness, goodness, faithfulness, gentleness, and self-control" (Gal. 5:22–23). He enables them to maintain "unity of the Spirit," to "worship by the Spirit," and to enjoy "fellowship with the Spirit" (Eph. 4:3; Phil. 2:1; 3:3). The Spirit distributes gifts to each believer for the common good "to equip the saints for the work of ministry, to build up the body of Christ" (1 Cor. 12:7; Eph. 4:12). The ministry of the Spirit is glorious and brings freedom (2 Cor. 3:8, 17). Over time, as believers gaze at the glory of the Lord, the Spirit transforms them into the image of Christ (2 Cor. 3:18). Finally, "the one who sows to the Spirit will reap eternal life from the Spirit," for the Spirit has sealed him or her "for the day of redemption" (Gal. 6:8; Eph. 4:30). In the meantime, the Spirit is the "firstfruits" of "the glorious freedom of God's children" (Rom. 8:21, 23); he is "a down payment" of their heavenly dwelling and their inheritance (2 Cor. 5:5; Eph. 1:14).

The Ministry of Prayer in the Epistles

How do disciples consistently walk in the Spirit? The Epistles underscore a strong link between walking in the Spirit and prayer. Jude ties abiding in God's love and growing in the faith to "praying in the Holy Spirit" (Jude 20). James observes that "the prayer of a righteous person is very powerful in its effect" (James 5:16). Paul connects being filled with the Spirit to singing spiritual heart songs and always giving thanks to the Lord (Eph. 5:18–19). Outlining instructions to Timothy, Paul stresses the priority of prayer: "First of all, then, I urge that petitions, prayers, intercessions, and thanksgivings be made for everyone. . . . [For this] pleases God our Savior, who wants everyone to be saved and to come to the knowledge of the truth" (1 Tim. 2:1, 3–4). Paul's frequent calls for prayer emphasize both their constancy and breadth: "Pray at *all* times in the Spirit with *every* prayer and request, and stay alert with *all* perseverance and intercession for *all* the saints" (Eph. 6:18). Even when believers do not know how to pray, the Spirit himself "intercedes for the saints according to the will of God" (Rom. 8:26–27). Jesus's revelation to John assures that all the prayers of all the saints are gathered and offered before the very presence of God (Rev. 8:3–4).

The subject matter of Paul's prayers reveals his heart for discipleship. He often prayed that the Lord would "sanctify [his disciples] completely" so they would "become fully mature" (2 Cor. 13:9; 1 Thess. 5:23). He asked God to give them "the Spirit of wisdom and revelation in the knowledge of him" and to enlighten the eyes of their hearts to know the hope, wealth, and power of this calling (Eph. 1:16–19). He requested that the Spirit strengthen them with power, that "Christ may dwell in [their] hearts through faith," and that they would know the magnitude of his love so they would be "filled with all the fullness of God" (Eph. 3:14–19). He prayed for their spiritual growth that they might "walk worthy of the Lord . . . bearing fruit in every good work" (Col. 1:9–10; cf. 2 Thess. 1:11). Paul also explained that the permanent high priest himself intercedes for maturing disciples (Rom. 8:34; cf. Heb. 7:25).

Paul's requests for prayer for himself tended to focus on evangelism. He asked others to pray that God would give him boldness and the words to say when he opened his mouth to speak the gospel (Eph. 6:19–20). He requested prayer that the Lord would "open a door" for him to speak about the gospel, that he might "make it known as [he] should" (Col. 4:3–4). Finally, he called for prayer "that the word of the Lord may spread rapidly and be honored" (2 Thess. 3:1).

Implications for Missional Living Today

The advance of God's kingdom through evangelism and discipleship in the first century was clearly grounded in the ministry of the Holy Spirit and prayer. The original disciples, no doubt familiar with the role of the Spirit in Hebrew Scripture, must have marveled at his ministry lived out before them in Jesus's life (Acts 10:38). But to personally experience the Holy Spirit's activity working in and through them in such powerful ways must have been absolutely astounding.

But what about today? The miraculous spread of the early church across the Roman Empire seems like ancient history. We may find it difficult to imagine a similar sweeping movement in our modern world. The Great Commission, however, still applies to every single follower of Christ in every generation. Jesus's command to make disciples of all nations remains just as compelling. And now, when the world population has mushroomed to eight billion people, the scope of the command appears even more staggering. Our minds may quickly jump to tools, methods, and programs. These have their place, but the priority still rests on the one thing Jesus said we need first and foremost—the power of his indwelling Spirit. Jesus's promise to accompany and empower believers is just as true today as it was for the original disciples. The reality of the Holy Spirit's ministry is just as breathtaking now as it was then.

Steps toward Appropriating the Presence and Power of the Holy Spirit Today

1. *Awaken to the reality that we are sanctuary people.* Like the Corinthians, we need repeated reminders that we are temple people, both as a corporate community (1 Cor. 3:16; 2 Cor. 6:16) and as individual believers (1 Cor. 6:19). Just as in the early church, the Father and Son have taken up residence in the life of every born-again believer through his Spirit. To be a disciple is to have the indwelling Holy Spirit. As Richard Foster points out, "This dynamic, pulsating *with-God* life" on display in the pages of Scripture should be the normal experience of every Christ follower.[16]

2. *Be filled with the Spirit.* We need to consciously obey "the ultimate imperative in the Pauline corpus": Ephesians 5:18–19.[17] This present-tense admonition and its attached participles—*speaking, singing, giving thanks*, and *submitting* to one another—indicate that worship and praise should continually well up in the lives of believers. The verb form is passive voice: God does the filling, but we do the yielding. Where we have crammed worthless substitutes into the Spirit's rightful place, we must repent. We ask him to empty us of our sin, shame, and selfishness; we invite him to fill us with himself—continually.

3. *Become a people who display the life of Christ.* Because God's temple is holy, we are called to be holy (1 Cor. 3:17).[18] Instead of conforming to the darkness that presses in on every side, we must allow the indwelling Holy Spirit to conform us to the very likeness of Christ. Practicing his presence, we live every moment

---

16 Richard J. Foster, *Life with God: Reading the Bible for Spiritual Transformation* (New York: HarperOne, 2008), 7 (emphasis original).

17 Gordon Fee, *God's Empowering Presence: The Holy Spirit in the Letters of Paul* (Peabody, MA: Hendrickson, 1994), 722.

18 Meditating on the somber preparations for the Day of Atonement (Lev. 16) helps us better appreciate the astounding access we have to God's presence through Christ (Heb. 10:19–22).

of every day as if Jesus is right beside us—because he is! Walking in the Spirit continuously allows him to produce in us an orchard of spiritual fruit (Gal. 5:22–23). Our spiritual transformation lends credibility to the reality of our message. As believers, we should radiate the life, love, and hope of Christ before a watching world.

4. *Recognize that "with-ness" is for witness.* As wonderful as it is to experience the fellowship of the Spirit, we must not think the Spirit-filled life is just for our own spiritual formation and edification. His power is in us for the spread of his kingdom (Acts 1:8).[19]

5. *Pray in the Spirit.* Not only is prayer communion with God; it is also partnership in God's mission. Prayer plays a crucial role in witness. We can ask God to show us where he's working and make a list of people for whose salvation we will pray on a regular basis.[20] We pray that the Lord would soften their hearts and make them curious about the gospel, that the Spirit would convict them of sin and bring them to repentance. We pray that the Spirit would give us wisdom, spiritual insight, the words to speak, and a life that reflects the God who lives within us. We need to develop the crucial habit of asking the Father—daily—to use *us* to share the gospel.

6. *Open our eyes to the harvest.* Recognize that people today are just as thirsty as ever, desperately trying to slake their parched longings with everything under the sun. We ask the Lord to give us his love for the lost and ideas about how to serve them. Mourning over the spiritual and moral decline of our day, we plead with the Father for a great outpouring of his Spirit. As Jesus commanded, we should

19 Sometimes believers emphasize one over another: spiritual formation or missional living. The truth, however, is that these two concepts dovetail closely, since the presence of God is the cornerstone for both. See Nathan Finn and Keith Whitfield, eds., *Spirituality for the Sent: Casting a New Vision for the Missional Church* (Downers Grove, IL: InterVarsity Press, 2017).
20 Think through specific categories of relationships: family, friends, coworkers, neighbors, and acquaintances.

pray for more laborers to join the harvest. Emulating Paul's prayers, which pulsate with the mission of God, we should ask for boldness; for open doors, open mouths, and open hearts; and for the gospel to advance rapidly throughout the world. We lift our eyes to the horizon, remembering that God's mission extends to the ends of the earth.

7. *Follow the Spirit's leading.* We must be intentional about looking for opportunities to share the gospel with individuals on our prayer lists, but we also anticipate that the Spirit will orchestrate divine appointments with people we haven't met yet. We request discernment to recognize people's functional idols and functional saviors; we ask for biblical passages and spiritual analogies that will resonate. It's imperative that we develop gospel fluency, but we also depend on the Spirit to give us words to speak in the moment. Just as the Spirit magnifies Jesus, our witness should also focus on Jesus—his life and teachings, his passion and his kingdom.

8. *Remember the goal of witness is "with-ness."* While "with-ness" is, in part, for witness (point 4, above), the ultimate goal is communion with God. Foster urges us not to reduce evangelism and discipleship to "formulas for admittance to heaven instead of a call to a rich, God-soaked life."[21] In place of a "gospel of sin management," Dallas Willard commends *"discipleship evangelism."*[22] In other words, sharing the gospel communicates not only what we are saved *from* but also what we are saved *for*: to be a temple of the living God. When we call people to repent and believe the gospel, we need to share that they receive forgiveness *and* the gift of the Holy Spirit (Acts 2:38). The Spirit gives them eternal life, *and* the Spirit-filled life starts immediately. We need to teach new believers to walk in

---

21 Foster, *Life with God*, 123.
22 Dallas Willard, *The Divine Conspiracy: Rediscovering Our Hidden Life in God* (New York: HarperCollins, 1998), 41, 304 (emphasis original).

the Spirit *and* equip them to share their faith as they become disciple makers who make disciples. Paul's prayers are helpful models for how to pray for new believers as they begin to grow and mature.

9. *Live as deployed people.* At this point we may be feeling a bit overwhelmed, somewhat like the original disciples who received the Great Commission. You may be thinking: *Who, me? This isn't what I signed on for! This kind of work is only for ministry majors!* It may help to remember that Jesus's original disciples were not rabbis; they were fishermen, a tax collector, a political zealot. Jesus intentionally selected ordinary people for his extraordinary mission. You don't have to change your career plans, but you do need to hold them in an open hand. As Christopher Wright has observed, "We ask, 'Where does God fit into the story my life?' when the real question is where does my little life fit into this great story of God's mission."[23] We need to close the Sunday-Monday gap by viewing all aspects of our lives in light of God's mission, because that truly is our mission!

So how can you leverage your job, your profession, your relationships for making disciples? The Lord may lead you to explore where occupational opportunities in your field intersect with great spiritual and physical needs around the world. Even our increasingly post-Christian / never-Christian setting in North America calls for an "infiltration strategy," one that capitalizes on the reality that "believers are already dispersed throughout the culture—embedded in schools, companies, and communities where they study, work, and live."[24] Observing that this army is dispersed but silent, Jeff Iorg argues for their deployment. They must be mobilized: sent on mission

23 Christopher J. H. Wright, *The Mission of God: Unlocking the Bible's Grand Narrative* (Downers Grove, IL: InterVarsity Press, 2006), 533–34.

24 Jeff Iorg, "Prioritize Personal Evangelism" (convocation sermon, Gateway Seminary, Fall 2019), *Baptist Press*, September 3, 2019.

to make disciples as they go. We are sanctuary people wherever God has placed us. The divine resident living within us will empower us to fulfill his Great Commission, just as he did the original disciples. Living as deployed people on mission with the indwelling Spirit of Christ is the most challenging and thrilling adventure imaginable.

The Ministry of the Holy Spirit and Prayer Today: Three Brief Examples

1. Some time ago, I invited a church visitor to a seekers' Bible study, but since Diana often worked out of town, time passed and she hadn't attended yet. One morning I woke up at 4:45 a.m. with a sense of urgency to pray for Diana. I knelt and prayed fervently until the burden lifted ten minutes later. Then I had a strong impression: I was supposed to call her. Nervously, I obeyed. "Diana, I hope I didn't wake you, but I feel the Lord wanted me to call you. He loves you and wants to forgive you, but you need to turn from your sin and trust in him." Long pause. She mumbled: "Umm, okay. Thanks. Goodbye." It all felt so awkward! A few days later, Diana showed up early for the study. When I started apologizing, she stopped me. Just before I'd called, she'd prayed for the first time in her whole life: "God if you're real, could you forgive me?" The Spirit had graciously moved me to call in answer to her sincere prayer.

2. The astounding spiritual harvest among Muslims today testifies to the global scale of the Spirit's ministry. Calling Christians to focused prayer, the Spirit has raised up laborers from every continent for this harvest. Over 25 percent of Muslim-background believers (MBBs) report that dreams and visions of Christ played a role in their conversion.[25] Thousands of MBBs, who now carry a burden for

25 Darren Carlson, "When Muslims Dream of Jesus," TGC, May 31, 2018, https://www.the gospelcoalition.org/.

their own people, demonstrate a Spirit-filled boldness right out of the pages of Acts as they share the gospel even under threat of death.[26]

3. On February 8, 2023, what started out as an ordinary chapel at Asbury University became a sustained outpouring of the Spirit. Like the previous campus revival in 1970, student testimonies sparked prayers of repentance and continuous worship beneath the lettering high above the platform: "HOLINESS UNTO THE LORD." Reflecting on the Spirit's activity mid-revival, New Testament scholar and faculty member Craig Keener noted that decades of prayer had preceded the unusual movement. He observed: "Hughes Auditorium feels like a holy place at the moment. But in Scripture, God's people are his temple. Whatever other places might be special to us in some respects, we are his most sacred place, and we don't have to be near campus to welcome and honor God's presence."[27]

Amazingly, the Spirit still invites us to partner with him as he makes his home in sanctuary people.

Questions for Reflection

1. How does seeing ourselves as sanctuary people impact everyday life?

2. How have you seen the Spirit of God involved in evangelism and discipleship?

3. Asking the Spirit to show you where he is working, draw up a list of people and begin praying for their salvation.

---

26 See, for example, "The Testimony and Defence of Mehdi Dibaj," *Banner of Truth*, January 5, 2015, https://banneroftruth.org/us/resources/articles/2015/testimony-defence-mehdi -dibaj/. Mehdi Dibaj died for his faith June 24, 1994.

27 Craig Keener, "What Is Revival—and Is It Happening at Asbury?," *The Roys Report*, February 16, 2023, https://julieroys.com/.

Resources for Further Study

Fee, Gordon. *Paul, the Spirit, and the People of God*. Grand Rapids, MI: Baker, 2023.

Foster, Richard. *Prayer: Finding the Heart's True Home*. New York: HarperOne, 2002.

Pippert, Rebecca Manley. *Stay Salt: The World Has Changed; Our Message Must Not*. Charlotte: Good Book, 2020.

13

Of Moths and Multiplication

Evangelism and Discipleship in
Symbiotic Relationship

Daniel DeWitt

THE JOSHUA TREE is an iconic symbol of life in the Mojave Desert.[1] It is a tree straight out of a Dr. Seuss story or transplanted from a Vincent van Gogh painting. With its porcupine-like bark, spiky leaves, and topsy-turvy, arm-like branches, it looks like a clumsy giant towering over the barren, brown, sun-drenched landscape.

Maybe you learned how to spell desert the same way as I did. It has one *s* because it is not the sort of place where you'd want to spend a whole lot of time. Dessert, on the other hand, the sweet after-dinner treat, has an additional *s* because you want

---

1 This chapter builds on Daniel DeWitt, "Of Moths and Multiplication," *Theolatte* (blog), September 21, 2023, https://www.theolatte.com/2023/09/.

a double serving. That little additional letter makes a world of difference.

For me, pictures of the desert recall movie scenes with stranded travelers or runaway prisoners covered in sweat, drowning in sand, chasing elusive visions of an oasis on the horizon. That is why the Joshua tree stands out. In an unforgiving environment, this tree means salvation. It offers shade and nutrition to a number of desert critters. Without it, they would not survive.

But as big of a deal as the Joshua tree is, it is dependent upon something very small. While the tree gives protection and nutrition to many, it would not live long were it not for a particular moth. Unlike other flowering trees, the Joshua tree does not produce nectar to attract pollinators. The Yucca moth, however, has reason to help the tree with pollination. The moth's babies eat the seeds from the flower of the tree for food in their first days of existence before they form cocoons.

Most pollination is incidental. Bees like the nectar they pick up from flowers. They just happen to take on some pollen and carry it with them to the next flower as they search for another sugary treat. Such pollination is a happy accident. Since the Joshua tree lacks nectar, this tree named for salvation is in need of some saving itself.

Enter scene, Yucca moth. Not only do the Joshua trees not have nectar; they have very little pollen. Were it not for the adept jaws of the female Yucca moths, with tentacles located near their mouths, the Joshua tree would not have a prayer. The Yucca moths intentionally and carefully take pollen from one flower and deposit it on another. But before they accomplish this important act of pollination, the female moths use a needle-like appendage to deposit their eggs. Charles Darwin called this "the most wonderful case of fertilization [*sic*]."[2]

The flower grows into a fruit, and the fruit provides nutrition for the Yucca moth eggs when they hatch. The Joshua tree and the moth share what is called an *obligate symbiotic relationship*. The two have a sort of obligation to one another. One could not survive without the other. Without the Yucca moth, the Joshua tree would have no method for pollination. Without the Joshua tree, the Yucca moth would lack an environment for its eggs to flourish in the desert.

There are, of course, other forms of symbiosis. There is the predatory type, where one species benefits at the expense of another. There is a mutually beneficial symbiosis, where both species benefit. And there are forms of symbiosis where one species benefits and the other does not. But the obligate kind of symbiosis is the sort that best illustrates the relationship between evangelism and discipleship as it relates to biblical multiplication.

The Relationship between Evangelism and Discipleship

In some ministries, discipleship and evangelism can look more like the other forms of symbiotic relationships. A ministry might pursue evangelism but neglect discipleship. It is a predatory kind of evangelism, advancing at the expense of discipleship. Or a church might emphasize discipleship at the expense of evangelism, a predatory discipleship unconcerned about reaching the lost.

You may have heard of ministries that are a mile wide but only an inch deep, because they focus on evangelism and not discipleship. The alternative, a ministry that is a mile deep but only an

---

2 Charles Robert Darwin, "Letter from C. R. Darwin to J. D. Hooker [7 April 1874]," in *Correspondence of Charles Darwin*, vol. 22, Cambridge University Digital Library, accessed November 27, 2023, https://cudl.lib.cam.ac.uk/view/MS-DAR-00095-00321/1.

inch wide, focuses exclusively on discipleship. It is my thesis that biblical multiplication requires both. To neglect either one is to neglect both. That is because evangelism exists for discipleship. And discipleship exists for evangelism. You cannot do one well while excluding the other. If you are discipling someone, it should be for the purpose of that person becoming a disciple who shares the gospel. If you are evangelizing someone, it should be with the goal that he or she will become a disciple. And the sequence goes on, which is where multiplication comes in.

However, as I will share later, biblical multiplication is not attainable through human efforts alone. It is a work of the Spirit, but the Spirit does not work contrary to the teachings of the Son, and Jesus clearly commanded his disciples to make disciples of all nations. That entails both evangelism and discipleship.

While there is much we can learn through common-grace, commonsense wisdom from successful leaders in the world, I fear we are sometimes guilty of thinking of multiplication in unbiblical ways. A lot of leadership theories use two low–high spectrums in order to create quadrants for classification. One common model looks at competency and willingness. It uses one low–high spectrum for competency and the other for willingness. If a person ranks high in regard to commitment to do a job but low in competency, he or she will have a poor result. The same is true if someone is high in competency but low in willingness.

When it comes to evangelism and discipleship, it is tempting to think along the same lines. You might think of churches or individuals who are high in evangelism and low in discipleship, or vice versa. And you could chart these differences in a military model, with quadrants. But we miss the mark in evangelical circles when we compartmentalize churches in these kinds of taxonomies.

Seeing churches that are great at evangelism, at reaching their communities, and at spreading the gospel, we sometimes validate an exclusive focus on evangelism as necessary for a particular community. For example, I have heard Christian leaders explain that discipleship-focused churches benefit from larger, more evangelistic churches. New believers reached by large evangelistic churches, it is reasoned, will seek environments more suited for discipleship, leading them to different churches. So one church reaches them and another church teaches them.

But what if both churches in this example are thinking wrongly about the relationship between evangelism and discipleship?

Note that I'm not saying one focus is better than the other, as though churches should prioritize one to the neglect of the other for some greater good. What we need is a realignment according to a more biblical vision of multiplication. We must pursue both evangelism and discipleship simultaneously. I believe biblical multiplication requires seeing evangelism and discipleship as an obligate symbiosis. The two need each other for survival. This sort of symbiosis creates a culture for Spirit-empowered multiplication.

The Commission of Christ Requires Both Evangelism and Discipleship

A foundational text for understanding the relationship between evangelism and discipleship comes from the final words of Jesus. The discourse in Matthew 28 provides a framework for thinking of biblical multiplication. Jesus didn't offer one command at the expense of the other, reaching versus teaching, but described them together as the integral mission of the disciples and, by extension, of the church collectively and individually today.

Now the eleven disciples went to Galilee, to the mountain to which Jesus had directed them. And when they saw him they worshiped him, but some doubted. And Jesus came and said to them, "All authority in heaven and on earth has been given to me. Go therefore and make disciples of all nations, baptizing them in the name of the Father and of the Son and of the Holy Spirit, teaching them to observe all that I have commanded you. And behold, I am with you always, to the end of the age." (vv. 16–20)

You can often tell whether a leader's emphasis is on either evangelism or discipleship by how he explains this passage. A more evangelistic pastor might prioritize the command to go and preach. A more discipleship-oriented pastor might focus on the command to "make disciples of all nations." But that sort of division is not in the passage itself. So we must avoid a false dichotomy. While the apostle Paul distinguishes between evangelists and teachers in Ephesians 4:11–13, their distinct gifts in the life of the faith community in no way undermine Jesus's command to all believers.

The process of making disciples requires growth and faithfulness of the disciples themselves. Their obedience to this command, the Great Commission, for example, is a requirement for their own growth. In other words, disciples cannot mature in their faith without heeding Christ's command to preach the gospel. And their preaching is empty if not aimed at making disciples.

In the process of growing as disciples, believers grow in their ability to present the good news. But in order to grow as disciples, they must simultaneously obey the command to preach the gospel. It's an obligate symbiosis.

John Calvin put it this way: "The goal of God's work in us is to bring our lives into harmony and agreement with His own righteousness, and so *to manifest to ourselves and others* identity as His adopted Children."[3] Our growing in harmony with God's design is crucial for manifesting God's saving purposes to the world. Calvin thus emphasizes the dependent nature of the two sides of this singular command to make disciples of all nations.

Fertile Soil and Biblical Multiplication

Mark's Gospel offers us another example of the inseparable nature of evangelism and discipleship for biblical multiplication. Using an agricultural analogy, Jesus illustrates for us what we might expect as we seek to obey the Great Commission:

> Listen! Behold, a sower went out to sow. And as he sowed, some seed fell along the path, and the birds came and devoured it. Other seed fell on rocky ground, where it did not have much soil, and immediately it sprang up, since it had no depth of soil. And when the sun rose, it was scorched, and since it had no root, it withered away. Other seed fell among thorns, and the thorns grew up and choked it, and it yielded no grain. And other seeds fell into good soil and produced grain, growing up and increasing and yielding thirtyfold and sixtyfold and a hundredfold. (4:3–8)

The sower is planting the same seed in each scenario. The variables in the story are the soils and the outcomes. Some seed falls on good soil, resulting in multiplication, while other seed falls on ground unfavorable for growth.

Jesus explains to the disciples that genuine and enduring multiplication is found in "the ones who hear the word and accept

3 John Calvin, *The Little Book on the Christian Life* (Orlando, FL: Reformation Trust, 2017), 3 (emphasis added).

it and bear fruit" (4:20). He contrasts authentic multiplication with a response to the gospel that is thwarted by intervention from Satan (4:15), opposition from the world (4:17), or sinful desires from within (4:19). Here we see that biblical multiplication is connected to both the preaching of the gospel—the sowing of seed—and the recipient's learning to observe all of Christ's commands (Matt. 28:20). This is at the very core of the Great Commission.

While the process of teaching believers to obey Christ's commands requires the discipline of theology, we must not make theology an end in itself. Scholar Michael F. Bird writes:

> Theology . . . is the way that we organize the content of discipleship training. Theology provides us with the substance and syllabus for Christian instruction. Theology is necessary to arrange and articulate Christian teachings, whether the basics or the more complex and contested elements of the faith.[4]

Without giving new believers a framework for thinking about the Christian faith, we limit their ability both to grow as disciples and to share their own faith in evangelism. This implies the need for other disciplines, like apologetics, polemics, and irenics, but all such disciplines are empty if not motivated by and aimed at the Great Commission.

The Role of the Spirit in Multiplication

In the context of seeking both to reach and to teach, we find fertile soil for multiplication. That is not to say that multiplication or

---

4 Michael F. Bird, *Evangelical Theology: A Biblical and Systematic Introduction*, 2nd ed. (Grand Rapids, MI: Zondervan Academic, 2020), 46.

growth is anthropocentric, a work of humans. While we are the ones learning, teaching, and planting seeds, Jesus's command to make disciples of the nations comes in the context of his authority and his presence. And as we see in John's Gospel and throughout the Bible, it is through the Spirit indwelling the believer that the disciples will fulfill the commission of Christ (see John 14).

We find a vivid example of this reality in an epic conversation Jesus shares with a religious leader. Nicodemus seeks Jesus out because of Jesus's authoritative teaching ministry. Jesus responds to what appears to be flattery on Nicodemus's part with a simple command to be born again.

In trying to understand Christ's words, Nicodemus seems to flip through the timeline of his past experiences. He was born once, and though he wasn't old enough then to know what was happening, he now understands something of the process. Perplexed, he asks how he might enter his mother's womb a second time. Imagine eavesdropping on this conversation and hearing this graphic misapplication of Jesus's words.

Jesus seems at first to compound Nicodemus's confusion. He talks about how the Spirit is like the wind, blowing wherever the Spirit so desires (John 3:8). Herein lies the problem. Nicodemus is not only unable to reenter his mother's womb; he's also incapable of controlling the wind. In other words, this kind of radical transformation of being adopted into God's family is far above his pay grade. On the other hand, Jesus points Nicodemus to the most helpful reality of all, the unstoppable work of the Spirit.

This of course touches on the great paradox of Scripture regarding God's sovereignty and human freedom. It's a mystery beyond what we can rationally reconcile. We see both truths in Scripture. Yet, wherever you might fall on the theological spectrum, one thing is certain: the Spirit is necessary for this kind of spiritual birth, as Joel Green and Scot McKnight point out: the "Spirit functions both as a witness and an advocate for Christ."[5]

Without the work of the Spirit, all evangelistic and discipleship efforts are destined to fail. While obedience to the Great Commission requires the disciples to actively engage in reaching and teaching, only the Spirit can bring about multiplication. You might think of this as a sort of bad news–good news scenario.

The bad news—it is not really bad, but bear with me—is that no human can control the work of the Spirit. The good news is that no person can stop the Spirit. In striving to obey the Great Commission, the believer may at times wish he or she could control the Spirit. That would make ministry much easier. I am reminded of Peter's exchange in Acts 8 with Simon the magician, who was rebuked for thinking he could purchase the Spirit (vv. 18–24). The Spirit does as the Spirit pleases.

Christians need not despair when the outcome to their reaching and teaching efforts is not as they might wish. Their confidence can be found in the reality that the Spirit, like the wind, will blow wherever the Spirit desires and bring life and fruit. No one can control or stop the Spirit.

The Christian's Dilemma

Church leaders often face difficult decisions—even criticism and conflict—related to which biblical command, evangelism or discipleship, they should prioritize in their ministries. In the middle of writing this chapter, I talked with a pastor who was navigating his church through what is sadly a common divide over the rela-

5   Joel B. Green and Scot McKnight, eds., *Dictionary of Jesus and the Gospels* (Downers Grove, IL: InterVarsity Press, 1992), 880.

tionship between evangelism and discipleship. As with all things, the challenges he was facing involved more than evangelism and discipleship, but they did not involve less.

The church leaders had recently dismissed an energetic staff member who possessed clear relational and evangelistic gifts. Through this man's ministry, scores of teenagers had begun attending the church, and many had made professions of faith and were baptized. One of the challenges leading to his dismissal was an unwillingness to align the student ministry with the discipleship aims of the church. The youth pastor felt the highest value was evangelism, with no parameters for biblical discipleship.

At the same time, another leader of a large Bible study in the church expressed frustration about what he felt was a lack of in-depth theological training from the pulpit. His concern was discipleship. He believed the church was too outreach oriented and thus he transferred his membership to another church. Sadly, many church members make such decisions in vain as no ministry will ever perfectly satisfy their expectations or priorities.

The pastor was caught between these seemingly conflicting values. One leader left because evangelism should be the priority, and another because discipleship should be the focus. What should a pastor do? Should the church focus on evangelism? Should it focus on discipleship? Is there a third way? This is a live issue because ministry leaders have to navigate this terrain every day. While there is no easy way to avoid church conflict entirely, knowing that they do not have to choose between these two concerns should encourage pastors and ministry leaders.

Biblical multiplication is the Spirit-empowered outcome of a dependent and symbiotic relationship between evangelism and discipleship. This obligate symbiosis reminds us that we must not sacrifice one at the expense of the other. In attempting to do so, we sacrifice both. One cannot survive without the other.

That, of course, raises the question of churches that reach large numbers of people with what seems to be no attempt to disciple those reached. One could question the validity of such multiplication, but it is important to keep in mind that God can indeed use flawed people and poor methods. Yet we dare not build our view of multiplication merely from what "works." If you were to study the history of churches in the area where you live, you would likely discover a number of ministries that once flourished in the sense of reaching a lot of people but today no longer exist.

It is also entirely possible to find churches in your region that, at some point, had wonderful biblical teaching and discipleship ministries but failed to reach their neighbors. It is possible to be a mile deep and only an inch wide. Though discipleship is of great importance, it does not exempt a church and individual Christians from seeking to reach those far from God. A church that only disciples believers will inevitably fail to pass the faith to the next generation.

If the Great Commission were a coin, its two sides would be evangelism and discipleship. It is impossible to think of a one-sided coin. No matter how thin a coin might be, it necessarily has two sides. A two-dimensional drawing may show only one side, but the coin itself has two.

In the same way, a one-sided Great Commission is impossible. Its two sides are evangelism and discipleship. Through the work of the Spirit, in the Spirit's time, and in the Spirit's way, this obligate symbiosis creates ecosystems for biblical multiplication.

Theologian Millard Erickson describes discipleship as the "second major function of the church," saying evangelism is "the very reason for [the church's] being."[6] While this might sound like a possible bifurcation of the two, it illustrates their dependence upon one another. The church is incapable of functioning as intended without seeking to reach and teach their communities and beyond.

What Hath Athens to Do with Jerusalem?

Multiplication looks different in every context. In Jerusalem, the promised Spirit turned the city upside down. Thousands came to faith in a single day. In fulfillment of Jesus's words, the Spirit blew in like the wind, overthrowing obstacles to belief of every kind and igniting faith among people from different nations who spoke different languages. This unique event was followed by believers meeting together to grow in fellowship and in their understanding of God's word, and God added to their numbers daily (Acts 2).

As the disciples were going and preaching and making disciples, multiplication subsequently looked different, at least from one perspective. Multiplication took longer and seemed more arduous the farther they traveled from Jerusalem. But seen in a different light, it was exactly the same. We do not see the same mass conversions, but we see the same means of multiplication. Conversions differed in quantity but not in quality.

Consider Paul's reaching and teaching ministry in the birthplace of Western philosophy, Athens. Paul's outreach did not have a Pentecost-like response in terms of immediate numbers. Yet he preached the same gospel. And as in Pentecost, there were those who believed. The Spirit, like the wind, blew through the city filled with idols and brought new life. While the number of converts was far smaller, it was still the same process. The same is true today.

6 Millard J. Erickson, *Christian Theology* (Grand Rapids, MI: Baker, 1998), 1061–63.

Preaching the gospel in an adverse context often requires what C. S. Lewis described as "pre-evangelism."[7] Paul used the cultural confusion of Athens to make room for, and frame, his presentation of the gospel. The apostle used a nearby shrine to an unknown god, and an acute understanding of the Athenians' own prophets and poets, to point his audience to Jesus.

Authors Scott Burson and Jerry Walls speak to this in summarizing the apologetic methods of C. S. Lewis and Francis Schaeffer: "Therefore, the inconsistency of the non-Christian is at the same time both a curse and a blessing. It causes the nonbeliever unpleasant cognitive and existential discomfort, but it also allows a point of evangelist contact, which can lead to the Christian solution."[8] This sort of apologetic uses the gospel as a lens through which to understand the human condition, a method increasingly described as cultural apologetics. Similarly, the late author and pastor R. C. Sproul described this process of learning the way a culture thinks in order to explain the good news: "Most ideas that shape our lives are accepted (at least initially) somewhat uncritically. We do not create a world or environment from scratch and then live in it. Rather we step into a world and culture that already exists, and we learn to interact with it."[9]

As the disciples moved from Jerusalem throughout Judea and into Samaria toward the ends of the earth, they encountered different ideologies and utilized different approaches.[10] Yet the content

---

7 See Brian M. Williams, *C. S. Lewis: Pre-Evangelism for a Post-Christian World: Why Narnia Might Be More Real Than We Think* (Cambridge, OH: Christian, 2021).

8 Scott R. Burson and Jerry L. Walls, *C. S. Lewis and Francis Schaeffer: Lessons for a New Century from the Most Influential Apologists of Our Time* (Downers Grove, IL: InterVarsity Press, 1998), 153.

9 R. C. Sproul, *The Consequences of Ideas: Understanding the Concepts That Shaped Our World* (Wheaton, IL: Crossway, 2000), 9.

10 My thoughts on this topic are indebted to New Testament scholar Christopher M. Hays, president of ScholarLeaders, whose conversation with me regarding his forthcoming chapter

of their message and their dependence upon the Spirit were the same. Like Jesus, they called upon their audience to be born again, to turn to Christ in faith. And yet they knew it was the Spirit who alone could bring new life.

In Paul's famous sermon in Athens, we find a helpful picture of what we can expect in our own efforts to obey the Great Commission:

> Now when they heard of the resurrection of the dead, some mocked. But others said, "We will hear you again about this." So Paul went out from their midst. But some men joined him and believed, among whom also were Dionysius the Areopagite and a woman named Damaris and others with them. (Acts 17:32–34)

Paul's sermon was met with three responses: Some mocked. Others inquired. Some believed. In our efforts to reach and teach, we can expect something very similar. Some will mock us. Some will invite us into conversations as they contemplate the claims of the Christian faith. Perhaps we will hear the wind of the Spirit rustling through our homes, villages, towns, and cities as some believe.

Back to the Desert

I really cannot get past the name the Joshua tree. What a great name. Through the heat of day and cold of night, it offers a life-giving ecosystem. And yet, it would quickly face extinction without that tentacle-mouthed moth. Together they flourish. Apart they perish. And through their dependent symbiotic relationship, they bless other organisms.

---

about Acts 17 helped me think through how multiplication "was more difficult and took longer the farther the disciples traveled from Jerusalem."

There is always a danger of taking a metaphor too far. But I think the relationship of the Joshua tree and the Yucca moth offers insights into the relationship of evangelism and discipleship. They need each other. Evangelism needs discipleship. Discipleship needs evangelism.

One of the interesting facts I discovered when looking into the Joshua tree and the Yucca moth is how female moths rarely lay their eggs in the same flower as other female moths. That would create competition for resources among the larvae. This symbiotic relationship is as strategic as it is intentional. It is designed by God.

God's good design for the world obviously goes far beyond the Mojave Desert. He has a good design for reaching the world. He has a good design for his disciples. It is not hidden. It is clear in the last words Jesus gave his disciples before his ascension. As we go, we are to make disciples, which entails evangelism, and teach them to obey Jesus, which is the very heart of discipleship.

Evangelism exists for discipleship. The goal of sharing the good news is to make disciples. Discipleship exists for evangelism. The goal of discipleship is to make disciples who make disciples. Like the moth and tree, evangelism and discipleship need one another. The two exist in an obligate symbiotic relationship. Together they provide fertile soil for Spirit-empowered transformation.

What God hath joined together, let no one separate.

Questions for Reflection

1. What is the relationship between evangelism and discipleship?

2. How are evangelism and discipleship included in Christ's Great Commission?

3. In what ways can it be said that evangelism exists for discipleship?

4. In what ways can it be said that discipleship serves evangelism?

Resources for Further Study

Burson, Scott R. and Jerry L. Walls, *C. S. Lewis and Francis Schaeffer: Lessons for a New Century from the Most Influential Apologists of Our Time*. Downers Grove, IL: InterVarsity Press, 1998.

Butterfield, Rosaria Champagne. *The Gospel Comes with a House Key: Practicing Radically Ordinary Hospitality in Our Post-Christian World*. Wheaton, IL: Crossway, 2018.

Williams, Brian M. *C. S. Lewis: Pre-Evangelism for a Post-Christian World: Why Narnia Might Be More Real Than We Think*. Cambridge, OH: Christian, 2021.

14

Christian Higher Education, the Church, Evangelism, and Discipleship

Freddy Cardoza

THE CHAPTERS OF THIS BOOK have sought to establish an essential truth: the world currently stands at a critical inflection point in its relationship with God. Where the people of the world and the people of God go from here will largely be determined by what happens in evangelism and discipleship through the church. Historically, Christian education has been consistently involved in this divine drama, and the challenges and complexities of today's digital age give Christian higher education a strategic role in supporting the church in her work. This chapter explores where we have been, where we are, and where we go from here.

The Beginnings of Higher Learning and Civilization

In the late sixth century BC, Athens developed the world's first democracy—a society of self-determining people. Though limited in scope and imperfect in application, democratic rule revolutionized human existence by creating a free society. This liberating spirit permeated the lives of its citizens, leading to the dawn of a golden age. That marvelous 150-year classical period became the peak of human civilization up to that time.

The classical age of philosophy was initiated by the so-called Age of Pericles, a time that began with the original philosophers. These included the powerful minds of Thales of Miletus and his contemporaries Anaximander, Anaximenes, and Pythagoras, followed later by the likes of Democritus and others.[1]

During this period, Plato founded his famed Academy in Athens. Established in 387 BC, the Academy was the world's first school of higher learning.[2] Plato's interest in establishing formal education was not merely intellectual curiosity in abstract and arcane ideas. He encouraged students to engage in serious intellectual pursuits to expand the boundaries of their understanding and enhance their existence and others. In *Phaedrus*, he wrote in the voice of Socrates to describe the simple purpose of his teaching—to help people live the "Good Life."[3]

Plato spent the remaining forty years of his life educating a growing number of students interested in that ideal. The practical relevance of Plato's school was so profound that it literally became an institution, enduring perpetually for centuries.

Plato's most famous student was Aristotle, who, like Socrates before him, became one of the most influential intellectuals in

1 Alvin J. Schmidt, *Under the Influence: How Christianity Transformed Civilization* (Grand Rapids, MI: Zondervan, 2001), 185, 189–90.
2 Thomas Brickhouse and Nicholas D. Smith, "Plato (427–347 B.C.E.)," *Internet Encyclopedia of Philosophy*, accessed November 27, 2023, https://iep.utm.edu/.
3 Jacob N. Graham, "Ancient Greek Philosophy," *Internet Encyclopedia of Philosophy*, accessed November 28, 2023, https://iep.utm.edu/.

human history. Aristotle remained in the Academy for two decades, leaving shortly after Plato's death to tutor Alexander, the teenage son of Macedonia's King Philip II. Following five years of tutoring, Aristotle returned to Athens. With Plato now gone and with the desire to start a different type of school, Aristotle launched what became the second institution of higher learning. The Lyceum was established just three miles from the Academy.[4] Though it did not gain the notoriety or endure quite like the Academy, it too became an influential center of learning, but with a different emphasis. Whereas the Academy focused on teaching, the Lyceum placed a greater focus on research.[5]

While living, Plato stimulated people with ideas using the teaching method of his mentor. His successors continued using that style of instruction, establishing the Socratic method as an ancient and master approach that continues to endure. Meanwhile, Aristotle invested time systematically building a library of precedent literature to foster knowledge through ongoing research.[6] In taking different approaches, the two schools defined the rudiments of what would become the essence of higher education today: scholarly centers of teaching and research for societal impact. Their work in the Greek trivium (grammar, dialectic, and rhetoric) and quadrivium (arithmetic, music, geometry, astronomy) gave the world the liberal arts and an embryonic version of the sciences that would flourish later in history.[7]

4 Google Maps, https://bit.ly/academytolyceum.
5 Olaf Pedersen, *The First Universities: Studium Generale and the Origins of University Education in Europe* (Cambridge: Cambridge University Press, 1997), 13.
6 John P. Lynch, *Aristotle's School: A Study of a Greek Educational Institution* (Berkeley: University of California Press, 1972), 75.
7 Kevin Clark, DLS, and Ravi Scott Jain, *The Liberal Arts Tradition: A Philosophy of Christian Classical Education* (Camp Hill, PA: Classical Academic Press, 2020), 26–28.

The merging of powerful political, educational, and cultural forces embodied in the classical age made Athens the cradle of civilization. Through inquiry and industry, Hellenism blossomed as knowledge grew. More sophisticated forms of geometry gave way to breathtaking examples of civil engineering, glorious architecture, and evocative sculpture. Powerful philosophical ideas unleashed the possibilities of linguistic expression, rhetoric, and poetry. In time, these facilitated the development of classical literature, art, and the performance arts, along with aesthetics and ethics. These superior hallmarks in the Greek way of life would be widely and enthusiastically embraced as society became cultured and civilized, leading people to a greater sense of meaning and quality of life.

Politically, with Alexander having completed his education under Aristotle, the young prince joined his father's army. Two years later, he ascended the throne to face a series of military hostilities requiring his attention. Through his legendary courage, mastery of leadership, and conviction about the superiority of Hellenism, Alexander became the great philosopher-king and champion who introduced this new way of living throughout the known world. By the end of his life, the Greek Empire spanned across parts of three continents, where rich expressions of human advancement abounded. Alexander's successors continued to promote the Hellenistic way of life across the wide expanse of the empire as Western Civilization flourished.

Though Athens gave the world the golden age, the Greek Empire ultimately fell three centuries later. The ascent of Rome as a global power brought the formation of the indomitable Greco-Roman Empire. Its enduring influence on what grew into Western culture now shapes the entire world as we know it. The name of the Greco-

Roman Empire speaks to Rome's nearly complete adoption of the ideals of classical Greece and the expansion of those values over an even larger geographical territory. This way of life soon stretched over an enormous land mass from modern-day Britain in north-western Europe, south to Morocco in Northern Africa, over to Iraq in the Middle East, and up to Azerbaijan in Asia. These lands comprised much of the known world at that time.

The Roman Empire by no means embodied all the lofty values of the Academy and Lyceum, but through its adoption of Greek ideas and culture, the die was cast. As a result, many of the principles that made great civilizations possible were enjoyed around the world as the Roman Empire expanded.

The Advent of the Master Teacher and Christian Education

Just prior to the time of Christ, the Roman Republic gave way to Imperial Rome (31 BC and following). Unlike the tumultuous political period of the republic that had been dominated by nearly constant strife, a new phase of Roman history involving the establishment of an empire under Augustus Caesar brought about a long season of internal peace and stability, the *Pax Romana*—the Peace of Rome. This was a time of unprecedented global peace when, through the unparalleled dominion of the empire, people enjoyed safe interstate travel, and global commerce began to develop. This included the Silk Road, that ancient trade route that united the Far East with the West. It led to tremendous economic growth that provided more goods, services, opportunities, and entertainment to the developed world as a result. It was during this time of history that Jesus was born.[8]

---

8 Jaś Elsner, *Imperial Rome and Christian Triumph: The Art of the Roman Empire, AD 100–450* (Oxford: Oxford University Press, 1998), 1–8.

In the broader Roman histories, Christ was originally little more than a footnote. Yet his teaching ministry, followed by his death, his resurrection, and the formation of the Christian church, changed that. Christ's Great Commission involved the proclamation of an evangelistic message calling for devoted discipleship, centering on the priority of teaching. These themes of evangelism, discipleship, and education would develop increasing prominence as the church took root and grew.

These developed robustly over a long period against the larger backdrop of the global Roman Empire. In time and despite its humble beginnings, the impact of Christian evangelism, discipleship, and education would be seen and felt on a global scale and would soon be interwoven into the fabric of Western Civilization itself.[9] So strong was the power of the gospel that it ultimately reshaped the whole of the Greco-Roman world, literally dethroning its pantheon of gods. At that time, the Romans were religiously inclusive and pluralistic. They proudly honored all gods, as the Greeks had before them. Meanwhile, Christians stood countercultural and rejected the pantheon on the basis of Christ's supremacy.[10] This ultimately resulted in the widespread recognition of Christ as Lord, a truth that helped reshape the mores and morals of the global empire. It was a turning point in history that changed human life in a fundamental way, resulting in the splitting of time by the incarnation of Christ.

During the Greco-Roman Empire's expansion, state-sponsored libraries were erected in substantial locations across its expansive landscape. These impressive buildings not only possessed vast holdings of preserved human knowledge but were also places of

9 Elsner, *Imperial Rome and Christian Triumph*, 7–10.
10 Schmidt, *Under the Influence*, 25.

rigorous instruction. These spectacular facilities included Egypt's Great Library of Alexandria, the Celsus Library in Ephesus, and Hadrian's Library in Athens.[11]

In the early days of Christianity, Christ followers suffered religious intolerance, and the church was a target of ostracism, attacks, and even martyrdom. In a very real way, Christianity *itself* was threatened. The church met the challenge with the help of strong Christian education. Believers responded in two ways: first, some withdrew to establish private monastic communities where they devoted themselves to prayer and rigorous study; second, others gathered in public centers to provide scholarly theological instruction.

While monasteries quietly grew in importance and intensity, the institutes offered studies in theology, polemics, and apologetics. These so-called catechetical schools became early examples of structured Christian education, as they gave instruction in catechesis—orthodox instruction in biblical teachings and the essentials of the faith. These schools would prove indispensable as they helped the church articulate doctrine, deconstruct heresies, and promote evangelism.[12]

Originally, Justin Martyr established catechetical schools in Ephesus and Rome. Then, the vast holdings of the Alexandrian Museum and Library contributed to the rise of the school at Alexandria, which became the single most important catechetical center of early Christian history. These institutes and the school of Syrian Antioch, however imperfect and error prone, made noble attempts to educate and equip believers. Generally, catechetical schools taught adults of both sexes, doubling their

---

11 Stuart A. P. Murray, *The Library: An Illustrated History* (New York: Skyhorse, 2009), 14–24.
12 Schmidt, *Under the Influence*, 171–75.

impact.[13] This was unlike the Greek school, the *gymnasium*, which excluded women from instruction.[14] Whereas catechetical schools were for adults, Christian boys and girls were educated in cathedral and, later, episcopal schools, parochial schools, and schools offered in monasteries or nunneries. Each had certain educational emphases, sometimes discipleship and sometimes including a full curriculum of diverse subjects.[15]

Ultimately, Christianity began to make an enormous cultural impact, and the Roman Empire began to splinter. In the third and fourth centuries AD, the empire declined, and enemy soldiers sought to diminish the influence of Hellenistic culture by destroying its centers of learning and dispersing its valuable library collections.[16] Christian education continued unabated, as catechetical schools gave rise to important intellectual voices in the church, which included the likes of Clement, Origen, Tertullian, and Chrysostom.[17] Meanwhile, St. Ambrose, the great doctor of the church, was instrumental in the conversion of Augustine. Following his baptism, Augustine left Milan and traveled to the city of Carthage, where he rose to prominence and became the greatest Christian educator until Aquinas. His writings were so powerful that he influenced St. Jerome, who was known as the greatest intellectual of the Latin fathers and the translator of the Latin Vulgate.[18]

---

13 William. M. Ramsay, *The Church in the Roman Empire before A.D. 170* (London: Hodder and Stoughton, 1893), 345, Internet Archive, https://archive.org/.

14 Kenneth. J. Freeman, *Schools of Hellas* (London: Macmillan, 1922), 46.

15 Schmidt, *Under the Influence*, 172.

16 Clare Graham, "Libraries in History," *Architectural Review* 203, no. 1216 (1998): 72–75.

17 Kevin E. Lawson, "Historical Foundations of Christian Education," in *Christian Education: A Guide to the Foundations of Ministry*, ed. Freddy Cardoza (Grand Rapids, MI: Baker, 2019), 20.

18 Saint Jerome, *On Illustrious Men*, trans. Thomas P. Halton, The Fathers of the Church (Washington, DC: Catholic University of America Press, 1999), xxix.

Through the intellectual traditions established by those and other believers across the northern span of the continent, and the New Testament's Apollos before that,[19] Africa figured very important in the early centuries of the church's efforts in evangelism, discipleship, and education.[20] Along with Antioch and Alexandria, the cities of Rome, Constantinople, and Jerusalem were the most influential centers of instruction in the church's early centuries.

Early Christian Higher Education

By the time the Roman Empire completely collapsed, the impact of Christian education had made the church a defining force in shaping "the culture of the world."[21] Meanwhile, Christian monastic communities had become important centers of learning. Due to the impact of both Augustine of Hippo and Benedict of Nursia in the Western Hemisphere, and Basil the Great in the East before them, these communities thrived. With time for devotion, reflection, and study, monasteries produced and housed books, as monks increasingly became known as respected intellectuals and scholars.[22] This was especially important during the rise of Islam and its centuries of attacks on the Byzantine Church. Though the Eastern church was weakened, its Greek monasteries housed rich scholarship and an intellectual heritage that would ultimately make a great impact on learning in the West.

With the demise of the Greco-Roman Empire, there was a de-emphasis of Hellenic studies throughout the West. Those were the Dark Ages, and the decline of the Greek language and classics

19 Acts 18:24–25.
20 Thomas C. Oden, *How Africa Shaped the Christian Mind: Rediscovering the African Seedbed of Western Christianity* (Downers Grove, IL: InterVarsity Press, 2010), 1–11.
21 Schmidt, *Under the Influence*, 172.
22 Graham, "Libraries in History," 72.

during that time led to the dominance of the Latin language in the Western church, which was increasingly dominated by the influence of Rome.[23] Ultimately, the establishment of the Holy Roman Empire by Charlemagne (AD 800) solidified the religio-political power of the church. Despite this, or perhaps because of it, much of the Christian intellectual tradition waned during this time, and historic biblical Christianity was again under siege. In a very real way, politicized religion in the form of the Holy Roman Empire greatly hollowed out the vitality of the church, leaving it largely impotent, ignorant, and even illiterate.

The dearth of state-sponsored centers of learning at this time was due to the fragmentation of civil authority and the disintegration of dynasties during the feudal period. This crisis was met as powerful monastic communities developed Christian higher education through the scholarly communities existing within Augustinian and Benedictine monasticism, including the giant intellectual work of Thomas Aquinas. Monasteries' scholarly demeanor and strong discipline[24] were singularly responsible for forming the most important category of higher education the world has ever known, the university.[25]

During this time, the Eternal City, Rome, was believed to hold all spiritual and secular authority through the Holy Roman Empire. As such, it was the fount of divine knowledge and truth. As for Christian education, theology was increasingly considered to

---

23 David C. Lindberg, "The Medieval Church Encounters the Classical Tradition: Saint Augustine, Roger Bacon, and the Handmaiden Metaphor," in *When Science and Christianity Meet*, ed. David. C. Lindberg and Ronald L. Numbers (Chicago: University of Chicago Press, 2003), 7.

24 Terrence G. Kardong, *Pillars of Community: Four Rules of Pre-Benedictine Monastic Life* (Collegeville, MN: Liturgical, 2010), iv.

25 Hastings Rashdall, *The Universities of Europe in the Middle Ages*, vol. 1, *Salerno. Bologna. Paris* (Oxford: Clarendon, 1895), 4.

be "the science of divine revelation." This concept was understood to give biblical truth the central place in learning and curriculum, thus establishing theology as "the queen of the sciences" and the university as the church's handmaiden.[26] This original service of the university to the church was a model that remains crucial even today.

A natural outflow of this conviction about the authority of truth was for the church to authorize ecclesiastically funded learning centers. It was believed that "ideals pass into great historic forces by embodying themselves in institutions."[27] The union of church and state made this possible, and the first such church school to be established was the University of Bologna in Italy, soon followed by the Sorbonne—the University of Paris.[28] These locations were chosen for their being the most intellectually progressive and impressive cities in the two most ecclesiastically important regions of the Western church. Soon other Italian cities near the Holy See were granted institutions as well. These included medieval universities in Naples, Toulouse, and Rome, with others put into place through the 1200s and 1300s.

The proliferation of these universities during the late Middle Ages produced such heightened inquiry, study, reflection, and learning in and around those respective cities that a renewal of learning ignited almost instantly. By the 1300s, the Renaissance had arrived and, with it, the transformation of society.

The idea of the *universitas* was that it was a gathering of scholars for the particular purpose of inquiry to know the truth of God. As universities developed, the curriculum was understood as a unified

---

26 Clark and Jain, *Liberal Arts Tradition*, 245.
27 Rashdall, *Universities of Europe in the Middle Ages*, 1:5–7, 10.
28 Rashdall, *Universities of Europe in the Middle Ages*, 1:17–20.

whole, and the concept of the university possessing a unity of knowledge in the diversity of disciplines, all under the authority of Scripture, was established.

Along with this departure from the Dark Ages came a renewed focus on classical learning. This fueled interest in the Greek language, the liberal arts, and other fields of burgeoning knowledge—the sciences. As Christian intellectuals and priests from the Eastern Hemisphere fled their Orthodox churches, which were being attacked during the Crusades, that influx of scholarship further enhanced the revolutionary nature of the Renaissance and of Christianity's contributions to the world. These contributions were not only great tomes of theology but also deep learning across the disciplines.

As a result, curriculum came to include the full scope of theological instruction: historical, philosophical, biblical, systematic, and practical theology. Along with this, courses of study began to develop across many fields of general revelation. Based on the earlier foundation of Plato's Academy and the Greek categories of the trivium and quadrivium, human knowledge grew exponentially.[29]

The misery of human existence during the Dark Ages began to be ameliorated through society's increasing insight of the divinely embedded knowledge within general and special revelation. This led to advances that blessed all of humankind in the generations that followed.

Christian Higher Education in the Renaissance to the Enlightenment

As the first universities came into being, the advance of human knowledge was breathtaking, especially in contrast to the lack of

29 Schmidt, *Under the Influence*, 173.

progress through parts of the Dark Ages. This phenomenon raised society's view of itself and of human potential. As knowledge increased, human pride swelled, and God was slowly de-emphasized in European society.[30]

The Renaissance

At the beginning of the Renaissance, study became focused on two areas: divinity and the classics. Because the classics focused on themes such as language, politics, education, philosophy, science, and the arts, the relevance of those subjects to contemporary human life was abundantly clear. At that point, the classics were renamed the humanities. Because the humanities comprised the liberal arts, those subjects would be an essential focus of education and learning in the Renaissance and beyond.

Over the next two or three centuries, constant reflection and reinterpretation of the classical subjects in the humanities remolded the idea of humanism as it underwent constant remodification throughout the Renaissance and on into the Enlightenment.

The focus on Renaissance humanities and the sciences naturally led to greater attention on the human body. Whereas art during the Middle Ages was directed upward, aspiring toward purity and acknowledging the supernatural, Renaissance art began to focus more on the human figure, as the ancient Greeks had done before. Almost immediately, nude portraits, murals, and monuments began to be produced. These included unclothed examples not only of unnamed female bodies but also of men—including biblical figures, such as Michelangelo's *David* (1504).[31] The field

---

30 See 1 Cor. 8:1.

31 See Michelangelo Buonarroti, *David*, Galleria dell'Accademia di Firenze, https://www.galleria accademiafirenze.it/opere/david-michelangelo/#.

of medicine also began to endure great change. The dissection of human cadavers from deceased criminals began occurring in medical schools, and empirical research on a growing number of subjects was launched.[32]

Human inquiry then turned its attention to humanity's place on the earth and in the universe, with an eye toward meaning and destiny. Thus humanism began as a philosophical position in the Renaissance and afterward.[33] Along with it came the development of modern astronomy, as Copernicus assigned the sun, rather than the earth, the central position of our galaxy. This forged new understandings about the fundamental structure of humanity's relationship to the universe, which led to the Copernican Revolution.[34]

The Reformation

The Renaissance was largely produced by the renewal of learning within universities and Christian public intellectual life. As scholars returned to the Greek classics, they began to study the Bible in its original languages. With society's new humanistic focus, common citizens wanted to become literate and informed, and to experience greater meaning in life. This led to a push to allow worship in people's native tongues and the development of Bibles in the vernacular. By the time printing presses were widely available, an enormous number of Bible translations and versions were being produced, along with informative tracts offering teaching on a host of topics. As people were personally exposed to ideas, they were able

32 Schmidt, *Under the Influence*, 189.

33 Charles G. Nauert, *Humanism and the Culture of Renaissance Europe* (Cambridge: Cambridge University Press, 1995), 8–24.

34 See Stephen G. Brush, J. Brookes Spencer, Margaret J. Osler, "Copernican Revolution," Britannica, https://www.britannica.com/.

to read and independently verify ideas. As a result, age-old truths were rediscovered, and new insights from God's word abounded.[35]

Meanwhile, the Roman Catholic Church could not withstand the fervent spirituality rising from the pews, and this allowed Protestantism and, soon, a variety of denominations to form. Not surprisingly, as the Reformation developed, new forms of religious intolerance between Catholics and Protestants developed. Even within Protestantism, church leaders began to encounter theological differences, and with the new emphasis on personal interpretation of Scripture, people began gathering in like-minded congregations. Thus, Christian denominations were born, which enjoyed varying degrees of religious freedom, depending on where they were located. Meanwhile, Roman Catholicism had a Counter-Reformation, leading to its own renewal movements.

The Reformation and Counter-Reformation represented one of the most intense periods of Christian history. The new movement of Protestantism promoted a strong commitment to ecclesiology and evangelism that had not been seen since the early church. Beyond this, inexpensive devotional literature available from printing presses led to stronger discipleship within churches. Much of this interest in learning was a direct or indirect result of the burgeoning Christian universities spawned during the fourteenth through sixteenth centuries. Despite this, internal conflicts flared up within movements and among their fiery leaders, leading to distrust and hostility between groups. Even worse, the Christian education that had been made available through universities during this time was increasingly shifting toward a new and different type of humanism that gave way to the Enlightenment. When the Eternal City of

---

35 Examples include, among others, the five *solas*: grace alone, faith alone, Christ alone, Scripture alone, and the glory of God alone.

Rome was sacked in 1527, the Roman Catholic Church lost much of its luster, money, and authority.

The weakening of Rome and the distractions and conflicts within the new Protestant movement gave secularism the opportunity to grow in power and popularity, which led to tremendous challenges for Christianity in Europe during the seventeenth and eighteenth centuries.

The Enlightenment

Rather than viewing the Reformation as a positive renewal movement that improved the church, the intellectuals of the day eyed it with derision and cynicism. They had tasted the freedom afforded by the Renaissance in the midst of a weakened church during the Dark Ages. They had seen nation-states form that had successfully challenged the authority of the Roman Catholic Church and the fledgling Protestant denominations, which were still in their infancy. These newly enlightened people were in no mood to surrender their newfound liberties and moral turpitude to those institutions. Instead, they frequently attacked them on the basis of the ever-evolving Enlightenment humanism.[36]

As society's attention continued to focus on this world rather than otherworldly concerns, the field of philosophy began to stray from its theological foundations. This led to inquiry detached from the knowledge of God and its relationship to metaphysics, epistemology, and ethics. This movement initially came to the forefront through the work of René Descartes. Descartes had become tormented by questions of knowledge and his dissatisfaction with

---

36 Colin Brown, *Christianity and Western Thought: A History of Philosophers, Ideas and Movements*, vol. 1, *From the Ancient World to the Age of Enlightenment* (Downers Grove, IL: InterVarsity Press, 1990), 191–92.

both the authority of Scripture and extant philosophical systems. He began to explore the nature of his doubts and concluded that the only thing that he could not doubt was his own awareness. That led to his grand conclusion, *Cogito, ergo sum*—"I think, therefore I am"—after which he celebrated by having a cognac.[37] Thus, the Cartesian revolution began.

Following these and other thinkers of the time, Europe exchanged a disengaged deistic being for the many "isms" that have become part of philosophical discourse. Whether it was through Descartes's skepticism; Spinoza's and Liebniz's rationalism; Bacon's, Hume's, and Locke's empiricism; or Rousseau's romanticism, the Enlightenment essentially banished Christian doctrine from education.[38]

These and other Enlightenment thinkers flatly rejected the idea of objective biblical authority in favor of a new type of anthropocentric subjectivism. This became the dominant view of seventeenth-century Europe. Christian higher education was thus secularized, and society began to believe that all authority had to be questioned, that all truth claims should be viewed with suspicion, and that God as the center and ground of being should be rejected. The intellectuals and aristocracy of the day accepted these ideas with great enthusiasm, as did commoners, as the newly enlightened European society began to feel justified in the belief that they were the center of the universe and that all mores and morals were henceforth self-defined.[39] The practical effect of the Cartesian revolution was that

---

37 Charles Colson, *Against the Night: Living in the New Dark Ages* (Ann Arbor, MI: Servant, 1989), 27.

38 Carl R. Trueman, *The Rise and Triumph of the Modern Self: Cultural Amnesia, Expressive Individualism, and the Road to Sexual Revolution* (Wheaton, IL: Crossway, 2020), 86, 106–28, 143, 160, 171, 381.

39 Colson, *Against the Night*, 27.

FREDDY CARDOZA

it began the movement to undermine notions about the existence of God and the truth of Scripture.

The implications of Descartes's skepticism went much further. Skepticism posed a serious challenge to the authority of the church, divine creation, the meaning of life, human ethics, morality, and destiny.[40] These slowly led to questions about the nature of Christ and the legitimacy of the gospel and evangelism, as well as suspicion toward the core concept of the university, with all of these defined by the individual, who was now considered the ultimate subjective authority.

By the end of the Enlightenment, European philosophy had effectively checkmated the public's belief in God by advancing a series of strategic metaphysical and epistemological views designed to expel God from the public consciousness. Thus Christian higher education had become compromised in Europe. Several other factors contributed to challenges the church faced. These included a decreased emphasis on theology, the weakening of the Holy Roman Empire, and the practical elimination of Christianity as a major force outside of Europe, due to the expanding Islamic caliphate known as the Ottoman Empire. As a result, many beleaguered Christians seeking a new life and religious freedom began to emigrate to the American Colonies. Christianity quickly began to flourish in the New World and, along with it, a new wave of Christian universities.

Christian Higher Education in Early America

As Christians reached Colonial America during the 1600s, they immediately began establishing churches and, along with them,

40 Trueman, *Rise and Triumph of the Modern Self*, 193.

262

institutions of higher learning. Not surprisingly, the schools being established were often aligned with particular faith traditions. Harvard, founded in 1636, was initially a Congregationalist institution with a Puritan heritage.[41] This emphasis on faith for education was also heavily influenced by Philipp Jakob Spener's Pietism, which focused on the need for spiritual nourishment over dead orthodoxy, like that which had taken over many European schools.

As each institution was started, each and every school was aligned with Christianity. This was true of Harvard, William and Mary, Yale, Columbia, Brown, Princeton, and essentially all others. In fact, "every collegiate institution founded in the colonies prior to the Revolutionary war—except the University of Pennsylvania—was established by some branch of the Christian church."[42] Even later, of the 182 colleges and universities started before the Civil War, 92 percent were founded by Christian denominations. What's more, surprisingly even state universities like the Universities of Tennessee, Kentucky, and California at Berkeley had roots as church schools.[43]

While these schools were launching, however, they had to face the onslaught of American thinking that had adopted post-Enlightenment philosophies. Despite that, Christian higher education in seventeenth-century Colonial America and the United States through the mid-1800s made great strides in ministry preparation. As these schools supplemented the ministry of the local church, evangelicalism emerged in the 1740s with the Great Awakenings during the ministries of Jonathan Edwards, George Whitefield, and the brothers Wesley. During this time, ministers trained in

41 James Tunstead Burtchaell, *The Dying of the Light: The Disengagement of Colleges and Universities from Their Christian Churches* (Grand Rapids, MI: Eerdmans, 1998), 2, 8, 46–47.
42 Schmidt, *Under the Influence*, 190, quoting Paul Lee Tan, *Encyclopedia of 7700 Illustrations: Signs of the Times* (Rockville, MD: Assurance, 1984), 157.
43 Schmidt, *Under the Influence*, 190.

these institutions were being placed in missions and ministries as church planting rapidly expanded through the Eastern Seaboard, the South, and parts of the Midwest. Roman Catholic Franciscan missionaries, Methodists, and Presbyterians were the first to push out to the American West as the notion of manifest destiny took hold in the American imagination.[44]

Christian Higher Education in Modern America

Some of the greatest challenges to the American church have come in the modern age. Having enjoyed an unprecedented surge in growth and expansion and powerful gospel impact through evangelism and the building of the single greatest Christian evangelical heritage thus far in world history, American churches and Christians began to face brutal threats.

In 1859, the ongoing attempt to undermine the essence of the biblical narrative continued with Charles Darwin's *On the Origin of Species.* That book laid down the gauntlet of an alternate explanation for the origin of human nature, one that was not created in the image of God but was accidental and exclusive of the need for a deity. Later, the German scholar Julius Wellhausen published an important work on higher criticism and the so-called documentary hypothesis in which he contended that the Bible had spurious sources that eliminated it from consideration as a book that could be taken literally.[45] In 1925, the infamous "Monkey Trial" with Clarence Darrow and William Jennings Bryan introduced a challenge to Christian creationism in the American legal system. The stunning release of the 1933 "Humanist Manifesto" argued for

44 "Missionary Activity in the American West," Library of Congress, accessed November 28, 2023, https://www.loc.gov/.
45 "Documentary Hypothesis," https://www.cs.umd.edu/~mvz/bible/doc-hyp.pdf.

the first time that matter was uncreated, eternal, and preexistent. These major challenges completed the adoption of secular humanism as a leading worldview in the United States.

Just as these ideological shifts were happening, two major government actions took place concerning American education. In 1852, Massachusetts passed a law requiring compulsory education for children.[46] Later, a landmark 1873 court case permitted public tax funds to pay for children's schooling.[47] By 1918 every American child was required to have a minimum amount of schooling. With this series of actions, public education ensured that not only the "three R's" but also secular dogma would become a part of every American child's educational curriculum.

This thoroughgoing secular humanism in schools was bolstered by a new cultural canon that included Nietzsche's and Sartre's nihilism, William James's pragmatism, Hegel's idealism, Marx's Marxism, and Freud's psychosexual development. Concurrently, Christian discipleship and evangelism were further undermined by ideas within liberal theological circles such as Kierkegaard's and Barth's anti-supernatural neoorthodoxy, Bushnell's and Schleiermacher's atonement-undermining liberalism, and Rauschenbusch's social gospel.[48]

These attacks formed an all-out assault on Christianity, as many of the original American Christian higher education institutions had flailed and failed. These challenges posed a serious theological threat to Christian churches, as the essentials of Christian faith

46 Stephanie Watson, "How Public Schools Work," Howstuffworks, accessed November 28, 2023, https://people.howstuffworks.com/public-schools.htm.

47 Elizabeth Timmerman, "The Kalamazoo School Case," Kalamazoo Public Library, January 2012, https://www.kpl.gov/local-history/kalamazoo-history/kps/kalamazoo-school-case/.

48 Stephen Law, *The Great Philosophers: The Lives and Ideas of History's Greatest Thinkers* (London: Quercus, 2007), 135–39, 176–78.

became the target of open ridicule. That notwithstanding, the secular optimism and sarcasm of the early twentieth century was tempered by two world wars, numerous other geopolitical conflicts, the Cold War, and the rise and fall of Communism, National Socialism, and Fascism. These humiliating failures on the global stage forced secularism to retreat, at least temporarily, into the humility of confused isolation and ideological disillusionment.

In the face of all this, Christian higher education met many of the challenges of the modern age heading into the twentieth century. Though the majority of sixteenth-to-eighteenth-century Christian universities had failed miserably in executing their historical mission statements, a new generation of fundamentalist and evangelical institutions came into existence. From the establishment of the original Bible institutes at the turn of the century (Moody, BIOLA, Tyndale, and Nyack) to the many dozens of other major theological institutions in the early to mid-1900s, Bible-believing and confessional Christian institutions rose to the occasion to help the church. Despite this, Christian higher education's greatest challenges would soon be made manifest.

Christian Higher Education Today

Little did the world know back in 1983 that engineers making a simple change in the way computers communicated with one another would revolutionize human life on earth. The World Wide Web, the Internet, was born and the digital revolution began.[49] The decades that followed have been among the most tumultuous in human history. The speed of change became supersonic as the world

49 Angelo Young and John Harrington, "World History: These Are among the Most Important Global Events to Happen Annually since 1920," *USA Today*, September 6, 2020, https://www.usatoday.com/story/money/2020/09/06/.

entered an altered reality that was both incomparable to anything before and incomprehensible to anyone until then.

Momentous world events have continued to unfold: the world-wide financial failure of Black Monday; the fall of the Berlin Wall and the end of Soviet Communism; the beginning of the European Union; the birth of Amazon, Facebook, and Google; 9/11; the introduction of the iPhone; ISIS; the COVID-19 pandemic.[50] As these historical events occurred, new philosophies surfaced or old ones resurfaced. Postmodernity and its associated "isms" went mainstream. Foucault, Derrida, and Lyotard became household names as life began to imitate art and the world began to become the theater of the absurd. Metanarratives and worldviews, including Christianity, were declared incredible. Words were rejected as having no essential meaning, and all language was said to be biased. The pragmatism of William James was accepted, and any view sincerely held was considered true "for me," and any action deliberately taken was considered inherently self-justified.

Nietzsche's nihilism convinced many that might equals right, that humans can be their own gods, and that nothing is objectively right or morally wrong. Law, order, and meaning began to suffer catastrophic cultural collapse as civilization itself unraveled. Finally, Max Horkheimer and the Frankfurt School's critical theory exploited Hegelian and Marxist theory further, leading many universities and societies to near-complete ruin. Critical theory has undermined the foundations of the concept of the university, maligned nearly all systems of thought, and infected entire academic disciplines with self-referential ideas. From critical theory comes the embrace of subjectivism and collectivism, and the radical rejection

50 Young and Harrington, "World History."

and brutal assailing of absolutes, individual agency, and objective truth. Today's narcissistic worship of self, sexuality, and identity are unique in the history of our world.[51]

In addition to all these, technological advances of this Fourth Industrial Era have wrought bewitching inventions and bedeviling consequences. Though some such advances in medicine, business, and recreation have improved human life and leisure, looming trouble abounds. Mixed or virtual reality blurs the line between virtual and actual. Artificial intelligence creates public-safety threats, identity-theft vulnerabilities, job-obsolescence possibilities, human-machine ethical challenges, and exponentially more direct and indirect possibilities to imagine.

Though the historical, philosophical, ethical, and technological challenges outlined are numerous, even the casual reader knows they hardly scratch the surface of the actual changes we face. Even so, these make it clear that the church has its work cut out for it, and the many connections these issues have to STEM subjects,[52] the liberal arts, teaching, evangelism, and discipleship make the relevance of today's Christian higher education abundantly clear.

Where Do We Go from Here?

Christianity has been the most influential force in the history of global education. It has made more contributions to society and the world than any other movement or religion, by far and bar none.[53]

---

51 Trueman, *Rise and Triumph of the Modern Self*, 284.

52 Science, technology, engineering, and mathematics.

53 Schmidt, *Under the Influence*, 191. Schmidt quotes D. James Kennedy and Jerry Newcombe, who present a convincing argument that "every school you see—public or private, religious or secular—is a visible reminder of the religion of Jesus Christ. So is every college and university." In D. James Kennedy and Jerry Newcombe, *What If Jesus Had Never Been Born?* (Nashville: Thomas Nelson, 1994), 40. Also, see Schmidt and Burtchaell in the bibliography.

This is fundamentally due to the preeminence of Jesus Christ and his pedagogical perfection, which he modeled as the greatest teacher in history.[54] Beyond that, the body of Christ, the church, has made a deep and positive impact on cultures, societies, and populations for the last two thousand years.

Because the challenges being faced by the church and Christian higher education pose an existential threat to all we know, believe, and hold dear, this is no time to be passive. In the classic words of the late Wheaton professor Lois LeBar, "A revolutionary Gospel in a revolutionary age calls for revolutionary teaching that revolutionizes lives."[55] Just as Christian higher education has played a critical role in the past, Christian colleges, universities, seminaries, and divinity schools must also play a role now—and in the future.

Here are ten recommendations on how professors and administrators can fight the good fight of the faith and aid the church in its work of evangelism and discipleship in the world:

1. *Demonstrate grace and truth.* Show the kindness of God without compromising the word of God.
2. *Present apologetics and polemics.* Apologetics defensively protects the faith from outside attacks, while polemics offensively disarms or negates false teachings from within or outside the church. Both are biblical.
3. *Build bridges and walls.*[56] Walls provide protection against danger and invasion, and form community to those who belong there; bridges provide smooth access and ease of connection. Both are biblical.

---

54 Schmidt, *Under the Influence,* 170.
55 Lois E. LeBar, *Education That Is Christian* (Colorado Springs: Chariot Victor, 1995), 287.
56 2 Chron. 14:7; Neh. 4; Prov. 25:28.

4. *Love God and love people.* Loving God and loving people are not contradictory. There is always a way to do both if we understand the biblical meaning of "love."

5. *Employ word and Spirit.* We must open our Bibles and also open our hearts. Avoid dead orthodoxy and conviction-free sentimentalism.

6. *Play offense and defense.* Some Christian leaders live and serve in a perpetual state of defense. Others are always armed to the teeth. Our armor includes a sword and a shield.[57]

7. *Use faith and reason.* Augustine and, later, Anselm spoke about the importance of believing so one could gain understanding. Faith is important in Christian education, but so is the life of the mind.[58]

8. *Stand alone and stand together.* Develop the mettle to stand by yourself for Jesus and his truth, but value the need to stand with other believers.

9. *Be a disciple and make disciples.*

10. *Live the gospel and share the gospel.* It is not enough to live it; we must also tell it. The gospel should be shown, but it must also be proclaimed.

Work and collaborate together to take the gospel to the nations for the glory of God.

Questions for Reflection

1. How can faculty and administrators preserve confessional Christian higher education and institutions if their mission, convictions, and

---

57 Eph. 6:10–20.
58 Mark A. Noll, *The Scandal of the Evangelical Mind* (Grand Rapids, MI: Eerdmans, 1994), 3–12.

identity are no longer protected or are outright persecuted by a government?[59]

2. How can Christian higher education fundamentally address challenges to its identity, convictions, and mission that arise from within its ranks (its own departments or schools, or in areas related to co-curriculum, finance, advancement, or the board of directors)?

3. What hinders or threatens your own institution's ability to make evangelism an important part of its on-campus efforts?

4. What are some appropriate responses to objections students, staff, administrators, or faculty may have to the idea that evangelism and discipleship are legitimate and necessary pursuits in your Christian institution?

5. The voices of those opposing the word of God and the message of Christ today will not be silenced. What are some necessary perspectives, convictions, or actions committed Christian students and institutional leaders must demonstrate in order to ensure the survival and missional integrity of Christian higher educational institutions?

Resources for Further Study

Barna Group. *Reviving Evangelism: Current Realities That Demand a New Vision for Sharing Faith*. Ventura, CA: Barna Group, 2019.

Chan, S. *How to Talk about Jesus (without Being That Guy): Personal Evangelism in a Skeptical World*. Grand Rapids, MI: Zondervan, 2020.

59 John David Trentham, "Christian Higher Education," in Cardoza, *Christian Education*, 338.

Richardson, Rick. *You Found Me: New Research on How Unchurched Nones, Millennials, and Irreligious Are Surprisingly Open to Christian Faith.* Downers Grove, IL: InterVarsity Press, 2019.

Schmidt, Alvin J. *Under the Influence: How Christianity Transformed Civilization.* Grand Rapids, MI: Zondervan, 2001.

Trueman, Carl R. *Strange New World: How Thinkers and Activists Redefined Identity.* Wheaton, IL: Crossway, 2022.

Contributors

Susan Booth, professor of evangelism and missions, Canadian Baptist Theological Seminary and College

Freddy Cardoza, professor of Christian ministry and leadership, and dean, Grace Theological Seminary; dean, School of Ministry Studies, Grace College

Anna Daub, director of special projects and partnerships for global theological initiatives, Southeastern Baptist Theological Seminary

Jim Denison, president, Denison Forum

Daniel DeWitt, executive director of worldview analysis and cultural engagement, Southwest Baptist University

Travis Dickinson, professor of philosophy, Dallas Baptist University

David S. Dockery, president, International Alliance for Christian Education; president, Southwestern Baptist Theological Seminary

David Gustafson, associate professor and chair, missions and evangelism, Trinity Evangelical Divinity School

David Kotter, professor of New Testament and dean, School of Theology, Colorado Christian University

Mark Legg, associate editor, Denison Forum

Tim McKnight, associate professor of youth ministry and director, Global Center for Youth Ministry, Anderson University

Christopher W. Morgan, dean, School of Christian Ministries and professor of theology, California Baptist University

Harry Lee Poe, Charles Colson University Professor of Faith and Culture, Union University

Robert B. Sloan, president, Houston Christian University

Erik Thoennes, professor and chair of theology, Biola University

General Index

Abolition of Man, The (Lewis), 165
Abraham, 36, 73, 129–30, 170
   God's covenant with, 11, 14–15
   "seed of Abraham," 14
Adam, 10, 46, 48
Aeneid (Virgil), 72
African Baptist Church of St. Louis, 84
African Bible Commentary (Kapolyo), 179–80
Alexander the Great, 247, 248
Allegory of Love, The (Lewis), 146–47, 154, 155, 165
Ambrose, 252
American Mission Board, 199
Anderson, Rufus, 178
Andrew, 97
Ansgar of Bremen, 72–73
anti-intellectualism, 134
apologetics
   aim of in evangelism, 139–41
   and arguing people into the kingdom, 141–43
   definition of the term *apologetics*, 135
   distinct roles of apologetics, 138–39
   misunderstandings of, 128–34
   Peter's call to, 132
   relevancy to discipleship, 138–39

   simple apologetics, 110
   as a way for Christians to love God, 138
   what is apologetics? 134–38
   See also apologetics, misunderstanding of
Apology (Tertullian), 68
Apology of Socrates, The (Socrates), 135
apostles, the, 4, 12, 23, 24, 26, 28–29, 64, 65, 67, 70, 75, 90, 91, 130, 134
Aquinas, Thomas, 155, 252
Aratus, 194
Aristotle, 147, 246–47
Asbury, Francis, 85
Athens
   as the cradle of civilization, 248
   and the development of democracy, 245–46
   See also Paul, in Athens
Augustine of Hippo, 71, 145–46, 155, 252, 253
Augustus Caesar, 249
Azariah, V. S., 177

Babylon, 15
Backus, Isaac, 117
Barth, Karl, 151
Basil of Caesarea (Basil the Great), 70–71, 253

Coleman, Robert, 44, 54
collectivism, 267
Colson, Charles, 163
compassion, 110–12
  marrying truth with compassion,
    123–24
Concerning the Glory of Christ (Proba),
  72
Confessions (Augustine of Hippo), 71,
  145–46
Constantine, 68–69
Cost of Discipleship, The (Bonhoeffer),
  120

Daniel, 16
Dark Ages, the, 253, 256, 257, 260
Dark Tower, The (Lewis), 159
Darrow, Clarence, 264
Darwin, Charles, 151, 229, 264
David, 16, 28, 58, 209
Denison, Ryan, 120
Derrida, Jacques, 108, 267
Descartes, René, 147–48, 260–62
Discarded Image, The (Lewis), 165
disciples, the, 49, 172
  boldness as a main trait of, 58
  the disciples' initial reaction to the
    Great Commission, 213, 222
discipleship, 138–39, 215
  "discipleship evangelism," 221
  as the "second major function of the
    church," 238–39
  See also evangelism, and discipleship
Domitian, 66
Dymer (Lewis), 153–54
Dyson, Hugo, 149

Edict of Milan, 68
Edinburgh Missionary Conference
  (1910), 177–78
education. *See* higher education
Edwards, Jonathan, 263
Elijah, 16, 58
Elliot, Jim, 59

*English Literature in the Sixteenth Cen-
  tury* (Lewis), 165
Enlightenment, the, 260–62
Erickson, Millard, 238–39
evangelism, 1, 25–26, 69, 172n6
  and faith, 3–4
  farming metaphor concerning,
    187–89
  global nature of, 207
  importance of in missions,
    172–73n7
  Jesus's intentions for, 63–64
  modern-day evangelism, 13
  of neighbors, 119–20
  in the post-Christian West, 105–7
  recommendations for today's Chris-
    tians concerning, 102–3
  as a summons to lifelong obedience,
    10–11
  what is evangelism? 9–10, 19–20
  work of, 4, 10, 11
evangelism, and apologetics
  of early Christians, 99–101
  New Testament practices of, 87–90
evangelism, and discipleship, 242, 245,
  265
  and biblical multiplication, 233–34
  the Christians' dilemma concerning,
    236–39
  the commission of Christ requires
    both, 231–33
  recommendations for professors and
    administrators, 269–70
  relationship between, 229–31,
    237–38
  and the role of the Spirit in multipli-
    cation, 234–36
evangelism, cultivating in, 189–90,
  194–95
  through contextualization, 193–94
  through love, grace, and respect,
    191–93
  through prayer, 190–91

evangelism, in the history of the church
in the 1700s, 82–84
in the 1800s, 83–85
in early Greece and Rome, 63–72
lay Christian evangelists, 72–73
in the medieval period, 74–76
and missionary monks in northern
Europe, 73
and the Pietist movement, 78–80
in the Protestant Reformation, 76–78
in the Renaissance, 75–76
evangelism, motivations of early Christians for
early Christians understood the
gospel message (six essential truths
of), 92–93
early Christians understood the heart
of Christ, 90–91
early Christians understood the power
of prayer and the Holy Spirit, 95–96
early Christians understood their
mission from Christ, 91–92
early Christians were glad to be
saved and grieved for the lost,
94–95
evangelism, planting in, 195, 200–201
and clarity, 200
and gospel conversations versus
gospel presentations, 196–98
planting good seed, 198–99
planting indiscriminately, 195–96
evangelism, practice of early Christians
concerning
early Christians were intentional in
apologetics, 99–101
early Christians were intentional in
evangelism, 97–99
early Christians were intentional in
perseverance, 101–2
evangelism, reaping in, 201
inviting others to respond to the
gospel, 201–2
and the next steps concerning, 203

Evangelism as Exiles (Clark), 113
Evangelism in the Early Church (Green), 4
Eve, 10, 46, 48
Experiment in Criticism, An (Lewis),
165
Ezra, 33–34

faith, 3–4, 32, 52, 129–31, 202
Christian evidence for, 131–32
and literature in medieval society, 155
Farrer, Austin, 156–57, 162, 163, 164
Finney, Charles, 85
First Great Awakening, 117, 175n11
forgiveness, 4, 14, 23–24, 25, 52, 63,
77, 80, 92, 120, 212, 213, 221
Foster, Richard, 219
Foucault, Michel, 107, 267
Four Loves, The (Lewis), 166
Fourth Great Awakening, 117
Frelinghuysen, Theodore, 116–17
Freundlich, Matthäus, 81–82
Fuller, Andrew, 2

Georgics (Virgil), 72
global church, the, 173
and the global mission, 179–80
the road to, 175–79
what it is, 173–75
See also global church, the, opportunities for students
global church, the, opportunities for
students, 180–81, 184
and considering nations after college,
183
to disciple and be discipled by
people of other cultures, 182–83
note for faculty and administration
concerning, 184–85
praying for the nations, 181–82
for studying abroad, 183
God
character of, 45
covenant lordship of, 39–40

revelation of God through Christ, 50
supremacy, sufficiency, and exclusivity of, 49–51
as the true and perfect prophet, 56
work of, 52
See also Great Commission, the
Jews, 13, 24, 33, 34, 65, 99–100, 112, 117, 130, 190, 193, 210
Joanna, 64
John, 33, 66, 98, 130
John Chrysostom, 252
John the Baptist, 17, 64, 67, 97
Joshua tree, 227–28, 241–42
Judson, Adoniram, 176
Julian, 71
Justin Martyr, 251

Kapolyo, Joe, 179–80
Ko Tha Byu, 176
Köstenberger, Andreas, 171n3

Latourette, Kenneth Scott, 176–77n16
LeBar, Lois, 269
Letters to Malcolm Chiefly on Prayer (Lewis), 166
Lewis, C. S., 116, 118, 141, 154n12, 240
on Aristotle, 147
conversion of, 153–54
criticism of by his brother Warren, 153–54
criticism of by Pittenger, 152
originality of, 153
Protestantism of, 155–56
See also Lewis, C. S., and apologetics
Lewis, C. S., and apologetics, 145–48, 166–67
approach of Lewis to apologetics, 157–58
formation of Lewis as an apologist, 148–50
preparation of as an apologist, 151–56

See also Lewis, C. S., distinct ways of presenting an apologetic for the Christian faith
Lewis, C. S., distinct ways of presenting an apologetic for the Christian faith, 156–58
little books about Christianity, 166
and philosophical argument, 163–65
and the testimony of experience, 162
works of fiction, 158–62
Lewis, Warren, 153–54
libraries, in ancient times, 251
Licinius, 68
Lion, the Witch and the Wardrobe, The (Lewis), 160–61
Lucas Cranach the Elder, 77
Luther, Martin, 76–78
Lyotard, Jean-François, 267

Machen, J. Gresham, 142, 143
Man Born to Be King, The (Sayers), 161–62
Manning, Brennan, 118
Martin, Friedrich, 80
martyrdom, 67, 251
"red martyrdom," 70
"white martyrdom," 70
Marx, Karl, 265
Mary (mother of James), 64
Mary Magdalene, 64
McKinion, Steven, 192, 196
McKnight, Scott, 236
Meachum, John Berry, 84
Mere Christianity (Lewis), 154, 162, 163, 164
Methodists, 85, 264
Miracles (Lewis), 146, 157, 163, 164
missions, 47, 172–73n7
Franciscan missionaries, 264
and the global mission for a global church, 179–80
polycentric mission, 179n25

Scripture Index

International Alliance
for Christian Education

The International Alliance for Christian Education (IACE)
is a global education network encompassing a variety
of educational institutions and organizations in the
evangelical tradition. Our mission is to unify, synergize, and
strengthen collective conviction around biblical orthodoxy
and orthopraxy, cultural witness, scholarship, professional
excellence, and resourcing of Christian education at all levels.

iace.education